Philosophy
of Physics

Dimensions of Philosophy Series
Norman Daniels and Keith Lehrer, Editors

Philosophy of Physics, Lawrence Sklar

Metaphysics, Peter van Inwagen

Theory of Knowledge, Keith Lehrer

Philosophy of Law: An Introduction to Jurisprudence,
Revised Edition, Jeffrie G. Murphy and Jules L. Coleman

Philosophy of Social Science, Alexander Rosenberg

Introduction to Marx and Engels: A Critical Reconstruction,
Richard Schmitt

FORTHCOMING

Philosophy of Biology, Elliott Sober

Philosophy of Science, Clark Glymour

Philosophy of Mind, Jaegwon Kim

Contemporary Continental Philosophy, Bernd Magnus

Political Philosophy, Jean Hampton

Normative Ethics, Shelly Kagan

Philosophy of Religion, Thomas V. Morris

Philosophy of Education, Nel Noddings

Also by Lawrence Sklar

Space, Time, and Spacetime
Philosophy and Spacetime Physics

Philosophy of Physics

Lawrence Sklar
UNIVERSITY OF MICHIGAN

Westview Press

BOULDER • SAN FRANCISCO

Dimensions of Philosophy Series

Copyright © 1992 by Westview Press, Inc.

Published in 1992 in the United States of America by Westview Press, Inc., 5500 Central Avenue, Boulder, Colorado 80301-2877

Library of Congress Cataloging-in-Publication Data
Sklar, Lawrence.
    Philosophy of Physics / Lawrence Sklar.
        p.   cm. — (Dimensions of philosophy series)
    Includes bibliographical references and index.
    ISBN 0-8133-0599-3 — ISBN 0-8133-0625-6 (pbk.)
    1. Physics—Philosophy.   I. Title.   II. Series.
QC6.S578   1992
530′.01—dc20   92-18759
                                                                                    CIP

Printed and bound in the United States of America

The paper used in this publication meets the requirements
of the American National Standard for Permanence of Paper
for Printed Library Materials Z39.48-1984.

10   9   8   7   6   5   4   3   2   1

For
PAT and RUBBY

Contents

Acknowledgments

For a work of this sort, designed to survey the current state of the field, the sources of intellectual influence are far too many to mention in an acknowledgments section. The suggested readings at the ends of the three major chapters will indicate to the reader where I have found the sources of many important ideas in the philosophy of physics.

Discussions with many people over the years have helped me to get my ideas in order on the topics presented here. Jim Joyce and Bob Batterman have been of great help, and I have learned much from John Earman, Clark Glymour, David Malament, Paul Horwich, and Michael Friedman.

Michele Vaidic provided invaluable help in putting the manuscript together. Spencer Carr and the two referees of Westview Press helped greatly in improving the early draft of the manuscript, especially with regard to style and organization. Marian Safran, copy editor, provided much-appreciated help in bringing the manuscript to its final form.

Research that contributed to the material in Chapter 3 was supported in part by the National Science Foundation, whose aid is gratefully acknowledged. Thanks are due also to the University of Michigan for a grant that helped defray some of the costs of manuscript preparation.

Lawrence Sklar

1

Introduction: Philosophy and the Physical Sciences

The Relation of Science to Philosophy

The demarcation of the natural sciences from philosophy has been a long and gradual process in Western thought. Originally, inquiry into the nature of things consisted in an amalgamation of what would now be thought of as philosophy: general considerations of the broadest sort about the nature of being and the nature of our cognitive access to it, and what would now be considered to be the specific sciences: the amassing of observational fact and the formulation of general and theoretical hypotheses to explain it. If we look at the fragmentary remains of the works of the pre-Socratic philosophers, we find not only important and ingenious attempts to apply reason to broad metaphysical and epistemological questions but also the first crude, if extraordinarily imaginative, physical theories concerning the nature of matter and its changing aspects.

By the time of classical Greek philosophy, we can already see some splitting of the two disciplines. Aristotle in his metaphysical works is plainly doing what would now be done by philosophers. But in much of his biological, astronomical, and physical works, we find methods of inquiry familiar to us now in the practice of scientists.

As the special sciences such as physics, chemistry, and biology have increased in number, commanded more and more resources, and developed highly individual methodologies, they have demonstrated ability to describe and explain the fundamental features of the world in which we live. Because of the success of the practitioners of the special sciences, many question whether there is anything left for philosophers to do at all. Some philosophers believe that there are areas of inquiry that are radically distinct from those of the particular sciences, for example, inquiry into the nature of God, of "being itself," or of something else again. Other philosophers have sought in varying ways for a remaining area of inquiry for philosophy more closely connected to the natural sciences in their latter-day, sophisticated, development.

An older view, waning in popularity over the centuries but never disappearing entirely, holds that there is a way of knowing the world that need not rest upon observational or experimental inquiry at its foundations, the method of the specific sciences. The older view was partly influenced by the existence of pure logic and mathematics, whose firmly established truths do not seem to rest for their warrant on any observational or experimental ground. The hope has endured—from Plato and Aristotle to Leibniz and the other rationalists, through Kant and the idealists, and even to the present time—that were we but smart and thoughtful enough, we could establish a body of propositions descriptive of the world, yet known with the certainty with which we claim to know truths of logic and mathematics. These would be believable independently of any inductive support from particular observed facts. Were such a body of knowledge available to us, would it not be the goal aimed at over the centuries by the discipline traditionally called philosophy?

A more contemporary view is that philosophy's role is to serve, not as some ground for the sciences or as some extension of them, but rather as their critical observer. The idea here is that the particular scientific disciplines use concepts and methods. The relationships of the concepts to one another, although implicit in their use in science, may fail to be explicitly clear to us. It would then be the job of philosophy of science to clarify these conceptual relationships. Again, the particular sciences use specific methods for generalizing from observational data to hypothesis and theory. It is the job of philosophy, from this perspective, to describe the methods employed by the sciences and to explore the ground for rationalizing these methods. That is, it is philosophy's job to show them to be the appropriate methods for finding the truth in the scientific discipline in question.

But is it clear from either of these two perspectives that philosophy and science can be differentiated from each other in any hard-and-fast way? Many have suggested not. In the specific sciences theories are sometimes adopted not merely because of their consistency with the observational data but also on such grounds as simplicity, explanatory force, or other considerations thought to contribute to their intrinsic plausibility. When we observe that, we begin to lose confidence in the idea that there are two quite distinct realms of propositions, those supported by data alone and those supported by reason alone. Many contemporary methodologists, such as W. V. Quine, would maintain that the natural sciences, mathematics, and even pure logic form a unified continuum of beliefs about the world. All, these methodologists claim, are indirectly supported by observational data, but all contain elements of "rational" support as well. If this is true, would not even philosophy, construed as the truths of reason, also form a part of the unified whole? That is, would philosophy not also be just a component of the body of specialized sciences?

When we ask for the proper description and rationalization of the methods of science, we seem to expect the specific results of the particular sciences again to come into play. How could we understand the ability of the methods of science to lead us to the truth without being able to show that these methods really had the reliability imputed to them? And how could we do this without employing our knowledge of what the world is like, revealed to us by our best available science? How could we, for example, justify our trust in sensory observation in science unless our understanding of the perceptual process, an understanding grounded in physics, neurology, and psychology, assured us that perception as employed in the testing of scientific theories was, indeed, a good guide to the truth about the nature of the world?

It is in the discussion of the most fundamental and general theories of physics that the indistinctness of the boundary between natural science and philosophy becomes most apparent. Given the bold ambition of these theories to describe the natural world in its most fundamental and general aspects, it is no surprise that the kinds of reasoning employed in developing these highly abstract theories sometimes seem closer to philosophical reasoning than to the methods employed when more limited and particular scientific investigation is being pursued. Later, as we explore the concepts and methods of physics when it deals with its most foundational questions, we will see again and again that it can be quite unclear whether we are exploring questions in natural science or questions in philosophy. Indeed, in this area of our exploration of the nature of our world, the distinction between the two disciplines becomes very unclear.

Modern Physics and Philosophy

It will be helpful to have a preliminary look at a few of the ways in which the results of modern physics have affected philosophical questions. This can happen when a theoretical study in physics pushes up against what have been thought to be the boundaries to its domain of inquiry. Consider, for example, current cosmology. The most widely accepted model for the very large-scale structure of our universe is the Big Bang. Here the evolution of the current universe is traced backward in time, with a shrinking of the spatial dimensions of the universe in that backward-time direction. Much of the current structure and dynamics of the universe can apparently be accounted for if we think of the universe as having evolved in an explosive way from a singularity at a finite time in the past. That is, it seems that at some time in the past (of the order of at most a few tens of billions of years ago), all the matter of the universe was concentrated "at a point" in space (or, better, space itself was so concentrated).

But such a model of the universe obviously gives rise to perplexing questions that seem to take us beyond the modes of seeking for an answer familiar to us in discussing issues of causality on the astronomical scale. If the current state of the universe can be traced back in a sequence of cause and effect to the initial singularity, what can we then do to continue the question-and-answer process of science and look for the causal explanation of the existence and nature of that initial singular state itself? It simply isn't clear to us what *sort* of explanatory answer we could give to a question like, "Why did the big bang take place and why was it the way it was?" We have, as it were, run out of room for explanatory answers of the familiar sort. The chain of regressive causal reasoning from state to earlier state posited as sufficient cause seems to come to a halt with the singular initial Big Bang.

This isn't to say that nothing in the way of an explanation of the Big Bang's occurrence and nature could be imagined, only that at this point, it seems the usual scientific modes of thinking must be supplemented by modes familiar to the philosopher. The very nature of our request for an explanation, the sort of answer we could expect in reply to such a request, is what is in question. Here physics and philosophy seem to merge, with specific questions about the nature of the world becoming inextricably entangled with questions of a more methodological sort about just what sorts of description and explanation of the world are appropriately expectable from science.

Another pressure to "philosophize" in contemporary physics comes about because changes in our physical picture of the world require a radical revision in our conceptualization of it. When we try to accommodate the puzzling observational data that forced the new scientific revolutions upon us, we soon find that many of our prized concepts for dealing with the world rely for their viability on the presence of certain structural features of our picture of the world. In some cases these are features whose existence we don't even notice until they come under challenge from the new revolutionary physical theories. But once these features of our theoretical picture become doubtful, the concepts dependent upon them can no longer function for us as they have before and we must revise our concepts. But such conceptual revision is just the sort of thing that imposes on us a typically philosophical investigation into the very meaning of the concepts we have been employing all along and into the revisions of meaning needed to accommodate the new conceptual understanding of the world.

Consider, for example, the revision in our concept of time implied by the special theory of relativity. For reasons that we will explore later, the adoption of this theory requires us to say many things about time that would appear to be manifestly absurd. Two events occurring at the same time for one "observer" can, in this theory, be nonsimultaneous for some other observer in motion with respect to the first. The very time order of some events (ones not causally connectable to each other) can be reversed relative to distinct observers. But our older concept of time supposes, almost unconsciously, that what is simultaneous for one is simultaneous for all, and that if event *a* is before event *b*, this is an "absolute" fact for one and all.

The nature of the new theory of space and time, bringing its revolutionary concepts with it, forces upon us a thoughtful reconsideration of just what made up our old theoretical presuppositions and conceptual apparatus. That reconsideration leads us to examine with care just what in our earlier conception was grounded in experience and what was presupposed without warrant or justification. And the revolutionary shifts impose upon us the duty of exploring with care the way in which concepts do depend upon the theoretical structure in which they are embedded, and how changes in that structure can legitimately demand conceptual renovation from us. As we shall see when we move beyond the special theory of relativity to the general theory, we will need even more-novel structures for space and time. It becomes possible to countenance at least the possibility of worlds in which, for example, a given event is, in a perfectly coherent sense, in its own past and future. Clearly this kind of a change counts as a conceptual revolution. The understanding of just how such conceptual revolutions can take place and of what exactly goes on when one does take place is the kind of problem well suited for philosophical investigation. Philosophy now becomes integrated into physical theorizing.

Yet another example of this kind of scientific conceptual revolution requiring that philosophical reflection become a part of ongoing science involves the impact of quantum theory on our traditional notions of causation. Presupposed in much of our science was the understanding that each event could be explanatorily associated in a lawlike way with some earlier condition of the world. Such an assumption was in many ways a guiding principle of the search for ever-more-encompassing scientific explanations of the phenomena of experience. If an event seemed uncaused, this could only be a reflection of our ignorance, of the fact that we had not yet found the cause whose existence could be assured to us by the general principle that "every event has a cause."

But, as we shall see, many have claimed that the principle can no longer be held to be true in a world described by quantum mechanics. What kind of a theory could inform us that there are uncaused events in the world, events for which the search for an underlying determining cause is guaranteed to be fruitless? The answer is no simple matter. The failure of universal causation implied by quantum mechanics is part of a much more profound conceptual upheaval forced on us by this theory. Indeed, few who have explored the issues carefully think that any account of the world yet constructed will do justice to the facts quantum mechanics tells us we will find in the world. Basic ideas of what constitutes "objective reality," as opposed to our subjective experience of it, become problematic in the light of this astounding theory. Once again (and this is the only point being made here), the revolutionary nature of the data of experience and of the theory constructed to account for it in modern physics forces upon us the kind of careful, critical examination of the role played (sometimes only implicitly and unconsciously) by certain fundamental concepts in our older theories. Moreover, that same revolutionary nature demands a careful philosophical examination of how revision of theory forces revision of conceptual structure upon us. The kinds of thinking and reasoning familiar in philosophical contexts become an integral part of science in the context of conceptual revolutions.

Philosophy has also been integrated into scientific practice in recent physics through the intrusion into scientific theorizing of a kind of epistemological critique previously found only in philosophy. Earlier physics rested upon assumptions about what could constitute legitimate data for grounding the inference to physical theories and what could constitute the legitimate rules of inference by which one went from summaries of observed data to generalized hypotheses and postulated theories. It was usually left to philosophers to puzzle over the implicit assumptions made in the sciences, to elucidate their nature and examine their legitimacy. But in recent physics, it has become necessary for theorists, as part of their scientific practice, to explore these basic issues concerning our ground for accepting and rejecting hypotheses. The work of Einstein in relativity theory and Bohr in quantum mechanics is particularly revealing of this new epistemological trend.

In his seminal paper on the special theory of relativity, for example, A. Einstein confronts a number of extremely puzzling observational and theoretical difficulties in existing physics. His attack on these problems is grounded in an extraordinarily original and brilliant discussion of the question, "How can we determine of two spatially separated events whether or not they occur at the same time?" This exploration into the evidential and inferential basis of our legitimate theoretical postulation leads Einstein to the fundamental core of his new theory, the relativity of simultaneity to the state of motion of the observer. Although Einstein does derive from his basic postulates some startling new and fundamentally important observational consequences, many of his predicted results were contained in the earlier theory of H. Lorentz. But even for these consequences, the work of Einstein constitutes an advance of fundamental importance. Seen in his new perspective, the older formulas take on a wholly different meaning. It is crucial to note that this new perspective is founded upon a critical, philosophical examination of the evidential basis for our theoretical inferences. Astoundingly, as we shall later see, a very similar critical, epistemological examination of earlier theories resides at the very heart of Einstein's other fundamental theory of space and time: the general theory of relativity.

Quantum mechanics provides us with another prime example of how epistemological critique plays a crucial role in modern physics. The question of the nature of the measurement process, the process by which a physical system is explored by an external observer to determine its state, becomes fundamental to an understanding of the meaning of the formulas at the core of quantum mechanics. From the very beginnings of this theory, questions about what is observable played an important conceptual role. Later, attempts to understand such curious consequences of the theory as the so-called Uncertainty Principle required, once again, a critical examination of what could be observationally determined. Ultimately, attempts at understanding the fundamental conceptual framework of the theory led Niels Bohr to claim that the new physical theory required an extraordinarily radical revision of our traditional ideas about the relation between what we know about the world and what is the case about it. The very notion of an objective nature of the world independent of our knowledge of it came under attack in Bohr's program. Once again, ideas previously familiar only in the context of philosophy became a part of physics. In philosophy, the denial of objectivity and claims in favor of various doctrines of relativity or subjectivity for the world are an old story.

The interaction of philosophy and physics did not begin with these twentieth-century theories. As we shall see, philosophical issues were intertwined with the early development of dynamics (especially in I. Newton). In the nineteenth century, philosophical debates played a crucial role in the development of the new molecular-atomic theory of matter. Other debates of a philosophical sort were important in establishing the conceptual basis of the theory of electromagnetism, with its invocation of the "field" as a fundamental component of the physical world. But modern physics has pushed its explorations to the very boundaries of the world. In doing so, it has strained the conceptual apparatus adequate for dealing with more limited questions. Physics, in its attempt to do justice to the puzzling and unexpected phenomena revealed by modern experimental techniques, requires the radical revision of previously unquestioned concepts. The novel theories necessitate an examination of the evidential and inferential basis behind their postulates. Therefore, recent theoretical physics has become an arena where philosophical modes of thinking are an essential component of physical progress. It is this intertwining of physics and philosophy that we shall be exploring.

Philosophy of Physics and General Philosophy

We have just seen some of the reasons philosophy has become important to those concerned with the nature of physical theory. It might be helpful to explain as well why the study of the foundations of physical theory and its philosophical aspects is worthwhile for philosophers not specifically concerned with the nature of physics. I would like to suggest that the problems investigated by philosophers of physics and the methods they employ to explore these problems can throw light on more general philosophical issues as well.

Philosophers of science are interested in such questions as the nature of scientific theories, how they explain the phenomena of the world, the evidential and inferential basis for these theories, and how that evidence can be taken as rationally supporting or discouraging belief in a hypothesis. We can gain insight by exploring these more general issues in the context of specific theories of contemporary physics. The broad scope of the theories and their highly explicit nature provide a context in which many otherwise rather vague issues of general philosophy of science become more "fixed" when we focus attention on these special physical theories.

Because the theories are highly formalized, the place played in them by crucial concepts is delineated easily and clearly. Questions about the meaning of the crucial concepts, their eliminability or irreducibility, their definitional relations, and so on, become subject to a rigorous examination. Such examination is more difficult to conduct with respect to the "looser" concepts of less well formalized sciences. As we shall also see, in many of the cases in formalized physics, the relation of the theoretically posited structure to the observational facts from which it is inferred is particularly clear. In theories of space and time, for example, the very context of scientific theorizing presupposes quite definite notions of what is to be counted as "facts amenable to direct observational inspection," which are to provide the totality of evidential support for the theory. Thus questions whether the totality of such facts could uniquely pick out a single viable theoretical competitor, supporting it above all its rivals, are treated in an illuminating way, one not available in the general scientific context. In the latter context, there is neither a clear notion of the limits of observability nor a clear delimitation of the class of possible theoretical alternatives to be considered. If we explore such issues as eliminability or ineliminability of theoretical concepts or the degree to which theoretical choices are constrained by observational facts in the context of fundamental theories in physics, we have a way of dealing with these general methodological issues: we look at specific cases that provide a special sharpness to the philosophical questions. Insights gained in this more formalizable and delimited area can benefit those involved in the broader issues.

These considerations can be somewhat generalized. Philosophers concerned with general issues in metaphysics, epistemology, and the philosophy of language will find that exploring questions in these fields as the issues are instanced in the particular concrete cases of physical theory will throw light on the appropriate ways of dealing with the general questions. One cannot make much progress in understanding the specific structures of the partial physical theories without using the resources provided by those exploring the most general and fundamental issues in philosophy. What is more, one can't make clear progress in these more general areas without seeing how general methods and solutions fare when applied to specific cases. And the specific cases of the philosophical foundations of fundamental physical theory are, again, particularly well suited as test cases for general philosophical claims.

A final related matter should receive a moment's attention. One frequently finds in the literature very bold claims that contemporary physics has decisively resolved long-standing philosophical debates once and for all. "Quantum mechanics refutes the claim that all events have a cause," is a frequent example. Sometimes, perplexingly, both sides of a philosophical debate claim that a theory resolves an issue in their favor. Thus it has been argued that the general theory of relativity decisively resolves the question of the nature of space. But some argue that it refutes substantivalism, whereas others argue that it resolves the debate in favor of that doctrine! Such bold and unqualified claims are deceptive because the issues are complex and the arguments sometimes frustratingly subtle and opaque. Under such circumstances, claims of decisive victory of any kind should be treated with at least some skepticism.

We will have to take one special caution about philosophical conclusions derived from physical results. In an analogy to the GIGO Principle of computer science ("garbage in, garbage out"), we can call this the MIMO Principle: "metaphysics in, metaphysics out." There is no doubt that any philosophical claim must be reconciled with the best available results of physical science. Nor is there any doubt that the progress of science has provided a useful antidote to much dogmatism in philosophy. But in looking at what physics tells us about philosophical questions, we must always be careful to ask if philosophical presuppositions have been built into the theory itself. If we find that such presuppositions *have* been embedded in the theory itself, we must be prepared to examine carefully the question whether that way of presenting the theory is the only way in which its scientific results could have been accommodated or whether there could be other presuppositions that would lead us to derive quite different philosophical conclusions were the theory to embed them instead.

The Aim and Structure of This Book

Finally, I shall offer a few remarks about the aim and structure of this book. The thorough and systematic inquiry into any of the major problems in the philosophy of physics is a lengthy and difficult task. A mastery of the contents of the fundamental theories of contemporary physics requires a previous study of a large and difficult body of mathematics, as the theories are often framed in the powerful, abstract language of contemporary mathematics. Study of the special physical elements of the theories must be added to the mathematical background. On top of this, the philosophical inquiry requires a firm grounding in many aspects of contemporary analytical philosophy: metaphysics, epistemology, and the philosophy of language.

An attempt to do full justice to any of the central problems in the philosophy of physics in an introductory work such as this is obviously out of the question. The aim here, rather, is to provide the reader with a road map of the central problem areas in the field. The book focuses on what, in my view, appear to be the most important questions of philosophy of physics. Many other interesting topics will be barely touched upon, and some are skirted altogether, in the interest of directing as much attention as possible to the most crucial and central questions.

For the topics covered, I provide a sketch or outline of the main features of the physical theories that interact most crucially with philosophy. My hope is to offer a sufficiently concise and clear treatment of the issues to lead the interested reader through the sometimes labyrinthian paths taken by the central debates. Chapters 2, 3, and 4 are supplemented by an annotated guide to the literature. The reader interested in following up in detail the issues outlined in the text will find in these reference sections a guide to the basic background materials in mathematics, physics, and philosophy, as well as a guide to the most important contemporary discussions of the specific problem. The reference sections are not intended as an exhaustive survey of the literature on any of the subjects treated (a literature of sometimes vast extent) but, rather, as a selective guide to the materials most helpful in carrying the reader further in a systematic way.

Although I have attempted to include in the reference sections material accessible to those without an extensive background in mathematics and theoretical physics, I have not excluded material that does require background in these areas for its comprehension. Material requiring a rather modest background of this sort (say at the intermediate undergraduate level) is marked (*). Material requiring a more extensive familiarity with the technical concepts and methods is marked (**).

The three main areas we shall explore in this book are those of space and time, of probabilistic and statistical theories of the "classical" sort, and of quantum mechanics. This will allow us to survey many of the most perplexing and fundamental of the current problem areas in the philosophy of physics. One other major area will be treated only incidentally, although it introduces many extremely interesting issues of its own that have been only partially explored. This is the general theory of matter and its constitution as described by contemporary physics. Issues arising out of the postulation of the field as a basic element of the world, out of problems in the theory of the constitution of matter out of microconstituents in the hierarchy leading us down through molecules and atoms to elementary particles (and perhaps beyond), and out of the fundamental theory of the elementary particles themselves will be touched on only in passing as we deal with the three central problem areas noted above.

2

Space, Time, and Motion

**Traditional Philosophical Problems
of Space and Time**

Issues About Knowledge

The great philosophers of ancient Greece set themselves the problem of understanding what it is to have knowledge of the world. What, they asked, are the grounds and the limits of our ability to know what is really the case about the world around us? Not surprisingly, this enterprise of trying to distinguish genuine knowledge from mere opinion began with an examination of current beliefs of what could be considered by the ordinary rational person to constitute well-grounded knowledge.

Of course there were many particular common beliefs about the existence and nature of individual objects in the world encountered in daily life. But were there also *general* truths about the world that could also be known, truths about every object or feature of a given kind?

Some general truths seemed to be establishable by generalizing from everyday experience. Thus, it seemed, it could be inferred from observation that the seasons of the year would perpetually follow their usual round. That rocks fell, that fire rose, that living beings generated progeny and then after a process of maturation died, and countless other general truths were part of the common stock of beliefs. But critical reflection showed that observation, being subject to illusion and perceptual error, was often unreliable. And general beliefs inferred from experience were often found not to hold when later experience came in. Further, the truths inferred seemed to lack exactness and precision, except in such limited spheres of observational experience as that of astronomy, where a more perfect and perpetual regularity was observed than was found in experience of ordinary earthly things.

Nevertheless, in seeking for general truths about the fundamental structure of the world, the Greeks also had the theories of the great early speculative philosophers. Among the many grand general theories proposed were that all things are made up of a small number of basic substances; that change is to be explained by the rearrangement of unchanging atoms; that the world is fundamentally unchanging or, alternatively, that it is constantly in flux. But although these fundamental theories of the universe were exciting and profound, they seemed to lack the kind of evidential support that could convince a skeptic to accept them as true. Their proponents did, to be sure, argue for them, sometimes invoking crude general truths derived from observation, at other times citing claims that they could establish belief by the process of pure reasoning. But no doctrine received universal acceptance; that is, there was no doctrine that could be shown to be true by indisputable evidence.

And then there was geometry. Here one seemed to have available a body of assertions whose meaning was completely clear, assertions about the nature of the world that were exact and precise and that could be known to be true with certainty. Examples of such truths are that doubling the length of a side of a square multiplies its area by four, and that the square of the length of the hypotenuse of a right triangle is the sum of the squares of the lengths of the other two sides. These and the other claims of geometry had a clarity and certainty not present in any other kind of assertions about the world.

This certainty existed because propositions of geometry could be *proved*, a fact that had been discovered by the Greeks sometime before the great era of classical Greek philosophy. The propositions could be derived by purely logical reasoning from first principles, axioms, or postulates that seemed self-evidently true to the reasonable mind. The reasoning used was intuitively certain never to take one from a truth to a falsehood. One started with such obvious truths as that two points fixed one and only one straight line containing both of them and that equals added to equals gave equals. One could then, by a chain of reasoning in which each step was a transition from proposition to proposition that self-evidently took one from truths to truths, ultimately arrive at a conclusion whose truth was then warranted with certainty. These were the truths about the complex geometric structure of the world.

So impressive is this feature of geometry, its ability to give us knowledge of the structure of the world certified by undoubtable inference from undoubtable, simple, basic truths, that all other kinds of putative knowledge seemed to the philosophers at best a kind of second-rate knowledge. Knowledge based on the senses was subject to the familiar types of sensory error—misperception and illusion. And knowledge that arose by leaps of generalization from the particular data of sensation suffered a double liability, the possibility of sensory error and the possibility that our generalizing inferences might themselves lead us from truth to falsehood. Whereas the purely logical inferences that took us from basic postulates to geometric theorems seemed to have their truth-preservingness guaranteed by intuition, the rules for going beyond experience of the senses to general claims about nature seemed to have no such intuitively certified warrant.

For many, belief grounded on sensory observation and inference from it became merely a useful preliminary to the establishment of genuine knowledge by the "geometric" method. Philosophers long held out the ideal that if only we were smart enough we could eventually construct an edifice of knowledge encompassing all fields of inquiry, the physics of nature, the psychology of mind, even the basic principles of morality governing the truths of good and bad and right and wrong, by discovering in all these fields their self-evidently true first principles that paralleled the axioms of geometry. We could then derive from these first principles the full range of truths in each area, just as the theorems of geometry follow by logic alone from the basic geometric postulates.

With the ever-increasing role played by observation and experiment in grounding the science that arose after the Scientific Revolution, and with the inability to frame a "geometry" of nature and morality, people became skeptical about the appropriateness of the geometric model for the structure of scientific knowledge. Instead, models of knowledge based upon observation and generalization from it became more appealing, at least to most philosophers.

David Hume suggested that there could, in fact, be no genuine knowledge of the world founded on intuitive self-evidence and logical derivation. Such infallible knowledge, he suggested, could only be knowledge of "empty" propositions, propositions true by the definitions of their terms alone (such as the proposition that every bachelor is unmarried). All genuine contentful propositions could be known, if at all, only by reliance upon the senses and by the generalizing from them that led us to beliefs in causal relationships in the world. In particular, Hume denied the very possibility of metaphysics, the branch of philosophy concerned with establishing deep and general truths about the nature of the world on the basis of pure reasoning alone.

Immanuel Kant's response to Hume was especially important. Although agreeing with Hume's skeptical rejection of most of traditional metaphysics, Kant reserved a small portion of it as consisting of genuinely contentful assertions established without reference to observation or experiment. That such contentful truths could be known by pure reason, he argued, was shown to us by the existence of the two branches of pure mathematical truth, geometry and arithmetic. Both disciplines consisted of truths that no rational person could doubt and that had been established by pure reason alone. Yet the truths of these disciplines, he thought, were plainly not of the "empty" sort. It is not part of the meaning of 'triangle' that the sum of the interior angles of a triangle is 180° in the same way that it is part of the meaning of 'bachelor' that a bachelor is unmarried.

Kant held that such contentful truths establishable by reason existed because they reflected the structure of the perceiving and cognitive apparatus of our minds with which we grasped the nature of the world. He said that a limited portion of traditional metaphysics, including such assertions as "every event has a cause," shared with geometry and arithmetic this nature of having genuine content yet being knowable without reliance on observation and experiment. What is important for our purposes about his general claims is the role played by geometry in them. Even if the hope of a physics, psychology, or ethics founded upon pure reasoning is vain, doesn't the theory of space—geometry—remain, along with arithmetic, as a body of knowledge not founded on generalization from the particular observed facts given us by the senses?

Many attempted in the years after Kant to justify Hume's contention that all the assertions that made genuinely informative statements about the world could be shown to be correct only by confronting them with the data of observational experience. The problematic status of geometry and arithmetic received a good deal of attention, for if Hume was right, the mathematical disciplines may be about the world or may be known by pure reason, but not both. Some tried to show that those disciplines could retain their status of knowability without reference to observational experience, but only because they were free of genuinely informative content. Various attempts to show that mathematical truth was the result of pure logic, combined with the definition of the mathematical terms in the purely logical vocabulary, were motivated in this way.

Others sought instead to retain the genuinely informative content of the mathematical sciences, but to reject the Kantian claim that they could be established by any kind of pure reasoning process that made them, unlike the ordinary sciences, immune to confrontation with observation as the ultimate test of their believability. J. S. Mill, for example, argued that even the propositions of arithmetic were established by the process of generalizing from the results of particular observations. It might appear that the basic laws of arithmetic had a kind of self-warranting certainty. But this was an illusion. We derive the laws of arithmetic from our sensory experience. This experience, however, is so familiar and so pervasive that we are misled into thinking that the arithmetic laws require no empirical confirmation at all. In fact, Mill thought, like the laws of physics and chemistry, the laws of arithmetic could only be established by generalizing from empirical experience.

Certain theorists of knowledge reflected on the way our beliefs form a complex network of assertions, some of which are invoked whenever the reasonableness of believing some of the others are in question. They also noted the degree to which our beliefs must be grounded on principles of inference, such as accepting as reasonable the simplest theory we can imagine consonant with the empirically relevant data. The theorists also argued that these principles seem intelligible and justifiable only if one assumes an already existing set of beliefs that remain un-challenged for the moment. They were skeptical of the usefulness of any rigid distinction between propositions knowable by pure reason and those knowable only by reliance upon experiential data. Indeed, many were skeptical of the possibility of sorting our beliefs, as Hume wished to do, into two groups: those that are true by convention (or by definition or by mere meanings of terms) and those with genuine informative content.

From this perspective, all our beliefs are part of a seamless web of theoretical belief. Each proposition contains elements of convention and elements of factuality. According to these philosophers, each proposition confronts sensory experience only when it is conjoined with a wide body of accepted beliefs. Only as part of a general theoretical structure can a proposition be tested by experience or confirmed by it. It is this body of accepted belief, they claimed, that grounds our principles of legitimate scientific inference.

It won't be our task in this book to explore the options in any depth. Instead we will later explore the impact of changes in the place of geometry in mathematics and in physics that influenced and were influenced by the more general problem of the grounds of legitimate scientific belief. We have already noted that the early existence of geometry as the ideal body of truly scientific knowledge of the world led many philosophers to limit genuine knowledge to that which could be established by impeccable logical derivation from self-evident and indubitable first postulates. Mathematicians' discovery and exploration of alternatives to the familiar Euclidean geometry, which had reigned as the unique mathematical geometry for many centuries, and their later application of the newly discovered alternative geometries to physical theories intended to describe the real world were key influences on philosophers who sought to come to grips with the issues posed by the conflict between Kant and Hume and carried on by others. These were the issues concerning the ultimate ground of our scientific belief about the world and the degree to which that belief was responsible to the particular evidential data of observation and experiment.

Issues About the Nature of Reality

Geometry is the descriptive science of space. But what sort of thing is space? Or rather, how can we fit the spatiality of the world into our overall conception of what sorts of things and properties exist? It is clear that spatiality is one of the most general and fundamental aspects of the world as we experience it and as we construct its nature by inference from that experience. In our ordinary language and practice, we are perfectly happy to use such spatial notions such as distance, spatial containment, and continuity and discontinuity in space when we deal with important structures governing the behavior of the material world about us. But when we try to reflect on what space is in and of itself we find ourselves puzzled.

Perhaps what comes to mind first is that space is some sort of "container" of the matter of the world. We think of all things as existing in space, indeed, in one and the same overall space, which contains all the material things of the world. But even this notion of containment is perplexing, for it seems that space contains objects by virtue of the objects' spatially coinciding with pieces of space itself. An object takes up a portion of space in which it resides. This certainly is a different kind of containment from that of, say, an object's being contained in a box.

The natural idea occurs to us that we can imagine a world devoid of all the material things but still having a kind of reality. It would be empty space waiting to be filled, or partially filled, with bits of matter. This idea of space as a kind of entity, the permanent and unchanging container of ordinary material things that can come into being and pass out of being and can change in their natures, is probably present in Plato's talk in the *Timeaus* about space as the "receptacle" of material being.

But what kind of peculiar thing or stuff is this ghostly entity, space itself? We certainly feel entitled to talk of "the empty space between the stars" or even to imagine the totally empty space of a world in which all matter was somehow magically destroyed. But what sort of thing is this stuff we want to call "empty space"? Is it a single particular object of which spaces like the space in a room are parts, just as a piece of bread is a part of the whole loaf? This thing, space, has features, for example, the features of it described by the truths of geometry. However, our intuitions tell us that space itself is too unlike ordinary matter, too insubstantial, to really count as a thing in the world, along with the ordinary things that are in space. But how else can we view the matter?

Aristotle spoke of "place." It is hard to decipher exactly what he had in mind, but it seems as though he thought of place as the bound or limit of a piece of matter. Motion is change of place, as an object changes one limiting surface of itself for another. But does this mean that space is some additional thing over and above the matter in it? One senses that Aristotle is trying to avoid that conclusion but is at a loss as to what conceptual scheme to put in its place. Soon we shall look at the main attempt by later philosophers to find a conceptual scheme that would do justice to the claims we wish to make about objects being in space, having a place, being able to change place, and so on, and also do justice to such intuitive notions as the possibility of space unoccupied by matter. That later proposal will also try to avoid the felt outrageousness of thinking of space as some additional component of being that can have a reality independent of the very existence of the matter in it.

If space perplexes us, time puzzles us even more. Once again our intuition tells us that all that happens in the world happens in time. Although we sometimes think that our subjective mental states might not be in space (where, for example, are thoughts located?), we think that even our thoughts must occur at some moment in time. We have the intuition that there is a single time in which all that happens happens, any extended process taking up some portion of the overall time of the world. Something like the container aspect of space seems to be true of time as well. Processes occupying time have their times coincide with moments of "time itself." And, we think, it is possible for us to imagine stretches of time in which no material happenings occur. Can't we imagine a world in which all matter and its transformations vanished, but in which time would go on as it always had?

But if it is peculiar to think of space as a "thing," how much more peculiar it is to think of time as an "entity" in the ordinary sense. Yet if there can be a going on of time even if matter ceased to exist, must we not credit time with some kind of being independent of the existence of the ordinary things of the world and their ordinary changes in time?

Other connections of temporality and being leave us even more perplexed. We seem to think the very existence of ordinary things is tied up with time in a way it is not tied up with space. If something existed in the past but doesn't exist now, we think of it as not, properly speaking, existing at all. And the same is true of future objects, which don't yet exist. But as St. Augustine pointed out, the present is a vanishingly small moment of time, leaving us to wonder how things can, given their temporal nature, properly be said to have any existence at all. In contrast to space, time seems to have an asymmetric aspect. Past and future seem very different to us, with the past as a fixed, if vanished, reality, but the future as something with, perhaps, no determinate kind of being at all until it occurs.

Other features of the temporality of things so puzzled the ancient philosophers that some became completely skeptical of the reality of time and its concomitant change. Zeno of Elea posed arguments trying to show that the ordinary notions of time were fraught with contradictoriness. How could there be such a thing as motion, for example, if at any particular moment an object was at rest in the space it occupied at that moment? It happens that some of Zeno's arguments purporting to reveal inner contradictions in the very notions of time and motion would now be judged to be fallacious. However, the quandaries he brought up in other arguments still provide a fruitful starting point to discussions concerning such matters as the correct conceptual schemes for dealing with the notion of space and time as continua and with the concept of motion. Rich achievements in philosophy and the development of the correct mathematics for dealing with motion have been inspired by attempts to solve the puzzles posed by Zeno.

Once again Aristotle strikes the modern reader as insightful, even if, from the modern perspective, what he has to say can be interpreted in a multiplicity of ways. Aristotle thinks of time as something distinct from the motion or change of material things, just as space cannot be identified with the objects in it. Yet, he points out, without motion or change, we would have no awareness of the passage of time. So in a manner parallel to his notion of place as the spatiality of bodies, distinct from the body but not existing as an independent entity apart from the bodies in the world, he speaks of time as a measure of motion and change. But it remains unclear just what time is, then, supposed to be. It is something that depends upon things and their motions and changes, yet it is not those motions and changes themselves. What then is it?

Underlying much of the puzzlement about the nature of space and time is their double role in providing an arena both for the play of physical phenomena and for the contents of what we intuitively take to be our own subjective or private awareness. Philosophers frequently argued that whereas physical objects and their processes took place in space and time, the mental contents of our minds existed only in time. Yet we feel that some spatial mode is appropriate even for describing, say, the visual contents of our dreams. The dream cat and the dream mat may be unreal as genuine objects, but the dream cat may very well appear to us as on the mat, in a manner that we feel is at least like the way a real cat can be on a real mat. So spatiality of some sort seems to be an aspect even of our mental phantasms.

Surely, moreover, the events of our dreams occur in a time order, even if we are convinced that it is an order in time of unreal happenings. Yet, again, there seem to be some differences between the space of the mental and its temporality. The space in which the dream cat and mat exist seems "nowhere" as far as real space is concerned. It seems to be a kind of space disjoint from the space of physical things. Yet the dream processes seem to us to occur in the same time as the time that encompasses physical events. My dream of the car crash occurred after I went to sleep and before I awoke, in the same time order that my lying in bed occurred. Yet the space of the illusory car crash can't be fitted into any real place at all, even the real space in my head where the mechanism of my dreaming, my brain, is located.

As we shall see, there is no easy solution to the problem of putting into one coherent scheme a model of the nature of time and space that will do justice to the intuitions we have just surveyed. Our account should explain in what the nature of space and time consists. What kind of being do they have, and how is their being related to that of the more ordinary things and processes that occupy space and take place in time? How does this nature of space and time do justice to our intuitions about the spatiality and temporality of both the physical happenings of the world and the contents of our subjective experience? Finally, what is it about the nature of space and time that gives us access to the knowledge we claim to have about its nature, a kind of knowledge that was thought by some to be the very model of the certainty we could have about the world generated by our pure reason alone?

The Debate Between Newton and Leibniz

In the seventeenth century, the philosophy of space and time became a central issue of metaphysics and epistemology. The discussion reached a high point in the important debate between G. W. von Leibniz, the great German philosopher-mathematician, and Newton, the great English physicist-mathematician. In their debate, two opposing theories of the place of space and time in the world were delineated, and many of the fundamental questions that in later years exercised philosophers concerned with space and time received their clearest formulation.

Leibniz offered an account of space and time that at last presented a clear understanding of how the theory could, in an Aristotelian vein, deny space and time a kind of independent being over and above the being of ordinary material things and material happenings but could retain for space and time a crucial place in the structure of the world. In Leibniz's "deep" philosophy, his true metaphysics, the existence per se of matter, as well as that of space and time, is denied. In this esoteric Leibniz, the world is constituted of mindlike fundamental entities, monads, that exist in total isolation from one another, not even interacting by means of causation. Each monad contains within its nature a full picture of the entire universe, which explains how, without interaction, they can show coherent evolution in time. We must leave to the side this "deep" Leibnizian view of the world, which is strange but argued for in ingenious and important ways. His less profound, exoteric, view on space and time has a kind of intermediate status between the view that matter, space, and time all exist and the final monadological view.

In this intermediate position, the existence of material objects and material events may be assumed. What then are time and space? Consider any two events, thought of as instantaneous happenings among the material things. The events have a temporal relation to one another, the first event being after, simultaneous with, or before the second event in time. We can go beyond this to a quantitative relation among the events, the first event being separated in time from the second by some definite time interval, which might be positive, zero, or negative. Leibniz's simple idea is that time just is the collection of all such temporal *relations* among events. Were there no events, there would be no relations, so time in that sense has no existence independent of the events in it. Yet the relations among the events are a real component of the world (in this exoteric perspective). Thus it would also be misleading to say that there is no such thing as time at all.

If we consider all the things of the world at a single time, we see spatial relations among them. They are at certain distances from one another and in certain directions from one another. The collection of all these spatial relations among the objects of the world at a time is what space is. Once again, there is no container, no space itself, waiting to be occupied by the objects. There just are the objects and the innumerable spatial relations they bear to one another.

The analogy with familial relations may make this clearer. Any extended family consists of a number of people. They are related to one another in the familiar ways. *A* might be the father of *B*, *C* the first cousin of *D*, and so on. What is the "stuff" of reality in an extended family? Answer: the people in the family. But of course, the relations these people bear to one another are perfectly real aspects of the world. Could we, though, think of the relations as existing independent of the people? Could there be a kind of "relational space" that exists in and of itself and waits to be occupied by people? Such talk is manifestly absurd. Well, says Leibniz, just as it is with "relational space," so is it with ordinary space. There are things and there are spatial relations among them. But there is no independently existing container thing, space itself, anymore than there is an independently existing thing, "relational space."

Every event that happens in the material or mental world is related in time to every other event. And every material object is spatially related to every other material object. These two families of relations, then, encompass all of reality. But they exist as a collection of relations among the substantial events and things of the world, not as independent substances themselves.

Alas, it isn't that easy. What about moments of time when nothing happens? What about unoccupied regions of space where nothing is located? Should we just deny their reality? Leibniz suggests a means whereby we can hold on to these notions as legitimate and yet remain relationists. Consider the empty space between here and a star. There is nothing that bears the spatial relationship to us of being halfway between us and the star. Yet something *could* have that spatial relationship to us and to the star. So we might think, then, of unoccupied places as spatial relations that something *might* have to the objects of the world but that nothing actually does have. Space is, Leibniz says, "as to possibility," the set of spatial relations among things. So the family of relations contains possible as well as actual spatial relations. We might even think of restoring the notion of totally empty space in this way. Even if there were no actual objects, there could be objects, and if there were, they would bear spatial relations to one another. So totally empty space, which the antirelationist thinks an intelligible notion, might become, for the relationist, the collection of possible (but not actual) relations that possible (but not actual) material objects could bear to one another if such objects existed. Whether tolerating such "relations in possibility" is giving the game away to the antirelationist remains a matter of philosophical debate.

Leibniz does not merely propose his relationist account of space and time dogmatically as an alternative to the view that space and time are some kind of independently existing things. The container view seems to look upon space as kind of substance. Things exist in space, on this view, by coinciding with a limited piece of the spatial substance. But, Leibniz argues, such a view is fraught with difficulties.

Imagine empty space existing and God's trying to decide where to place the material universe in space. There is no reason for putting the universe in one location rather than another. Because every point or region of "space itself" is like every other point or region, there could be no ground for choosing one location for the material world over another. But, Leibniz believes, every fact must have a sufficient reason for being the case. Because location in space itself of the material universe cannot have such a sufficient reason, there can be no such thing. But the view of space as container, and not as mere set of spatial relations among things, entails the existence of location in space itself. Therefore such a container space cannot exist.

He further argues that there would be no observational difference between the material world's being located at one place in space itself rather than another but maintains that such a fact (location in space itself) with no observational consequences is not really a fact at all. Indeed, using the principle that one possible world that is exactly like another possible world in all its features must be the same possible world, he argues that the very notion of space itself is incoherent. If space itself existed, there could be two possible worlds exactly alike, except for a different location in space itself of the material world in each such possible world. But such difference in location in space itself is no real difference at all. So there cannot be two such possible worlds. Therefore, the theory of space itself as container, which implies that there could be two such possible worlds, must be wrong.

The Leibnizian relationist position is, then, that viewing space as a thing in its own right leads to incoherency. Further, viewing it as the collection of all spatial relations among material things allows us to say all we need to say that is coherent about the spatiality of the world. So it is this relationist account we should adopt. And a similar view of time as the family of temporal relations among material events is alleged to do away with any talk of "time itself" as some constituent entity of the world.

But there are straightforwardly philosophical objections to relationism, especially to the sort that invokes possible relations. For the relationist, the structure of space, as revealed by geometry, is the structure of the collection of all possible spatial relations among objects. But what is the "ground" of this structure of possibilities? By this I mean the following: If we think of most physical possibilities, they are understandable only because of some underlying actual structure. A piece of salt, for example, is, even if not dissolved, possessed of the "possibility" of going into solution. It is, we say, soluble. But this solubility rests upon the piece of undissolved salt having an actual constitution out of ions. In the case of the structure of space itself, which the relationist takes to be the structure that describes the collection of all possible spatial relations, what is the underlying reality that grounds this order among possibilities, if it is not the structure of "space itself" as the antirelationist envisions it?

Leibniz's opponent, the great physicist Newton, was an antirelationist. Newton takes space and time to be something more than mere spatial and temporal relations among material objects and events. What, exactly, it was, he wasn't sure. He considers it something like a substance, but in places prefers to think of it as an attribute or property, in fact a property of God. Although he offers some purely philosophical arguments against Leibnizian relationism, he is most famous for arguing that the results of observation and experiment can conclusively refute the relationist doctrine.

In the physics developed by Newton from the earlier work of Galileo and others, there is a clear contrast between inertial motions and noninertial motions. Inertial motions are taken to be motions of an object with a constant velocity, that is, with an unchanging speed and in a fixed direction. Now for a relationist such notions as "unchanging speed" and "fixed direction" can be understood only relative to a framework fixed by some material objects. Something at rest relative to the earth's surface, for example, is in rapid motion in a constantly changing direction relative to a reference frame fixed, say, in the sun. But, Newton argues, the notion of noninertial motion is not that of some "merely relative" motion, but of a motion that is "absolute."

Why? Noninertial motions generate "forces" that reveal themselves in demonstrable effects. Water in a spinning bucket sloshes over the side of the bucket. Passengers lurch forward or backward as a train accelerates or brakes to a halt. If two trains are in relative acceleration, the passengers in one train might feel the acceleration while those in the other might feel nothing at all. For example, one train may be at rest in the station while the other is rapidly braking. Yet the trains are both accelerating relative to each other. The only explanation there can be for the asymmetry between the trains is that there is an "absolute" acceleration, acceleration that is change of velocity not merely relative to some arbitrary material reference frame.

Newton argues that such inertial effects will be everywhere and at every time the same throughout the universe. After all, it is just such inertial effects that, for example, keep the planets from falling into the sun. So acceleration, absolute acceleration, generates observable effects. But acceleration, even absolute acceleration, is acceleration relative to *something*. If it cannot be understood as acceleration relative to the ordinary material objects of the world, it can only be understood as acceleration relative to "space itself." So space itself is not merely the "container" of objects, perhaps a clumsy way of referring to the fact that material things are spatially related to one another. It is an object that enters into a causal relation with material objects. Just as relative motion of brick and window causes the brick to shatter the window, so relative acceleration of passengers and space itself reveals itself in the inertial forces generated as a result of that relative motion.

Although time is less plausibly thought of as some kind of "object" than is space itself, it must, according to Newton, be also absolute in an important sense. For the relationist, the measure of the lapse of time is some change or motion in a material thing. Relative to one clock, a process might be regular, with some event recurring in equal time intervals. Relative to some other chosen clock, however, the same process might appear irregular. This will be the case unless the second clock is "regular" by the first clock's standards. For the relationist, there is no "absolute" measure of lapse of time, merely the choice of some clocks as preferred for the simplicity of our description of the world in their measure of time. Now accelerated motion gives rise to effects that nonaccelerated motion does not. And this acceleration is absolute. But accelerated motion in a straight line can be represented as unaccelerated if a peculiar enough measure of time is chosen, one that makes the speed appear uniform by speeding up and slowing down the time measure in conformity to the objects' changing speed. But real acceleration is absolute, so the measure of time must be absolute as well. There is a time "in itself," which "flows uniformly irrespective of the measure of particular clocks." Good clocks conform to this absolute time; poor clocks do not.

We have in Newton, then, a new element introduced into the old philosophical debate between those who would take space and time as autonomous constituents of the world and those who would take them to be merely the compendia of collections of relations among the fundamental things of the world, material objects and their changes. For the Newtonian, space and time are posited theoretical elements whose existence must be presupposed in order to explain phenomena available to us at the experimental-observational level.

Reactions to Newton's transformation of the old philosophical debate were many and varied over the two centuries following his arguments. Early proposals that tried to find an explanation for the Newtonian phenomena and that posited only the relationists' material things and their relations to one another floundered. Even Leibniz admitted that a notion of "which object is moved" in relative motions was essential. He sought for an explanation for the distinction in the object on which the cause of motion acted.

It was realized quite quickly that Newton's doctrine had peculiar consequences. Because "space itself" existed, the position of an object in space itself and the uniform motion of an object with respect to space itself were real features of the world, even though they, unlike the acceleration of the object with respect to space itself, gave rise to no observational phenomena. Some results of physics suggested that absolute uniform motion might entail phenomena of an optical, rather than a mechanical, sort, being detectable; as we shall see, these conclusions proved misguided. Later proposals, coming after the innovations in our thinking about space and time inspired by relativity theory, posited notions of space and time that would allow absolute acceleration to be defined, whereas absolute spatial position and velocity were not.

In the nineteenth century, the physicist-philosopher E. Mach tried, once again, to reconcile the results of Newtonian physics with the relationist approach to space and time. He noted the important fact that the rotation rate of the earth, determined by observing the fixed stars, and the absolute rate of rotation of the earth, determined by purely mechanical experiments that relied on the forces generated by rotation, were the same. Might this suggest an origin for the inertial forces, one not imagined by Newton? Suppose the acceleration of one material object with respect to another generates forces, just as the relative velocity of two charged particles generates a magnetic interaction. Suppose this force is highly independent of the separation of the objects, but dependent on their masses. Might not the forces generated by accelerations, which Newton credited to the causal interaction of test object and space itself, be credited instead to the relative acceleration of the test object with respect to the fixed stars or, more appropriately, with respect to the average "smeared out" remaining matter of the universe? If this were so, might not we be able to reconcile the observational facts Newton used to argue for the existence of a kind of substantival space with a Leibnizian relationism that took all positions, velocities, and accelerations to be these features of one material thing relative to some other material thing?

At the end of the nineteenth century, then, the situation was more or less like this: Everyone agreed that there were two broad dimensions to reality—all material things existing in space and all happenings, material or mental, taking place in time. The structure of these arenas of the world was known. Time could be viewed as being a simple one-dimensional continuum. Space was a three-dimensional structure described by the familiar Euclidean geometry. It seemed that we could know this structure by inferring it from first principles, whose truth was, in some sense, indisputable, that is, whose truth was given to the rational person by some kind of pure reason. The nature of these containers of all things and happenings was, from a philosophical perspective, unclear. Substantivalists in the Newtonian mold contended with relationists following out the ideas of Leibniz. Others, such as the philosopher Kant, who thought that space and time were organizing structures of the mind by which we put sensation in a comprehensible format, held different metaphysical views.

Space and time could be mathematically described, as could the motion of material things in space as time went on. The lawlike characterization of this motion in terms of kinematics (the description of motion) and dynamics (its explanation in terms of forces) constituted the central discipline of physics. One aspect of this physical theory was the necessity in it of distinguishing the preferred classes of inertial motion from accelerated motions that generated inertial forces. This provided the core of the Newtonian scientific argument of the substantivalist view of the nature of space.

Whereas acceleration with respect to space itself had observable consequences, position in space itself and uniform velocity with respect to space itself had no such observational concomitants. But there was hope that, by means of optical phenomena, the state of rest in space itself could be determined. The attempt to determine the state of rest with respect to space itself by means of experiments with light is what led to the astonishing revisions of our ideas of space and time, through the work of the great physicist Albert Einstein. The possibility of further purely philosophical insights into the nature of space and time had existed prior to his work, but it was in the light of his accomplishments and with the insights provided by them that the bulk of contemporary philosophy of space and time was explored. In "From Space and Time to Spacetime" and "Gravity and the Curvature of Spacetime" I will outline the novel theories of space and time he proposed and then return to the philosophy of space and time in the context of these new physical theories.

From Space and Time to Spacetime

The Origins of the Special Theory of Relativity

We have seen that whereas Newton posited "space itself" as the reference object relative to which accelerations generated observable inertial forces, uniform motion with respect to space itself was deemed to have no observable consequences. This followed from Galileo's famous observation that in an enclosed laboratory, one could not tell which state of uniform motion the laboratory was in by performing any mechanical experiment. But it remained conceivable that some other, non-mechanical, phenomena would depend upon the uniform motion of the apparatus with respect to space itself in some way. This motion would then reveal itself in an observational consequence.

In the nineteenth century, hope for this came out of the reduction of light to electromagnetic radiation. According to J. C. Maxwell's theory of electricity and magnetism, electromagnetic waves, of which light waves are a species, are predicted to have a definite velocity with respect to an observer. This velocity should be the same in all directions and independent of the velocity of the source of the light with respect to the observer. An observer at rest in a tank of water will determine a speed of sound in the water that is the same in each direction. This speed of sound will be completely independent of the motion of the source of the sound in the water. Once the water wave is generated, its speed depends only on the properties of the water in which the wave is traveling. So it should be for light, with the medium of transmission of light (the stuff that is for light as water is for the sound) called the "aether."

An observer who himself moves through the water in the tank will not see the speed of sound the same in all directions, as he will be catching up to the sound in one direction and running away from it in the opposite direction. So an observer in motion with respect to the aether should be able to detect this motion, even if it is uniform, un-accelerated motion, by measuring the velocity of light in all directions. If we assume that an observer at rest in the aether will be at rest in one of the inertial frames of mechanics in which no mechanical, inertial forces are generated, it becomes plausible to identify the aether with Newton's space itself. The assumption was always made in the nineteenth century, and in a reinterpreted version, it remains correct in relativity theory. We could then use experiments with light to determine our uniform motion with respect to space itself.

An ingenious series of experiments was designed to detect which state of uniform motion was the state at rest in the aether or in space itself. These worked by sending light out from a point along different paths and then bringing the light back to its point of origin. The light should take different amounts of time to traverse the different paths, depending on the length of the paths and on the state of motion of the apparatus in the aether. Changing the orientation of the apparatus, or letting the motion of the earth do that for us as the earth rotated on its axis and traveled in its orbit around the sun, would change the relative times taken by the light to travel the different paths. Such a change in times could be detected at the origin of the light by an observer, who would see a shift in the position of the interference lines, alternating lines of light and darkness that are generated when the two returning beams of light meet and have regions of varying intensity add or subtract from one another. (See Figure 2.1.)

When the experiments were performed, much to the astonishment of those performing them, no detectable difference in travel times for the light could be discerned. It was as if the light traveled with the same fixed speed, the speed predicted for light by the theory in the rest frame in the aether, in every laboratory frame that was in uniform motion. (These "null results" don't hold, incidentally, when the apparatus is in nonuniform motion. Rotation can be detected, for example, by a ring laser gyro, which detects the change in speed of light in opposite directions around a circular path as the laboratory rotates.) Now it might seem that this surprising null result might be due to some peculiarity of light or electromagnetism. If one thinks about why the speed of the signal should vary when the laboratory in motion with respect to the medium of transmission of the signal, however, one quickly sees that a very fundamental intuition about motion is being challenged here. That intuition is that, for example, if we run after a moving thing, it will be moving more slowly with respect to us than it will be to someone who didn't join in the chase.

One could try to explain away the surprising results in a number of ways. One suggestion was that the earth in its motion dragged the local

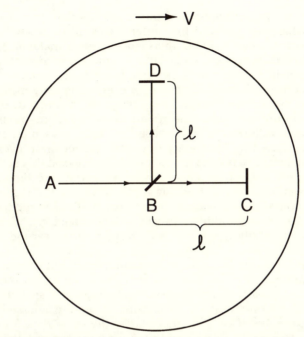

Figure 2.1 The Michelson-Morley experiment. A beam of light is split into two beams at the half-silvered mirror *B*. One beam goes to mirror *C* and is reflected, the other to mirror *D*. If the apparatus is moving through the aether, the medium of transmission of light hypothesized by the older wave theory, in the direction shown by arrow *v*, the light should take longer to travel path *BCB* of length *l* than it does to travel path *BDB*, also of length *l*. If the apparatus is then rotated 90 degrees, the difference in time along the paths is reversed. But no such change is detected when the experiment is carried out. This remains true even if the path length *BC* is made different from length *BD*. In general no round-trip experiment reveals motion through the aether of the laboratory.

aether with it, so that the portion of aether near the earth was always at rest with respect to the earth and the apparatus. Such a claim would, however, result in conflict with well-established astronomical observations.

A series of compensatory theories were invented to explain the unexpected null results. If we assume that the apparatus shrinks in its length in its direction of motion with respect to the aether, and further assume that all physical processes measured by apparatus clocks slow down when these clocks are put in motion with respect to the aether, one could then explain away as appearance the seeming sameness of speed of light in all directions. Although the light actually was moving at different speeds with respect to the apparatus in different directions, the observational consequences expected from this were exactly canceled out by the changes induced (by the motion of the apparatus through the aether) on the components of the apparatus that one used to determine speeds—lengths and time intervals as measured by rods and clocks. The net result would be, then, once more to make uniform motion with respect to space undetectable by any experimental means!

It was Einstein's brilliant suggestion to take the appearance that light has the same velocity in all directions in every uniformly moving state of motion as indicative of reality. Why not posit, he argued, that what appears to be the case from the round-trip experiments really is the case? For each uniformly moving observer, light in vacuum travels at the speed predicted by the theory of electromagnetism in every direction. It is important to note just how radical a proposal this is. If a light beam is moving away from an observer in a given direction at speed c, and a second observer is traveling in the direction of the propagated light with, say, speed v, with respect to the first observer, we take it to be the case that the light is traveling with speed c, and not with speed $c - v$ as intuition tells us, with respect to the second observer as well.

How could this be? The core of Einstein's argument is an insightful critique of the notion of simultaneity for events at a distance from one another. What does it mean for two happenings at a spatial distance from each other to occur at the same time? In pre-Einsteinian thought, we just assume that if two events occur at the same time for one observer, they will occur at the same time for all observers. It is a challenge to this last notion that provides the main difference between space and time as earlier understood and spacetime as understood in Einstein's so-called special theory of relativity.

Einstein argues that if we are to determine the speed of light in a given direction, we might think to get around the null results of the round-trip experiments by directly measuring the speed of light from one point, A, to another, B. But we could only do this if we could determine the distance between the points and the time taken by the light to get from A to B, speed being the distance divided by the time. But to get the time interval between emission and reception of a light signal requires that we be able to synchronize clocks at the two points so that they read "zero" at the same moment. How could this synchronization be done?

If we could transport a clock instantaneously from A to B, we could establish synchronization by synchronizing two clocks at A and instantly shifting one to B. But, Einstein assumes, objects cannot be transported from one place to another in no time at all. He assumes, in fact, that the speed of light in a vacuum is a limiting speed faster than which nothing can travel. Well then, why not synchronize two clocks at A, move one at some speed or other to B, and assume that when a clock at A reads value n and the clock at B reads n the two events are simultaneous?

At this point we must remember the point of trying to establish simultaneity for distant events. We wanted to do this so that we could determine the speed of light from *A* to *B*. And we wanted to do that so that we could get around the problem of the round-trip experiments' giving null results, a phenomenon explained by combining the idea that the light had different speeds in the different directions with the compensatory claims about how rods shrink and clocks slow down when moving with respect to the aether. Remember that the point of the round-trip experiments in the first place was to determine in which state of motion the speed of light was really the same in all directions in order to determine which state of motion really was at rest in the aether or in space itself.

But if the compensatory theory is correct, clocks transported from *A* to *B* won't, in general, be synchronized at *B* even if they were at *A*. For when in motion from *A* to *B*, they will, in general, be traveling at different speeds with respect to the aether and, hence, suffering different amounts of "slowing down." Clearly, the right clock to use to determine synchronization of clocks at *A* and *B* will be one moved very slowly with respect to the aether and hence suffering minimal distortion as it is moved. But to know which clock that is, we would have to know which state of motion was the rest state in the aether, which is what we were trying to determine in the first place!

Suppose we knew which state of motion was at rest in the aether. Because light, relative to the aether, travels with the same speed in all directions, an easy way to synchronize clocks at *A* and *B* would be to send a light signal from *A* that was reflected at *B* and returned to *A*. As the light took the same time to get from *A* to *B* and from *B* to *A*, the event at *A* simultaneous with the reflection at *B* could be taken to be the event at *A* midway in time between the emission and reception of the light signal at *A* as determined by a clock at rest at *A*. But, says Einstein, as far as the round-trip experiments go, it is as if light had this same speed in all directions no matter what is the uniform state of motion of the observer. Assume light really does travel at the same speed relative to any observer in uniform motion. Then each such observer can use the reflected-light method to determine which events take place at the same time as which other events.

It is easy to see that taking this as our definition of simultaneity for distant events will result in observers' disagreeing about *which* pairs of events take place at the same time, as can be seen from Figure 2.2 and its explanation. Well, which observer is *right* in his attributions of simultaneity? According to the aether theory, only the observer at rest in the aether. The others are being deceived by their taking light to travel at the same speed in all directions relative to their laboratories, when it really does not. According to Einstein, all the observers are correct in their attributions of simultaneity. It is just that there is no such thing as "occurring at the same time," only "occurring at the same time *relative* to a particular state of uniform motion." We can reconcile the null results of the round-trip experiments with the Galilean assumption that all uniformly moving observers see the same physical

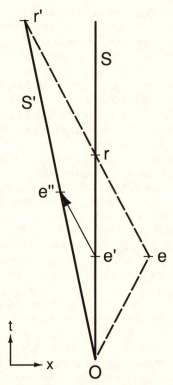

Figure 2.2   The Einstein simultaneity definition and the relativity of simultaneity.
OS represents the events in the life history of one observer, an observer who stays
at a constant *x* position as time, *t*, goes on. *OS'* the life history of another observer
moving (relative to *OS*) to the left. Because *e'* is halfway in time from *O* to *r*, the
events of emitting and receiving a light beam reflected at event *e*, *S*, taking the speed
of light to be the same toward and back from *e*, takes *e'* to be simultaneous with *e*.
S', reasoning similarly, takes *e"* to be simultaneous with *e* because it is halfway in
time from *O* to *r'*. Yet because a causal signal can leave *e'* and arrive at *e"*, both *S*
and *S'* agree that *e'* and *e"* cannot be simultaneous. In relativity, events are or are
not simultaneous only relative to a chosen "inertial frame of motion" like that of *S*
or that of *S'*.

phenomena by simply dropping the intuitive notion that there is an
absolute, nonrelative notion of "occurring at the same time."

We can mitigate some of the strangeness of this conclusion if we look
at the concept of "being in the same place." Imagine two observers in
motion with respect to one another. The first observer is hit on the
head at two different times. Did the blows occur "at the same place"?
"Yes," says the struck observer, "they both occurred in the place where
the top of my head was located." "No," says the other observer, "one
occurred near to me and the other far away." Which claim is correct?
Unless one believes in Newton's "space itself," relative to which one

and only one of the observers can really be at rest, why not say that "at the same place" is just a relative notion? Two events can be at the same place relative to one observer and at different places relative to another in motion with respect to the first. And, if Einstein is correct, it is just the same with "at the same time."

To get the full picture of space and time proposed by Einstein requires one further assumption. It involves the claim that all places and directions in space and time are alike but goes beyond this in making an assumption that amounts to a posit that the spatiotemporal structure of the world is "flat." We will examine this notion of "flatness" in more detail in "Gravity and the Curvature of Spacetime." The assumption needed is the linearity of the relations of spatial and temporal separations for one observer with respect to those of another observer. With this additional posit, a structure of space and time is constructed in which observers in motion with respect to each other will attribute quite different spatial separations of events from each other and will also attribute quite different temporal separations between the events. The spatial and temporal separations attributed to a pair of events by one observer can, however, be calculated from those attributed to the pair by another observer moving with respect to the first, by means of the so-called Lorentz transformations, formulas originally derived in the context of the earlier compensatory theories.

Although the spatial and temporal distances between two events will vary from observer to observer, it is important to note that a consequence of the basic postulates of the theory is that another quantity, the so-called square of the interval between the events, will have an invariant value: It will be the same for all uniformly moving observers. It can be calculated from the time separation between the events in one observer's frame, t, and the spatial separation in that same reference frame, x, and the velocity of light, c, by means of the formula: $I^2 = x^2 - c^2t^2$. Whereas t and x will vary from observer to observer, I^2 will remain the same for all of them. A crucial step in this proof relies on the fact that all observers are attributing to light the same invariant speed, c.

Minkowski Spacetime

All the consequences of Einstein's theory for a new conceptualization of space and time can be summarized in the notion of Minkowski spacetime, the arena of all physical processes in the theory of special relativity. The basic idea here is to start with point-event locations, as the fundamental constituents out of which spacetime is built. One can think of these as the possible locations of happenings that are instantaneous and unextended spatially. These point-events take the place of the spatial points and moments of time of the prerelativistic theory. It is the basic structures imposed on the set of these spacetime points, the events or event locations, that constitute the framework of the new picture of space and time. (See Figure 2.3.)

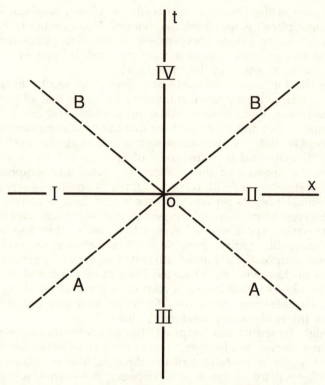

Figure 2.3   Some elements of Minkowski spacetime. The line *t* represents an inertial observer with *o* an event in that observer's life. The line *x* represents the events simultaneous with *o* for the observer. *A* and *B* represent light signals coming from the past to *o* and leaving *o* into the future. The events in regions *I* and *II* are so far from *o* in space and close to it in time that a signal would have to travel faster than light to connect such an event to event *o*. It is generally assumed that there are no such signals. The events in regions *III* and *IV* are events connectable to event *o* by causal signals traveling at less than the speed of light.

Pairs of these event locations have a definite interval between them, invariant and absolute in the structure. For a given observer in a particular state of uniform motion, a definite spatial separation and a definite time interval between the events can be derived, but the values of these are relative to the particular observer's state of motion.

Two events whose interval separation has value zero are such that a light signal in vacuum emitted at one place-time could arrive at the other place-time. Notice that "interval" is unlike spatial distance in that distinct events can have zero-interval separation. Such events are said to have null or lightlike separation. Events whose interval squared is negative are close enough together in space and far enough apart in time so that signals propagating slower than light can get from one to the other. They are said to have timelike separation. Event pairs whose interval squared is positive are too far apart in space and too close together in time for any signal traveling at the speed of light or less to connect them. If we assume that light is the limiting fastest signal, the events are unconnectable by any causal process whatever and are said to have spacelike separation. If we pick one event as origin, the class of events null separated from it divides the spacetime into interior and exterior regions of events timelike and events spacelike separated from the origin event. This separating class of events lightlike separated from the origin event consists of a future and past component. Together these are called the "light cones" of the origin event. (Actually they are cones only in a spacetime of two rather than the actual three spatial dimensions.)

In the usual flat space of Euclidean geometry, straight lines exist. Minkowski spacetime also has straight-line paths. If the intervals between the points on the geodesic path are spacelike, the path represents a straight spatial line. The latter is a straight line in the space at a time generated from the spacetime by picking some uniformly moving observer and taking as space at a time for him a collection of events all of which are simultaneous in his reference frame. Straight lines whose events have null separation represent the paths of light rays traveling in a vacuum. Timelike straight lines represent the path through space in time of some particle in uniform motion.

On a diagram we could represent some observer at rest in a frame of uniform motion by a vertical straight line. Any other uniformly moving observer who coincides with our first observer at the origin event would be represented by a straight line at an angle to the vertical. It is important to recognize that which line is vertical carries no physical significance. Only if we had a Newtonian notion of who is really at rest in space itself would there be some real significance to representing one observer as always at the same place and the other uniformly moving observers as changing places over time. But Minkowski spacetime has no such notion of which uniformly moving observer has zero real velocity, for all uniform velocities are physically on a par in this spacetime picture.

Having chosen some uniformly moving observer, we can also represent on the diagram by a straight line all of those events simultaneous to the origin event relative to that observer's state of motion. Diagrammatically, this straight line really represents "space at a time" for the observer, which is, of course, three dimensional. But we must suppress two spatial dimensions to get the diagram on a plane; therefore, a whole infinite, flat, Euclidean three-dimensional "space at a time" is represented by a line. For the observer in motion with respect to our first observer, a different straight line will represent all the events simultaneous to the origin event relative to this new observer's state of motion. A different line is needed because for the two observers different events are classed as simultaneous to the origin event, and what counts as space at the time of the origin event depends on an observer's state of motion. It can easily be shown that the simultaneity line (space at a time) for the second observer represented in the diagram would have to be tilted with respect to the first observer's simultaneity line.

We noted that in the compensatory theories originally designed to explain the null results of the round-trip experiments, it was posited that objects in motion with respect to the aether shrank in their lengths, and that clocks in motion with respect to the aether slowed down. In Minkowski spacetime, there is, of course, no aether. Yet length contraction and time dilation do occur. Let a meter-long stick be at rest in a uniform motion reference frame. That meter stick will be declared to have a length less than one meter in any other uniformly moving frame. Let a clock be at rest in one uniformly moving frame. That clock will be declared to be "running slow," i.e., taking more than one second to tick off one second on its face, by an observer in any other uniformly moving frame.

What is striking is that this contraction of length and dilation of time is perfectly symmetrical. Meter sticks at rest in your reference frame are taken as shortened by me (the two of us in relative motion), but meter sticks in my frame are taken as shortened by you. And the slowing down of clocks is equally symmetrical. Despite the appearance of inconsistency here, there is none, for length and time interval are now relative to an observer, and the assertions made are perfectly consistent. Direct evidence of the real existence of these phenomena is available, for example, in the life span of unstable particles—inexplicably overlong in prerelativistic terms—created in the upper atmosphere and observed on the surface of the earth. Only the relative slowing down of their decay process, because of their high velocity relative to us, can account for the phenomenon.

This consequence of relativity gives rise to a wide variety of paradoxes, apparent contradictions that really aren't contradictions, some of which can be found in any standard text on relativity. For example, a man carrying a pole runs into one end of a barn and out the other. When the pole is at rest with respect to the barn, it has the same length as the barn. Because the pole in motion is shorter than the barn, someone can close both doors on the runner while he and the pole are in the barn. But to the runner the barn is shorter than the pole, so this is clearly impossible. The key is to think about the time order in which processes occur from the differing perspectives of the runner and of the observer at rest on the barn. For the man at rest on the barn, both doors are shut while the runner is in the barn with the pole. The runner sees the farther door open and his pole protrude from the barn before the nearer door is ever closed behind him.

The spacetime of special relativity, Minkowski spacetime, requires us to make another distinction about time that doesn't occur in the prerelativistic theory. We have noted that any observer will attribute a certain time interval between two events, and that this interval will vary from observer to observer. This is called the coordinate time interval between the events relative to the observer in question. Another notion of time arises when we consider someone who moves from one event (one place at a time) to some other event (a different place at a different time) along some spacetime path, through a succession of places-at-a-time. Let this agent carry a clock with him set at zero at the first event. This clock will read a definite value at the final event. Surely all observers will agree on what that value is because the coincidence of the clock's reading that value with the final event will be agreed upon by all, as these are events at the same place and there is no relativity of simultaneity in that case. This time is called the proper time between the two events.

But the elapsed proper time between two events will vary depending upon the spacetime path by which the clock is carried from one event to the other. This phenomenon is without precedent in prerelativistic physics. In fact, it can easily be shown that the time elapsed on a clock carried from one event to another will be maximal if the path followed from the first event to the second is one of unaccelerated, uniform motion. This is the source of the famous twin paradox, according to which if one twin remains in a frame of uniform motion while the other takes a course through space and time that involves accelerated motion but that brings him back into coincidence with his stay-at-home twin, the adventurous twin will be younger—will have shown, for example, less biological aging—than his twin when the two meet once again. Evidence that this consequence of relativity is real comes from unstable particles sent around the circular paths of accelerators. Fewer of them decay than their compatriot particles in a group remaining at rest in the laboratory between the first moment when they coincide and the second moment at which they coincide. As usual there is no contradiction in the theory here, just phenomena we hadn't expected, a result of the surprising nature of spacetime. (See Figure 2.4.)

We noted that Newtonian mechanics conformed to Galileo's principle that all physical phenomena would appear the same to any observer in a state of uniform motion, although the fact that one's laboratory was in accelerated motion would reveal itself in observable consequences. The old theory of mechanics, when put in the new, relativistic spacetime, no longer would satisfy that principle. Hence, a new mechanics was developed by Einstein that reconciles the Galilean relativity of mechanical phenomena with the new spacetime picture. The source of this theory is simple. The older mechanics obeyed such principles as the conservation of energy, the conservation of momentum, and the conservation of angular momentum. These are now realized to be the consequences of fundamental symmetries of the spacetime structure (in particular, the fact that all spacetime points are structurally alike, as are all spacetime directions). These symmetries obtain in the new spacetime as well, so we may hold to the old conservation rules and derive the new mechanics from them. In the new me-

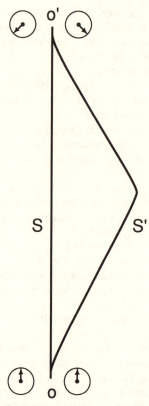

Figure 2.4 The twin paradox. *S* is an observer who remains inertial and carries a clock from event *o* to event *o'*. The time elapsed on the clock is represented by the left-hand clock faces. *S'*, originally at rest with respect to *S*, accelerates off to the right, travels to the right at a uniform speed, reverses direction of relative motion, returns to *S*'s location and again accelerates so as to come to rest relative to *S* at the location *o'*. The elapsed time on a clock carried by *S'* is represented by the right-hand clock faces. Special relativity predicts that less time will have elapsed on the clock carried by *S'* along the accelerated path from *o* to *o'* than will have elapsed on *S*'s clock.

chanics is found the famous consequence of relativity, for example, of the equivalence of mass and energy, i.e., that the more kinetic energy an object possesses, the greater will be its resistance to further acceleration by a force.

We also noted that Einstein assumed that the speed of light in a vacuum was a maximal speed of propagation of any signal whatever. Such a posit fits in nicely with the new spacetime picture.

We can, for example, find pairs of events, *A* and *B*, and observers *O1* and *O2*, such that *A* is before *B* relative to *O1* and *B* is before *A* relative to *O2*. But these will always be events that have spacelike sep-

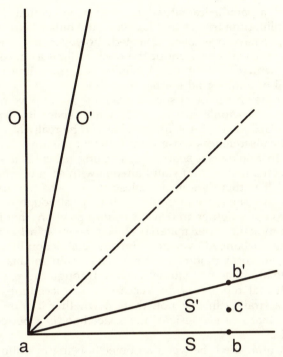

Figure 2.5   The relativity of time order of events in special relativity. *O* is an inertial observer. *O'* is another inertial observer moving to the right relative to *O*. The line *S* is the class of events *O* takes as simultaneous with event *a*. The line *S'* is the class of events *O'* takes as simultaneous with *a*. For *O* event *c* is after event *b* and hence after event *a*. But for *O'*, event *c* is before event *b'* and hence before event *a*. Such a reversal of time order can occur only for events, like event *a* and event *c*, that are not causally connectable to one another.

aration. This means, assuming the limiting velocity of light, that events will have different order in time relative to two observers only if the events are not connectable by any causal signal whatever. Events that are connectable by a causal signal, traveling at or at less than the speed of light, will appear in the same time order to all observers, although the amount of time between them will vary from observer to observer. (See Figure 2.5.)

It has been pointed out that one need not hold to the posit of the limiting velocity of light in order to have a consistent theory in which spacetime is Minkowski spacetime, the spacetime of special relativity. If one simply insists that conditions of the world are such that causal paradoxes are avoided, one can tolerate "tachyons," causal signals at higher than light speeds. The consistency constraint is needed because positing tachyons in Minkowski spacetime would allow for closed causal loops, in which one event causes itself. If initial conditions could be freely chosen, a paradoxical situation could be generated (I shoot my-self before pulling the trigger that launches the bullet). No such above-luminal speeds have ever been detected, however, and the standard versions of special relativity adopt the posit of light as maximal causal signal along with the structure of Minkowski spacetime with its in-variant speed of light for all inertial observers.

Nothing in the spacetime of special relativity, as we have noted, plays the full role of Newton's space. For Newton, space itself provided a genuine standard of what it is for an object to be really at rest, even if no empirical consequences arose from uniform motion with respect to space itself. In Minkowski spacetime, nothing provides a standard of when two events that are not simultaneous with each other are "at the same place." It is therefore meaningless to ask whether an object re-mains at one and the same place through time, although it is perfectly meaningful to ask whether an object's *relative* position, that is, position with respect to some other material objects taken as a frame of refer-ence, remains unchanged over time. But the distinction between being genuinely in uniform motion or not does remain in this spacetime. Whether the path of some material particle through the spacetime, the timelike path that represents the succession of place-times the object occupies, is a straight line or not, that is, whether it is one of the ti-melike paths that is a geodesic of the spacetime, is a perfectly mean-ingful question.

The distinction, then, between an object's being in uniform motion or being in accelerated motion—represented by a curved timelike path in the spacetime diagram—remains absolute in the sense that this dis-tinction has nothing to do with the motion of the object in question relative to other material objects. Instead, this distinction is determined by an object's motion relative to the structures of the spacetime itself. In Newtonian physics, genuinely accelerated motion revealed itself by the presence (in the accelerated laboratory) of inertial forces, acting on objects and generated, allegedly, by the acceleration of the objects rel-ative to space itself. In special relativity, real acceleration shows up in this way and in other ways as well. We noted, for example, that it was only when one of the round-trip experiments was performed with light in a laboratory in uniform motion that the null results were obtained. In an accelerated apparatus the light will take times around the paths that reveal the existence of the absolute acceleration of the experimental device. Although there is no such thing, then, as "being in the same place" in any sense other than relative to some material standard, there is, in special relativity, as much real significance to "being in uniform motion" in an absolute sense as there is in the Newtonian theory.

Neo-Newtonian Spacetime

Once the Minkowski spacetime of special relativity had been con-structed, it was noted that one could go back and construct a spacetime appropriate for the earlier Newtonian theory, a spacetime that had some advantages over the notion of space itself traditionally postulated in Newtonian physics. The main insights come from the realization that taking event locations as primitive and then constructing the spacetime by imposing structure on the set of event locations is the best systematic route for constructing a spacetime appropriate for what are taken to be the observable quantities posited by any given theory.

In Newtonian physics, the notion of simultaneity for distant events is presupposed as an absolute notion. So to construct our new spacetime for Newtonian physics, we impose on the collection of event locations a definite time interval between any pair of events. When this interval is zero, the events are simultaneous. In the Minkowski spacetime of special relativity, spaces are collections of events simultaneous relative to a given observer. It is assumed that these "relative" spaces have the ordinary three-dimensional structure described by Euclid's geometry. In the revised Newtonian spacetime, with its absolute notion of simultaneity, we can, again, take spaces to be collections of simultaneous events. Thus each event will be in one and only one space, and space is, again, assumed to be three-dimensional Euclidean space.

In the Newtonian context, as in special relativity, what counts as a path of uniform motion of an object is a well-defined notion. So we impose on this new Newtonian spacetime a demand similar to the one imposed on Minkowski spacetime: There must be a definite notion of straight-line paths representing the possible paths of motion through space in time of freely and uniformly moving particles. Now Newton assumed that there was such a thing as one event's being "in the same place" as some other nonsimultaneous event. If we impose that structure, a definite notion of same place for nonsimultaneous events, on the spacetime we are constructing, we build up Newton's absolute space picture of space and time. But this would give us features of the world without empirical consequences, such as the magnitude of the uniform speed of an object with respect to "space itself." If we leave that "same place at different times" structure out, however, we obtain a new spacetime, sometimes called Galilean spacetime, sometimes called neo-Newtonian spacetime. In this spacetime, absolute uniform motion is well defined, but absolute sameness of place through time is not.

In this new spacetime picture, absolute accelerations exist and have observable consequences, but there is no such thing as the absolute velocity of an object. This is just what we want. The physicists' need for a new approach to space and time in order to confront the startling and puzzling results of the optical round-trip experiments led to deep insights into what the components were of the picture of space and time that we held intuitively and that, in a refined version, underpinned the physical picture of the world of Newtonian science. By confronting the new experimental facts and constructing the conceptual apparatus to do justice to them, physicists came up with new ways of looking at possible theories to account for the older posited observational facts. As we shall see, the existence of these new structures for describing and explaining the spatiotemporal features of the world had an important effect on our philosophical understanding of the nature of space and time and of our access to knowledge about their nature as well. But before taking up those issues, we will look at a second revolutionary change in our views about the nature of space and time, once again generated out of the fertile scientific imagination of Einstein.

Gravity and the Curvature of Spacetime

Gravity and Relativity

In his greatest work, the *Principia*, Newton proposed a theory that would, among other things, explain the motion of the planets around the sun in the elliptical orbits that had been so carefully described by J. Kepler. The theory accounting for this motion has two components. One is Newton's theory of dynamics, his general theory relating motions to the forces acting upon the objects in motion. Based on a background assumption of absolute space and a definite absolute rate of time, the theory incorporates Galileo's principle that objects not acted upon by any forces remain in a constant state of uniform motion. It then posits that change of motion (acceleration) will be proportional to the forces acting upon a body and inversely proportional to the intrinsic propensity of a body to resist changes of motion, its so-called inertial mass.

The other component of Newton's theory concerns the force responsible for the observed motions of astronomical bodies (and for many other phenomena, such as the way in which bodies fall toward the surface of the earth and the tides). Once again building upon Galileo's important observation that, air resistance to the side, all objects suffer a uniform acceleration toward the earth when they are in free-fall near the earth's surface, Newton posits a general force of gravity acting between all material objects. Gravity is always an attractive force. The magnitude of the force exerted between the bodies is taken to be proportional to the inertial mass of each body and inversely proportional to the square of the distance between them. Newton's Third Law of Motion asserts that the force exerted by the first body on the second will be matched by a force of equal strength—but oppositely directed—exerted by the second body on the first.

The facts that the force increases in proportion to the inertial mass, but that the resistance of the body to acceleration is also proportional to the inertial mass, immediately produce Galileo's result that all bodies accelerate equally when subjected to the gravitational force exerted by some fixed body if the test objects are at the same location relative to the object exerting the gravitational force. Newton demonstrated that the combination of the laws of dynamics and the law of gravitational force that he postulates will lead to Kepler's laws of planetary motion or, rather, to a slightly corrected version of them.

It should be no surprise, then, that Einstein, having demonstrated the necessity for a new dynamical system and having constructed one consistent with the new spacetime of special relativity, takes up the problem of the construction of a new theory of gravity. This theory, which is clearly needed, must be consistent with the new spacetime ideas. Newton's theory, for example, takes the gravitational interaction between bodies to be instantaneous, but relativity takes all signals to propagate at a speed less than or equal to that of light. Quite a variety of alternatives to the Newtonian theory can be constructed that are compatible with the new relativistic spacetime. Indeed, a continuing program in experimental physics amounts to testing these alternatives against one another, looking for possible observations to rule out some of the possibilities. But the novel gravitational theory that has stood up best against experiment, and the one of greatest theoretical elegance, is Einstein's own. This is called the general theory of relativity. It is also the theory that posits to the world a nature that is of great interest to philosophers. I will spend the rest of this section sketching some of the ideas that led Einstein to this novel theory of gravity, which, as we shall see, constitutes a novel theory of the structure of spacetime itself. I shall outline some of the basic components of the theory and explore a few of its consequences that are of importance for the philosopher.

Einstein begins with Galileo's observation that the acceleration induced in an object by gravity is independent of the object's size and of what it is made of. Gravity is unlike any other force in having this universal effect. Consider the case in which the object is forced into acceleration by a distant enough gravitating object so that the gravitational field is effectively constant within the laboratory. Einstein observes that a small test object in a laboratory would accelerate relative to that laboratory in just the same manner as it would if no force were acting on the test object but, instead, the laboratory itself were being uniformly accelerated in the opposite direction to that of the particle's acceleration. In the latter case, any test object of any mass or composition would appear to accelerate uniformly with respect to the laboratory. It is the universality of gravity that allows us to replace the gravitational force by a reference frame acceleration.

Perhaps, Einstein suggests, all the effects of gravity could be duplicated by such a laboratory acceleration. This leads to the hypothesis that gravity will have effects on things other than particulate matter. If we shine a light beam across a laboratory in accelerated motion we expect the beam to follow a path that is not a straight line relative to the laboratory. Shouldn't gravity, then, deflect beams of light that pass near a gravitating body?

Perhaps more surprising is the conclusion that we ought to expect gravity to have an effect on measurements of time and space intervals, as revealed by idealized clocks and measuring rods. The argument in favor of the temporal effect is the easier one to construct and follow. Imagine an accelerated laboratory with a clock at its upper end and an identical clock at its lower end. Signals are sent from the lower clock to the upper and the rate of emission of the signals, as determined by the lower clock, and of their reception, as determined by the upper, are compared. By the time a signal released from the bottom has gotten to the top, the top clock is in motion with respect to the uniformly moving reference frame in which the bottom clock was at rest when the signal was released. Arguing either from the time-dilation effect of special relativity or from the so-called Doppler effect, which, even pre-relativistically, shows that a signal released from a source with a given frequency will appear to have a lower frequency when observed by someone relative to whom the source is in motion, it becomes plausible to claim that the lower clock will appear to be running slow as determined by the upper clock. That is, the frequency with which the signal is received by the upper clock is lower than that with which it is emitted as determined by the lower one. (See Figure 2.6.)

But now consider the laboratory not accelerated, with the apparatus all located at rest in a gravitational field. By Einstein's argument (often called the Principle of Equivalence), we ought to expect that the clock lower down in the gravitational field will appear, to the clock located higher up, to be running slow. Notice that this has nothing to do with the gravitational *force* felt by the two clocks but, rather, is determined by how much further down the gravitational "hill" one clock is than the other. So we ought to expect gravity to have an effect on our measurement of time intervals. Similar, but somewhat more complicated, arguments can be given that lead us to expect gravity to affect spatial measurements as well.

Taken together, these arguments led Einstein to the astonishing suggestion that the way to deal with gravity in a relativistic context was to treat it not as some force field acting in spacetime but, instead, as a modification of the very geometric structure of spacetime. In the presence of gravity, he argued, spacetime is not "flat" but is "curved." To know what that means, however, we must look briefly at the history of geometry as treated by the mathematicians.

Non-Euclidean Geometry

Standard geometry as formalized by Euclid derived all the geometric truths from a small set of allegedly self-evident, basic postulates. Although Euclid's axiomatization of geometry is not, actually, complete (i.e., sufficient in itself to allow all the derivations to be carried out without presupposing other underlying and hidden premises), it can be so completed. For a long period of time, puzzlement existed about Euclid's so-called Parallel Postulate. It is equivalent to the claim that through a point not on a line, one and only one line can be drawn that is in the common plane of given line and point and that will not intersect the given line in either direction no matter how far the lines are extended. It seemed to the geometers that this postulate lacked the self-

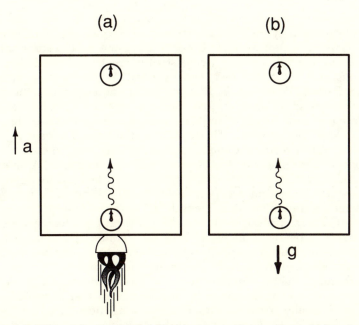

Figure 2.6 The gravitational red shift. (a) represents an accelerated laboratory with a clock on the floor and one attached to the ceiling. Because a signal emitted from the floor clock is received at the ceiling clock when the laboratory is moving with a velocity relative to the frame of motion in which the signal was emitted (because of the acceleration of the laboratory), the floor clock will be recorded as "running slow" by the ceiling clock in much the manner a whistle moving away from an observer is heard by that observer with a lower pitch than it would be if the whistle were stationary with respect to the observer. General relativity posits that a similar result will be obtained in a laboratory not accelerated but fixed in a gravitational field—as in (b). A clock lower down in the gravitational field will be recorded as "running slow" by a clock higher up in the gravitational potential. This is called the gravitational red shift. It indicates one way in which gravity can be taken to affect the metric structure of spacetime.

evidence of the other, simpler hypotheses (such as "Equals added to equals are equal," and "Two points determine a straight line between them"). Could this "suspect" postulate be derived from the other postulates, making it unnecessary as an independent assumption? If one could show that the denial of the Parallel Postulate was inconsistent with the other postulates, one could show this derivation to hold by the method of *reductio ad absurdum*. But could this be shown?

Denying the Parallel Postulate can go in two directions. The postulate says that one and only one parallel line through the point exists, and to deny that, one could affirm that no such parallel line existed or that more than one did. In 1733 G. Saccheri showed that the No Parallels Postulate was, in fact, inconsistent with the remaining axioms, at least if these were understood in their usual way. He was unable to show that the Many Parallels denial was so inconsistent. By the nineteenth century, J. Bolyai, N. I. Lobachevsky, and K. F. Gauss had realized that one could construct consistent geometries that adopted Euclid's postulates but that had a Many Parallels Postulate in place of Euclid's Parallel Postulate. B. Riemann then showed that if the other axioms were slightly reinterpreted, a new geometry with a No Parallels Postulate replacing Euclid's Parallel Postulate could be constructed that was also logically consistent. The reinterpretations needed are that "Two points determine a straight line," must be read so that sometimes more than one straight line contained a given pair of points and "A line may be extended arbitrarily in both directions," must be read to assert that a line wouldn't meet an end point if extended but not to imply that a fully extended line had infinite length.

Later it was realized that when these new non-Euclidean geometries were taken to be two-dimensional, plane, geometries, they could be understood in a Euclidean fashion as the geometry of shortest distance curves (geodesics) on curved two-dimensional surfaces. In particular, Riemannian axiomatic geometry was just the geometry of figures constructed by arcs of great circles on the surface of a sphere. But what could the logically consistent three-dimensional non-Euclidean geometries be taken to be about, or were they, even if logically consistent, absurd for other reasons?

Gauss carried geometry further by developing a general theory of arbitrarily curved two-dimensional surfaces. These are characterized by a number—known as the Gaussian curvature—at each point. How this curvature varies with distance as measured along curves drawn in the surface determines the shape of the curved surface. Gauss thought of these curved surfaces as embedded in ordinary Euclidean three-dimensional space. An important result of his work, however, was that one could characterize some of the aspects of curvature ("intrinsic" curvature) by means of quantities that could be determined by an imagined two-dimensional creature confined to the curved surface and not even aware that the embedding three-dimensional space existed. From this new perspective, it turned out that the geometries described by the older axiom systems could be understood as special cases. Euclidean two-dimensional geometry, the geometry of the plane, is the geometry of the surface whose Gaussian curvature is everywhere zero. Riemannian geometry, the geometry of the two-dimensional surfaces of spheres, is just the geometry of a surface whose Gaussian curvature is constant and positive. Lobachevsky-Bolyai geometry is the geometry of a two-dimensional surface whose Gaussian curvature is the same at each point and negative. Negative curvature characterizes a point like that in the center of a mountain pass at which the surface curves "in opposite directions" along different paths through it.

Riemann then went on and generalized Gauss's theory of curved surfaces to spaces of any dimension whatever. Whereas Gauss presupposed that the surfaces in question were embedded in a flat Euclidean space, Riemann made no such assumption. After all, it was a result of Gauss's work that some aspects of curvature would be available to a two-dimensional creature ignorant of the embedding space. General Riemannian geometry deals with these aspects of curvature, the intrinsic aspects. (This general Riemannian geometry of curved n-dimensional spaces is not to be confused with the earlier axiomatic Riemannian geometry.) The basic assumption of this geometry is that the curved n-dimensional space is approximable in small enough regions by a Euclidean, flat, n-dimensional space. For curved surfaces in flat three-dimensional space, these approximating surfaces can be represented as planes tangent to the curved surface at a point; the planes are also located in the embedding three-dimensional space. For a general Riemannian curved n-dimensional space, these "tangent planes" are posited to exist only in the sense that as far as intrinsic n-dimensional features go, the n-dimensional curved space can be approximated at a point by a flat, n-dimensional Euclidean space.

What are some aspects of curved spaces? How, for example, could a three-dimensional creature living in a curved three-dimensional space find out that the space was, in fact, curved? Intrinsic curvature reveals itself in distance measurements. An n-dimensional creature can make enough distance measurements between points to assure itself that there was no way these points could be located in a flat n-dimensional space and have the minimal distances between them along curves that the creature's points do. For example, a check of shortest airline distances between cities on the Earth could tell us that the Earth had not a plane surface but, instead, a surface approximating that of a sphere. In a curved n-dimensional space, shortest-distance curves, called the geodesics of the space, fail to be the straight lines that they would be were the space flat. These lines are also the lines of "least curvature" in the space. Intuitively, this means that the lines, although they cannot be straight, given the curvature of the space, deviate from straightness no more than they are forced to by the curvature of the space itself.

Curvature can reveal itself in other ways as well. For example, if we take a directed line (a vector) and move it around a closed curve in a flat space, all the while keeping it as parallel to itself as possible as we move it, when we return to the point of origin, the vector will point in the same direction at that point as when we began. But in a curved space, such parallel transport of a vector around a closed loop will, in general, change the direction of the vector so that it will point in a direction at the end of the transport that is different from its original direction when the journey started.

A flat three-dimensional space is of infinite extent and has infinite volume. A Euclidean plane is of infinite extent and has infinite area. But the intrinsically curved surface of a sphere, although it has no boundaries, has a finite area. A two-dimensional creature living on a spherical surface could paint the surface. It would never encounter a boundary to the surface. But after a finite time the job would be done, with the whole surface painted. Similarly, a three-dimensional creature living in the three-dimensional curved space that is analogous to the spherical surface, living in a so-called three-sphere, could fill the region with foamed plastic. Although never encountering a boundary wall to the space, it would, in a finite time, finish the job, with all the volume of the three-dimensional space filled by a finite amount of plastic foam.

It seems clear, then, that the notion of a curved n-dimensional space, including a curved three-dimensional space, is not only logically consistent but manifestly nonabsurd. As long as we are sticking to intrinsic features of curvature, we are not making the assumption that the space is sitting in some higher-dimensional, flat embedding space. And the features of curvature intrinsic to the space are manifestly ascertainable by straightforward techniques to a creature living in the space. Could it not be the case, then, that the actual three-dimensional space of our world was curved and not the flat space characterized by the basic postulates of three-dimensional Euclidean geometry? Such speculations naturally accompanied the discovery of the new geometries.

Using Non-Euclidean Geometries in Physics

There was some speculation in the nineteenth century about the possible reality of curved space. W. Clifford, for example, suggested that it was conceivable that matter was actually little regions of highly curved space in a three-dimensional space that was flat in the large. It was clear that a large-scale curvature of space could be detected only on the largest, astronomical, scales, for generations of experience had shown us how well Euclidean flat three-dimensional geometry worked in our descriptions of the world. Certainly it worked well for measurements of the ordinary sort and even in the description of such things as the structure of the solar system.

It was only with Einstein's new relativistic theory of gravity, however, the general theory of relativity, that curved geometry became an essential part of a plausible physical theory. We have seen that one could argue with plausibility that gravity would affect all objects dynamically in the same way, independently of their size and constitution. Thus a material object, which would, in the absence of gravity or other forces, follow a path of uniform direction and speed would, in the presence of gravity, follow a different path. But the change in this path would depend only upon the gravitational field and the initial place and velocity of the object. It wouldn't depend on the mass of the object or the material out of which the object was made. It is this independence of the effect of gravity on the object's size and structure that makes a "geometrization" of the gravitational field possible.

When combined with the arguments in favor of a gravitational effect on metric features of the world as determined by rods and clocks, the idea of treating gravity as curvature becomes plausible. But it is not, at least fundamentally, curved space that Einstein posits but, instead, curved spacetime. In the Minkowski spacetime of special relativity, free particles traveled timelike straight lines, the timelike geodesics of the spacetime. Now, Einstein suggests, we are to think of particles that are acted upon only by gravity as "free" particles, traveling, not timelike straight lines, but the curved timelike geodesics of a spacetime that is curved. A fundamental result of Riemann's geometry is that through a point in a given direction there passes a single geodesic path. In Riemannian spaces, the geodesics are both the paths of minimum curvature and of (locally) shortest distance. With the new metric of spacetime, it is best to think of the "least curvature" definition of geodesics as the fundamental one. In spacetime, if one specifies a direction at a point one will simultaneously specify a spatial direction and a speed in each direction. So the timelike geodesic through a point in a given direction will correspond to specifying the initial place and the initial velocity of a particle. The path specified by the geodesic will then be unique. And this is just what we want for gravity because, given an initial place and velocity, the path of any particle in a gravitational field is the same. Light, which in special relativity follows the straight-line null geodesics of Minkowski spacetime, is now taken to follow null geodesics in the curved spacetime, geodesics that will, in general, not be straight lines. (See Figure 2.7.)

One could determine the curvature of a spacetime by following out the paths of the "free" particles and light rays, that is, the particles and light rays acting only under the influence of gravitation, now taken to be simply the curvature of the spacetime. But one could also, at least in principle, determine the curvature structure by making enough measurements of spatial and temporal separations of events and combining these measurements into the interval separation, which is the metric for spacetime. General relativity posits that the spacetime so determined will agree with that determined by following out the geodesic motions of particles and light rays, the clocks and rods being used to make the temporal and spatial measurements also being affected by the gravitational field, in the sense that they properly measure these metric qualities in the curved spacetime.

Traditional gravitational theory had two parts: One specified the action of gravity on test objects; the other specified the kind of gravitational field that would be generated by a source of gravity. In the older theory, gravity was a force that accelerated all material objects at a place in the gravitational field to the same degree. In the newer theory, gravity is the structure of curved spacetime. It affects particles and light rays in that they now travel curved timelike and null geodesics in the spacetime, and it affects idealized temporal and spatial measuring instruments.

What about the second aspect of the theory, that which specified what kind of gravitational field would be generated by a source of gravity? In the older theory, any massive object generates a gravitational

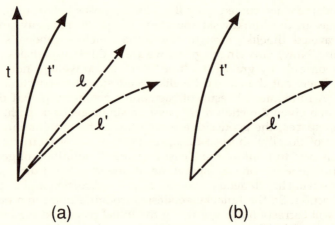

(a)   **(b)**

Figure 2.7   Motion in a gravitational field as following curved geodesics. In (a)
spacetime is viewed as "flat." The straight line *t* represents the path a "free" particle
would travel through the spacetime and the straight line *l* the path of a "free" light
ray. Under the influence of a force like gravity, the particle and light ray will travel
curved paths such as *t'* and *l'*. But these are viewed as deviating from the straightest
paths in the spacetime. In (b) the straight paths have vanished. Instead the spacetime is viewed as "curved" in the presence of gravity, with *t'* and *l'*, the paths of
"free" particles and light rays (that is, particles and light rays acted upon by no
nongravitational force), now considered geodesics, or straightest possible paths in
the curved spacetime.

field. In the new relativistic theory, gravity is associated with the mass-
energy of the material world. The field equations of general relativity
have on their left-hand side a mathematical expression characterizing
the curvature of spacetime. On their right-hand side they have an
expression characterizing how mass-energy is distributed in spacetime,
the so-called stress-energy tensor. It is this equation that relates gravity,
now curved spacetime, to its sources in nongravitational mass-energy.
(The "nongravitational" is important because the gravitational field itself, curved spacetime, also possesses mass-energy.) It would be a mistake to think of the matter as "causing" the gravitational field in any
simplistic sense, because to know the right-hand side of the equation,
which describes how mass-energy is distributed in spacetime, requires
positing a spacetime structure. The equation tells us whether a given
spacetime is compatible with a posited mass-energy distribution in that
spacetime. Only when the equation is satisfied by both the posited
spacetime structure and the posited distribution of mass-energy in that
structure is the world posited a possible world in the new theory.

   It is interesting that given the field equation, the dynamical law of
gravity—that pointlike material particles when "free" travel timelike
geodesics—follows. Unlike the Newtonian theory, the dynamical law

of gravity need not be posited as an independent law but is itself derivable from the basic field equation.

If we accept this new curved spacetime theory of gravity, we then confront the task of trying, as inhabitants of the world, to determine its actual spacetime structure. The theory tells us that the geometry of spacetime must be correlated with the distribution of matter and energy in that spacetime. And the spacetime structure in question reveals itself in terms of the curved geodesic paths of unimpeded light rays and "free" particles and by means of spatial and temporal intervals measured by ideal measuring rods (or tapes in a curved world) and clocks. Naturally, if spacetime shows curvature, it will be on astronomical scales, for we have a vast empirical experience to assure us that in local small-scale measurements, Minkowskian flat geometry works adequately.

Some effects of this newly understood "gravity as spacetime curvature" do show up in the scale of the solar system. The planets are taken to be traveling geodesics in the spacetime curved by the presence of the massive sun. This introduces slight changes from the Keplerian motion of the planets explicable by the Newtonian theory. We know that the spacetime curvature even of the solar system is small. The paths of the planets in spacetime deviate little from straight-line geodesics (not to be confused with the spatial, obviously curved, ellipses they travel). But the effect of the curvature is to superimpose on the familiar elliptical paths of the planets small additional effects, such as a motion (relative to an inertial frame fixed in the sun) of the nearest point of approach of the planet to the sun in its orbit, a motion detectable in the case of the planet Mercury.

Other metric effects of gravity can also be observed on a fairly small scale, in particular, the slowed rate of one clock relative to another if the former clock is lower down in a gravitational potential than the latter. But it is on the grand cosmological scale than the theory gives rise to its most interesting new predictions and to the possibility for the most fascinating appearances of observational consequences of spacetime curvature. Here one deals with highly idealized model universes, for which theoretical conclusions can be drawn. The hope is, of course, that at least some of these idealized pictures of the world on the cosmological scale will be close enough to reality to provide insight into the world we discover in our astronomical observations into deep space. For example, it is usually assumed that the matter of the universe can be considered as distributed uniformly and that the distribution is the same in all directions in space in the cosmological world. This assumption is now under intensive observational scrutiny.

A wide variety of possible spacetime worlds has been explored by the theorists. In many of these, the continuity structure of the world differs from that of the worlds of Newtonian or special relativistic physics. In some worlds, for example, there can be closed timelike paths, collections of events such that when an observer follows them from later to later event, he eventually returns to his initial event. Other

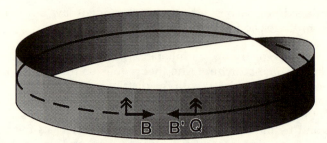

Figure 2.8   A non-orientable space. The Mobius band is the simplest example of a nonorientable space, in this case of dimension two. *B* and *B'* represent oriented figures that could not be transformed the one into the other by a rigid motion were the figures drawn on a normal plane surface. But if we take *B* and move it around the twisted Mobius band, we can eventually bring it back to *Q* so that it coincides with *B'*. This reveals the nonorientable nature of the surface. In spacetime, a nonorientability can be spatial, temporal, or spatiotemporal.

spacetimes, although not that causally pathological, can be close to having such closed, causal paths embedded in them. Other peculiar spacetimes have a nonorientability built into them. They are twisted like the familiar Mobius band, a twisted two-dimensional surface embedded in three-space. (See Figure 2.8.)

In such a nonorientable spacetime world, it may be impossible to make a global distinction between right-handed and left-handed objects, a right-handed object being transformable into a left-handed one at the same place by a voyage around the spacetime. Or there may be a lack of time orientability, which makes it impossible to say globally what is the "past" and what is the "future" direction of time at a point-event.

In some spacetimes, it is possible for observers to have spacetime split into spaces-at-a-time. That means that in these worlds, for an observer in a particular state of motion, the spacetime can be sliced into three-dimensional spaces of events that all can be assigned a specific time in a time order that can hold globally. For other spacetimes, such a splitting of spacetime into "simultaneity slices" of three-spaces-at-a-time is impossible. When such a cutting up of spacetime into spaces-at-a-time is possible, the spaces can themselves be curved three-dimensional spaces of the sort studied by Riemann in his generalization of Gauss's geometry of curved surfaces. One such universe, the Einstein model, has time going on forever in past and future. To an observer at each time the spatial world exists as a closed, three-dimensional sphere of constant, finite size. The Robertson-Walker universes have spaces-at-a-time of constant curvature, but the curvature may be positive, zero, or negative. The size parameter of these spaces can change with time, leading them to be plausible models of Big Bang universes that have, as, on the basis of the observational data, our universe seems to have, a singular point at which all the matter of the world is compressed to one spatial point.

Moreover, spacetime curvature helps to explain the possible data of experience in another area: the description of the singularities generated by the collapsing matter of massive stars. These are the famous black holes, regions of spacetime so curved up by the presence of highly dense matter that light cannot escape to the outside spacetime from the inner spacetime region immediately surrounding the point of singular collapse of the star. Models of such locally highly curved regions of spacetime corresponding to electrically charged and/or rotating collapsed stars, as well as the original kind studied, provide fascinating case studies of the peculiar effects gravity as spacetime curvature can have. Although the evidence from observation is still inconclusive, it seems that some of the generators of highly energetic radiation in the cosmos, for example, quasars and the centers of so-called active galaxies, may very well be such black holes.

Curved Spacetime and Newtonian Gravity

When we discussed the move from space and time to spacetime when the foundations of the special theory of relativity were formulated, we noted that after Minkowski spacetime had been constructed as the spacetime appropriate to special relativity, scientists realized that one could use the spacetime notion to construct a spacetime in some ways more appropriate to the physics of Newton than was his own absolute space and time. This was the Galilean or neo-Newtonian spacetime. In light of the curved spacetime account of gravity, the general theory of relativity, it became clear that one could redescribe gravity even in the prerelativistic picture by means of a curved spacetime as well. In this prerelativistic picture, gravity doesn't have the effects on distance and time measurements it has in the relativistic version, nor is any account taken of the effect of gravity on light. Instead, it is the familiar dynamical effects of gravity that are transformed into curvature of spacetime.

In this picture, time is just as it was for Newton. There is a definite, absolute time interval between any two events. Events that are all simultaneous form spaces-at-a-time. These are, as they were for Newton, flat, three-dimensional Euclidean spaces. As in the neo-Newtonian spacetime, there is no nonrelative notion of two nonsimultaneous events being at the same place; therefore this spacetime lacks Newton's absolute notion of sameness of place through time and absolute velocity. But just as in the neo-Newtonian view there were timelike geodesics corresponding to possible paths of freely moving particles, so are there timelike geodesics in this new spacetime picture. However, whereas the timelike geodesics of the neo-Newtonian picture were the straight-line paths of uniformly moving particles (particles not acted upon by forces and, following the law of inertia, keeping their velocities constant), now, the timelike geodesics are curved lines. They are now taken to be the paths of particles "free" in the new sense made familiar from Einstein's theory of gravity, that is, acted upon by no forces other than gravity.

Once again, gravitational force is eliminated from the theory in favor of gravity as the curvature of timelike geodesics, so that particles feel the effect of gravity not by being deflected from their geodesic motion by the force of the gravitating object but, instead, by following the "free" geodesic paths in the spacetime, paths now curved as a result of the presence of the gravitating object, which serves as a "source" of space-time curvature. Just as in Einstein's theory, it is only the uniform effect of gravity on a test object, the fact that all objects affected by gravity suffer the same modification in their motion independently of their mass or constitution, that allows for this "geometrization" of the gravitational force. This curved spacetime of Newtonian gravity is not, like Minkowski spacetime or the curved spacetime of the general theory of relativity, Riemannian (or, rather, pseudo-Riemannian) spacetime, because unlike the spacetimes of special or general relativity, it has no spacetime metric structure. There is a definite time interval between any two events. For simultaneous events, there is a definite spatial separation between any two events. In this sense, this spacetime has a metric of time and one of space. But there is, in contrast to the relativistic case, no spacetime interval between a pair of events. Curvature shows up only as the nonstraightness of the timelike geodesics, not in any metric feature of the spacetime.

Summary

So the development of the elegant theories of Einstein, which attempt to do justice to the surprising observational facts about the behavior of light, free particles, and measuring rods and clocks, provides us with two revolutions in our views of space and time. First, space and time are replaced by the unified notion of spacetime, relative to which spatial and temporal aspects of the world become derivative. Second, the notion of curvature is invoked to find a natural place for the effects of gravity in such a spacetime picture of the world.

Surely such revolutions in our scientific perspective on what space and time are actually like should result in a profound rethinking of the typically philosophical questions about space and time. How should we view the status of our claims to knowledge about the structure of space and time in this new context in which, for the first time, a variety of possible and distinct proposals about the structure of space and time are available for our scientific inspection? And what effect should such novel structures of space and time have on our views about the metaphysical nature of space and time? In particular, what effect should these revolutionary scientific views have on the traditional debate between substantivalists and relationists? It is to those philosophical questions that we now turn.

How Do We Know the True Geometry
of the World?

Changing Views About Our Knowledge of Geometry

We noted earlier the changing attitude in the philosophical and scientific community toward the issue of the ideal foundation for our knowledge of the world that followed the Scientific Revolution of the seventeenth century. First, it was thought that a proposition could be known with a kind of certainty that followed from pure reason alone; later, the idea gradually gained dominance that our knowledge of the world—general and theoretical truths about the nature of things—could only be inferred from basic truths about the world. This inference was trustworthy but fallible. Belief in these basic truths rested upon the data provided by the senses through observation and experiment.

But geometry remained a thorn in the side of this empiricist approach to the theory of knowledge. Suppose that geometry gives us truths about the nature of the world that can be known to be the case because they follow by certain logical inference from basic truths whose truth is self-evident and knowable to pure reason. Then geometry can be known to be true without reliance on observation and experiment. Isn't there then at least some domain of knowledge about the world that does not have to be secured by reliance upon the data of the senses, but that could be secured by pure thought alone? And if geometry was such a discipline, did it not remain possible that eventually all of our physical knowledge would rest upon such a superior epistemic basis?

The discovery of the non-Euclidean geometries tended to undermine claims of this sort. If Euclidean geometry was not the only possible geometry, then how could one affirm that the truths of geometry could be known independently of experiment? Was not the structure of space revealed in geometry, just like any other physical structure, describable by any one of a number of alternative, incompatible theories? In such a case, must we not rely on observation, as we do in the other sciences, to tell us which of the possible theories truly describes the structure of the world?

Defenders of the view that Euclidean geometry described the nature of the world sometimes tried to challenge the very logical consistency of the non-Euclidean geometries. That tack soon failed, as relative-consistency proofs for the axiomatic non-Euclidean geometries were soon produced. These proofs showed that we could be assured by pure logic that if the non-Euclidean geometries were inconsistent, then so was Euclidean geometry. Therefore, the non-Euclidean geometries were at least as logically respectable as the Euclidean. Kantians could continue to argue on other grounds that Euclidean geometry was the certain geometry of the world, holding as they did that there was a kind of necessity to the truth of Euclidean geometry that went beyond the necessity of truths made true by logic alone. We shall see, shortly, a reply to them. By and large, however, those familiar with the existence of the new geometries were convinced that the geometry of the world, like its chemistry or physics, was something that only experiment could tell us about.

As we have seen, it was only in the relativistic context that the non-Euclidean geometries actually began to play an important role in theoretical physics. The route went from Newtonian space and time through the spacetime of special relativity and then to the curved spacetime of the general theory of relativity. At each transitional state, empirical facts, the results of observation and experiment, played a decisive role. The postulation of Minkowski spacetime, the spacetime of special relativity, rested upon the surprising discovery that, as far as the round-trip experiments went, the speed of light seemed the same in all inertial states of motion and in all directions. In addition, the fact that the speed of light was the maximal speed of propagation of causal signals also played an important role in the foundation of the theory, and this too was a fact of observational experience. Furthermore, there were all the predicted facts relating to the special theory, such as those having to do with the apparent lifetimes of unstable particles in motion with respect to the observer, the apparent increase in inertial mass with increased velocity, and so on, which again and again were taken as experimental confirmation of the new spacetime picture.

In the move to general relativity as well, facts revealed by observation played a role first in suggesting the new theory and then in confirming it. The observational facts, known to Galileo, about how gravity acted on objects independently of their constitution and size initially suggested to Einstein the idea of treating gravity as a geometric feature of the spacetime. The predicted facts about the curving paths of light near gravitating objects and the relative rates of ideal clocks in different places in a gravitational potential are taken as confirming the theory. Additional factual confirmation comes from the predicted subtle changes in the orbits of the planets from the paths predicted by the Newtonian theory. In the long run, one hopes for observations on the grander astronomical scale, say, of black holes, or even on the cosmic scale, say, of the observational effects of the overall curved structure of the geometry of the universe, to further test the predictions of the theory and, if they are found to be as predicted, to confirm its truth.

Isn't it clear, then, that the empiricists are right? One can imagine innumerable theories about the nature of the world. Only observation and experiment can tell us which theory is correct. This is just as true for geometry as it is for physics, chemistry, biology, or psychology. What the geometry of the world really is like, then, is for observation to decide. Any hope of knowing the geometry of the world with certainty and independently of observation and experiment is an idea whose time has long gone. But are things so cut-and-dried?

Poincaré's Conventionalism

That they are not was suggested by the great mathematician Henri Poincaré in a brilliant examination of the status of geometric knowledge. His study preceded the revolutions of relativity but would throw great light on the status of geometry in these new theories. In a series of essays, Poincaré begins by presenting a relative-consistency proof for a non-Euclidean geometry, refuting any claim that such new geometries must be dismissed as logically inconsistent. Next he takes up the Kantian claim that Euclidean geometry is the necessarily correct geometry of the world. According to that claim, geometry's necessity rests upon the fact that space is a component of our perception of the world, and Euclidian geometry describes the structure of the perceived that is contributed to perception by the perceiving mind. Poincaré argues that the space of physics, the space in which material happenings take place, must be distinguished from any "perceptual space," such as the so-called visual field of visual perception. He argues, in fact, that we don't know of the existence or nature of physical space by any direct perceptual acquaintance at all but, rather, by inference from what we directly perceive. It is, he claims, the order and regularity of the bits of our phenomenal, perceptual, experience that lead us to posit that this experience has a causal origin in physical happenings that are themselves not immediate components of perceptual awareness. We infer the existence of the physical world, including physical space, and its nature as an explanatory hypothesis to account for the order and regularity we experience in our direct perceptions. Such an inference is, then, inference to a hypothesis. And no such hypothesis can have a necessity to it generated out of some alleged "structuring principles of the directly perceived," because the hypothesis is about the physical and inferred, and not about the content of direct perception at all.

At this point, one expects Poincaré to propose that geometry rests for its support on reasonable inference from the data of observation and that one could, in fact, discover that the non-Euclidean geometries fitted the observational data better than the Euclidean. But he surprises us, instead, by an argument to the effect that the Euclidean geometry cannot be refuted by any experience whatever. He argues, in fact, that Euclidean geometry will always be taken by us to be the geometry of the world. It has, then, a kind of necessity, but the necessity is only a matter of conventional determination on our part, not a reflection of some metaphysical fact about the world.

Poincaré's argument rests on a famous parable. Imagine two-dimensional scientists confined to a finite Euclidean plane disk. They try to determine the geometry of their world using transported measuring rods. But we fool them. We give them measuring instruments that expand and contract with changes in temperature—all at the same rate—and so arrange the temperature of the disk that the rods shrink to zero length at its periphery. With a suitable falloff of temperature from cen-

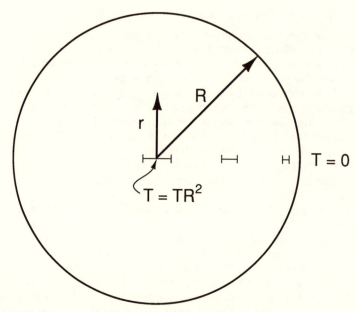

Figure 2.9 Poincaré's parable. Two-dimensional inhabitants are confined to the interior of an ordinary disk on the Euclidean plane. They are equipped with measuring rods that change length with temperature in a linear way. The temperature at the center of the disk is TR^2, where R is the radius of the disk and T is a constant. At any point on the disk the temperature is $T(R^2 - r^2)$ where r is the distance of the point in question from the center of the disk. At the rim of the disk, then the temperature goes to zero and the measuring rods shrink to zero length. It is easy to show that if the inhabitants take their measuring rods as having constant length, they will come to the conclusion that they live on a nonflat Lobachevskian plane that has constant negative curvature and extends to infinity.

ter of disk to edge, it is easy to deceive them into thinking that they are living on an infinite Lobachevskian negatively curved two-dimensional surface. If they try to use light to map out the geometry of their world, we put a medium with a variable index of refraction on the surface, so bending the paths of light rays as to deceive them once again. They are fooled into thinking their geometry is non-Euclidean when it isn't. (See Figure 2.9.)

Now consider us in our three-dimensional world. No matter what measurements we make using rods and light rays (or free particles or clocks if it is spacetime whose geometry we are determining), could it not be the case that any appearance of non-Euclideanness in the geometry was due to fields of stretching and shrinking and to fields that bent light rays and particles from their geodesic paths, rather than to genuine deviation of the space from Euclideanness?

Now in the case of the two-dimensional creatures, we posit ourselves as the ultimate authorities on what is *really* going on. But in the case of our trying to determine the geometry of our world, what is to count as the difference between a real non-Euclidean geometry and a Euclidean world with distorting fields that affect even idealized measuring devices? Poincaré's suggestion is that nothing in the facts of the matter determines which hypothesis is "correct." It is up to us to *choose* which description of the world to give. The "true" geometry of the world is a matter of decision or convention on our part. As we shall see, many different interpretations might be given to such a claim. He goes on to suggest that because Euclidean geometry is simpler than non-Euclidean, we would always choose the former as the "true" geometry of the world, restoring Euclideanness to a necessary feature of the world, but one that is only "conventionally necessary." Of course many people since then have noted that it might be simpler to describe the world in non-Euclidean terms if that made the remaining part of one's theory simpler, and that this is the choice (if choice it is) in, say, general relativity with its curved spacetime.

But Poincaré's main point is clear. The evidence we can accumulate by observation and experiment requires a theoretical explanation. But the hypotheses we offer to explain the observational facts have a structure with a number of elements in them. We can hold fast to a posit about the constitution of one part of this structure in the face of any data whatsoever, as long as we are willing to posit enough changes in another part of the structure. No matter what our experiments show, we can hold on to Euclidean geometry, for example, as long as we are willing to posit enough in the way of a physical field to stretch and shrink rods, deflect light waves, and so on. Therefore, Poincaré claims, it is a matter not of fact but of convention that one geometry rather than another describes the space (or spacetime) of the world.

Responses to Poincaré

There have been a very wide variety of responses to Poincaré's claim, a claim that would threaten not only the idea that we could determine the geometry of the world by inference from observation and experiment but also the general possibility of coming to definitive conclusions about the structure of the world remote from direct observation. One class of responses denies the fundamental premise of Poincaré's argument, that is, that one can separate out a set of alleged facts about the world as the facts of pure observation and then put these facts into some realm of "percepts in the mind," leaving all physical assertions to be knowable, if at all, only on the basis of some kind of inference. Some would deny that any such realm of the immediately perceived is intelligible, arguing that all our perceptions are not of some "sense data in the mind" but of the physical world. They would deny the existence of any such thing as items knowable to perception independently of a posited theory of the world. Can we seriously believe that the space in which we see tables and chairs is not physical space but some "visual space" not in the domain of physical science at all?

More important, these people would usually deny the claim that there are facts about the world in principle immune to being checked up on by "direct observation" or "direct experiment." It is crucial to Poincaré's thesis that such facts as whether the space of the world really is flat or curved is something that can only be known by an inference. It cannot be determined by any sort of direct inspection. This immunity of the geometric facts to observability allows the alternative theories, which "save the observable phenomena." And this immunity is at the core of Poincaré's argument that we could never legitimately claim to know the geometry of the world (except, of course, by conventionally stipulating it).

But many have expressed skepticism that any such realm of being forever immune to direct inspection can be postulated. If we once deny a realm of the directly inspected "in the mind," taking such things as tables and trees as seeable by us, doesn't a slippery slope argument convince us that in principle everything can be "observed"? Can we not see bacteria by using microscopes, viruses by using electron microscopes, and nuclei by using particle accelerators? How then can Poincaré be assured that we could never simply observe whether our space is flat or curved?

Yet Poincaré's presupposition that we can't, that geometric structure is part of a realm of being forever immune to direct observability, seems to have persuasive force. What would it be to observe, not light rays or particles, rods or clocks, but "the structure of space itself"? Obviously there are puzzles galore here. For example, don't we "directly observe" time intervals between our experiences? Are they to be dismissed as nothing but "mental time intervals," to be distinguished from real, physical time in the material world?

One line of argument in Poincaré's favor is that much of contemporary physics dealing with space and time seems to rest on just the sort of assertion of immunity of some facts about the world from direct observation that Poincaré is presupposing. Einstein's arguments for the special theory of relativity, for example, in his critique of the notion of simultaneity for distant events, presuppose that such simultaneity must be determined by light, by causal signals of some kind, or by transported clocks. It cannot be taken as something open to direct inspection. Again, the arguments for the "geometrization" of gravity in the foundations of general relativity rest upon the assumption that the gravitational field can be known only by its effects. It is the behavior of light rays and particles, rods and clocks, that we observe, not the gravitational field itself. In particular, in the relativistic theories, two assumptions seem to be built in to the foundations of the theories: (1) What we observe is the behavior of material things—light rays, particles, clocks, and measuring rods—not the structure of spacetime itself; (2) it is only the behavior of material things at a point that we can determine observationally, that is, such things as whether the ends of two rigid rods are coincident with each other. We cannot take as an observational fact that two rigid rods at a distance from each other have or fail to have the same length, any more than we can take distant simultaneity as an observable feature of the world in the sense of direct observability.

It may well be that such assumptions of classes of features of the world forever immune from direct observational determination are misguided. But they are presupposed in the analysis that grounds our acceptance of the contemporary spacetime theories. Let us, then, for the moment, assume Poincaré is right about these unobservable structures' being part of our theories.

Poincaré is claiming that our posited structures must go beyond the observable facts. It is this fact that introduces into theories the "duality" that allows numerous alternative accounts to have the same observational consequences. How do the theories of Einstein outrun the observable? In the special theory, whereas coincidences of events are observable, simultaneity for distant events is obtained by positing the uniformity of the velocity of light in all inertial frames and in all directions, a "fact" not open to observational check. Again, to get the full spacetime structure of special relativity, one has to add the Linearity Postulate, which amounts to positing spacetime as flat. Once more, this is a theoretical posit that outruns direct checking. Only if these posits are made, do we obtain the standard theory and not, for example, the old theory of an absolute aether with compensating "real" shrinking of moving rods and slowing down of moving clocks. In the general theory, it is posited that the curved light rays and "free" particles influenced by gravity map out the null and timelike geodesics of the spacetime respectively. And local rods and clocks are taken to be correct indicators of the metric intervals of space and time where they are located. Only with these assumptions do we get the observations of the effects of gravity to tell us that the spacetime has curvature. With other posits, we could retain the flat spacetime structure of general relativity, taking gravity to be, as in Newton's theory, a superimposed force field that has metric effects as well as dynamical effects on particles in motion and on light.

Poincaré's model seems, then, to describe nicely the context in which the relativistic theories were constructed. Novel observational facts are obtained. They are restricted to the material and local facts about our measuring instruments. To account for and explain these facts, a spacetime structure is posited. Yet the structures posited outrun in their richness the totality of possible observational facts that support them. And just as in Poincaré's parable of the two-dimensional creatures on the disk, a variety of possible spacetime structures will do justice to what we take to be the totality of observational facts we could encounter. This will be so, at least, if we are prepared to make the necessary changes in other parts of our physical theory.

Realist Options

If, then, we take the Poincaré problem seriously and refuse to dismiss it as resting upon illegitimate notions of what is and is not observable or on illegitimate notions that the realm of the theoretical outruns, in principle, the realm of the observable, how should we go on? One class of responses takes the positing of the theoretical spacetime structure quite straightforwardly, assuming that the theories of space and time genuinely propose real but unobservable structures of the world. Are we then, as Poincaré claimed, reduced to conventionality to choose the correct theory?

One response would be simply to adopt an attitude of skepticism. Assume one of the many possible spacetime theories compatible with the observational data is the correct one. Argue that nothing but observational facts can legitimately lead us to choose one theory in preference to another. Argue, then, that we must simply withhold judgment, if we are reasonable, about which of the alternative spacetime theories really describes the world. Perhaps we are just limited in what we can know about the world. Ought we not, then, to face up to these limitations honestly and refuse to claim knowledge of that which simply can't be known?

To avoid this counsel of despair, many have suggested that we ought to rely on those features of theories that we use and, they think, ought to use, to select the best, most believable, theory from a set of alternatives, the choice among which can't be made on the basis of differential compatibility with the observable facts. It is argued that there are many considerations we bring to bear on theory choice that outrun mere comparison of the observational consequences of the theory with the observed facts. These are considerations that can legitimately help us to decide which theory is the one most believable. Often it is argued that some theories have greater intrinsic plausibility than others. In other cases the relation of a theory to the background science in which it is being considered is alleged to serve as something that can discriminate between more believable theories and those less worthy of belief.

As an example of the second sort of approach, we might consider the allegation that methodological conservatism can play a role in guiding us to one theory as preferred to others observationally indistinguishable from it. Here it is claimed that there is a rule of scientific method to the effect that in choosing a new theory, we select, and ought to select, the one that deviates least from the older theories we had accepted but now reject because of their incompatibility with the evidence.

How would that rule apply in, for example, the case of general relativity? We are looking for a new theory of gravity. Newton's theory is incompatible with relativity and must be rejected, but the theory we put in its place ought to be the one that is compatible with the new observational data and closest in what it says to what the old theory said. Could such a methodological rule lead us to choose Einstein's theory over the "stretching and shrinking plus force field" alternatives to it? It is certainly true that in the older theory we took rods and clocks to correctly indicate spatial and temporal intervals. This holds true in general relativity but not in its flat spacetime alternative. So doesn't methodological conservatism lead us to select general relativity as the preferred alternative?

However, in the older theory spacetime was flat. It remains so in the field alternative, but in general relativity, the radical suggestion of curved spacetime is made. From that point of view, it looks as though the "flat spacetime plus a gravitational field" alternative is the more conservative, hence preferred, choice. The problem is, of course, that the instruction to be conservative with respect to the older theory is ambiguous. There are many aspects of the older and newer theories. Being conservative with regard to some of those aspects might lead to one alternative's being chosen, and being conservative with respect to other aspects might lead us to a quite different choice.

But it is worse than that. Even if conservatism led us to one choice rather than another, couldn't it be the case that the older theory itself could be retrospectively replaced by an alternative to it? Take Newton's gravitational theory, for example. Suppose we take it that the "flat spacetime plus forces" alternative is the relativistic theory most conservative with respect to Newton's and therefore to be preferred. But, as we have noted, it is possible to replace Newton's theory with a curved spacetime theory of gravity that would have the same observational predictions as Newton's theory. Wouldn't the curved spacetime theory, general relativity, then be the most conservative change from that revised version of Newtonian physics? Isn't the rule of conservatism with respect to how theories actually developed, then, full of arbitrariness? Doesn't it just tell us to project older arbitrary decisions, accidents of history, into the future? How can that be a guide to *truth*?

As an example of the other suggestion, that we rely on intrinsic features of theories to make the choice between the alternatives, we might consider the notion of theoretical simplicity. It is a common assertion that scientists, given two theoretical alternatives between which the observational data are not decisive, will choose the simpler of the two, revealing their intuition that the simpler hypothesis is more likely to be the true hypothesis.

The notion of simplicity is, however, one fraught with puzzles. In some versions, it is dependent on how the theory is formulated. In one language or representation, one theory might seem simpler than a second, but the simplicity ordering might be reversed if the theories were expressed in a different manner. Other notions of simplicity that depend upon the structural features of the theory, the logical form of its basic premises, might avoid some of this apparent relativity of simplicity to form of expression. There are, indeed, intuitive senses of simplicity that make special relativity simpler than the alternative aether theories or the alternative theories that don't assume spacetime to be flat. Similar intuitions about simplicity make general relativity seem simpler than the "flat spacetime plus imposed fields" theories alternative to it. In both cases, the idea is that the Einsteinian theory lacks some unnecessary and problematic structure that contaminates the alternatives to it.

To see this, first compare Einstein's special relativistic spacetime to one of the aether theories. Einstein takes it that the velocity of light is the same in all directions in every inertial reference frame. The aether theories deny this. They hold that light has uniform velocity in all directions only in the frame at rest in the aether. In the other reference frames, light only seems to have the same speed in each direction because of the effect of the motion of the laboratory with respect to the aether on such measuring instruments as rods and clocks. So whereas Einstein explains the null results of the round-trip experiments by the uniformity of the velocity of light in all directions along the paths, the aether theory explains it by putting in first a variation in the speed of light in different directions and then a compensating variation in the laboratory instruments, with each variation dependent on the velocity of the laboratory through the aether. The effects of these variations exactly cancel out. Surely the aether theory explanation of the observed results is unnecessarily complicated. To get the observational results, we need to specify a parameter of the theory, i.e., the velocity of the laboratory with respect to the aether. Yet whatever value we specify for this quantity, we get exactly the same observational predictions, because the effects of the velocity cancel out. For this reason no experiment we can perform could determine the velocity of the laboratory with respect to the aether. Surely Einstein's theory, which simply denies that there is such an aether frame or such an undetectable velocity, is simpler as an explanatory hypothesis and therefore to be preferred.

A similar situation holds in the general relativistic case. Einstein explains the curving paths of light and particles by the claim that they are following the geodesics of a curved spacetime. Positing a "flat spacetime plus forces" alternative would take this curvature to be the result of the forces' deflecting the particles from the true, straight-line, geodesics of the actual flat spacetime. Careful examination of the theories shows that to each single world described by the curved spacetime theory there corresponds an infinite number of "flat spacetime plus fields" worlds, just as an infinite number of "aether frame plus compensation" worlds corresponds to a single "special relativistic Minkowski spacetime" world. And just as each of the aether frame worlds is indistinguishable from the others by observation, so each of the new "flat spacetime plus fields" worlds is indistinguishable from all the other such worlds. This is a generalization of something that J. Maxwell and others realized about the prerelativistic theory of gravitation. Suppose there existed in the universe a gravitational field that was constant everywhere (i.e., at each point the gravitational force would have the same magnitude and point in the same direction). The entire material universe would, then, be falling with constant acceleration in this world. Although every object was being accelerated, this acceleration would not, contrary to normal acceleration, be detected. This is because all the measuring devices would suffer the same acceleration as the world itself. So which, if any, constant gravitational field exists is an undetectable fact about the world.

But in general relativity, there is no gravitational field, and all the observationally indistinguishable worlds of the older theory become assimilated to a single curved spacetime world. This is exactly parallel to the way in which special relativity replaces an infinite number of possible aether frames with a single Minkowski spacetime. Then, in an important sense, the standard, Einsteinian, theories are simpler than their observationally indistinguishable alternatives. Some theories of theoretical confirmation have used facts like this to generate new notions of data confirming a theory. The older notions of confirmation tend to give the same confirmation to any two theories that are observationally indistinguishable, unless some antecedent distinguishing intrinsic plausibility has been plugged in. The newer notions of confirmation allow theories like special and general relativity to be confirmed by the data but give only zero confirmation to any theories like the aether theories or the flat spacetime gravitational theories that contain parameters undeterminable by observation.

But, of course, there are those who object to this way out of Poincaré's puzzle. Why should we believe that the simpler theory, even if the notion of simplicity can be made coherent, is the one that we ought to accept as true of the world? What assures us that simplicity, no matter how construed, is to be taken as a mark of the truth of a theory? Of course we might prefer the simpler theory for its aesthetic appeal, but why should complexity be taken as a mark of falsehood, to be viewed on a par with the theory's failing to conform to the observational data? Should such considerations as the simplicity of a theory count toward its believability for someone who takes the realist stance that there is a world independent of our theories about it and that theories either do or do not genuinely describe this world?

Reductionist Options

Contrasting with all these approaches to Poincaré's problem are the approaches that try to undercut the skeptical challenge by denying that there really are alternative theories among which we must choose. If we take the very identity of a theory to be determined by its observational consequences, then won't we come to the conclusion that all the alleged alternative theories are really but one and the same theory, and that they appear to differ from one another only because they have chosen to express the same claims about the world in varying *language*?

The underlying idea is clear. Surely, it is said, we can understand cases where two expressions of theory apparently conflict with each other so that it seems that both cannot be correct, but where the conflict is only apparent: It is the result of terms' being used with different meanings in the two theory expressions. If, for example, someone proposed a theory of electricity exactly like our current theory except that the words "positive" and "negative" referring to charges were interchanged, we would immediately realize that no new theory had been proposed. Instead, the same old theory had been repeated, with the meanings of two key words interchanged. Suppose, then, we posit that the entire real content of a theory is contained in its observational consequences, and that any two theories with the same observational consequences amounted to a single theory. The apparent differences between the two theory expressions would really be due to mere differences in the meanings of some of the terms involved.

A variety of such "positivist" accounts of theory and theoretical meaning have been proposed. Sometimes it is suggested that the terms of a theory, in order to have genuine meaning at all, must receive individual definitions framed entirely in the vocabulary referring to the observables. When we have two apparently incompatible theories with the same observational consequences, we could localize which terms in the two theory expressions differed in meaning. For example, it might be claimed that the fact that light rays travel null geodesics in general relativity amounts to a definition in that theory of "null geodesic" as the path of a light ray. In the "flat spacetime plus forces" theory light rays don't travel null geodesics. So, it is claimed, "null geodesic" must mean something different in this new theory expression. Some other versions of the account demand translatability of any sentence of the theory into one expressed solely in observational terms. Still others find these demands for either strict term definability or sentence-by-sentence translatability too severe. For these theorists it is the theory as a whole that has meaning, and its meaning is exhausted by its totality of observational consequences. In the case of the curved versus flat spacetime theories of gravity, then, they would argue that it is pointless to ask which terms have changed meaning from one theory to the other. Alternatively, they claim, you might say that all of them have, except those referring to the observable phenomena. What one can say, though, is that because the two theories have the same observational consequences, taken as a whole they "say the same thing."

Reductionist approaches of this sort certainly do undercut the skeptical problem of the theory outrunning the data. From this point of view, the outrunning of the observable is only illusory. Sometimes it is said that choosing one theory in preference to another that is observationally equivalent to it is really only choosing a manner of expressing a theory. It is sometimes alleged that it is like choosing one coordinate system to describe the location of events rather than another. To the realist, who asserts that the theories may differ in simplicity, hence, in what they say and, perhaps, in their degree of intrinsic believability, these people would reply that such a difference in simplicity is only a difference in simplicity of manner of expression. It is not a real simplicity difference like that, say, between a linear and a quadratic function relating observable to observable. To choose one of the observationally equivalent alternatives over another, then, is a mere choice of how to express one's theoretical beliefs. According to this view, theoretical beliefs really are nothing but linguistically convenient summaries of the totality of their observational consequences. Although it isn't completely clear what Poincaré meant when he said the choice of geometry was conventional, perhaps this is what he had in mind.

The gravest objection to this approach to theories is where it takes one when it is pushed to its—almost inevitable—limit. As two theories that apparently say quite incompatible things about the structure of the unobservable are taken to be actually fully equivalent to each other, it is plain that one ought not to take what they say about unobservables in a straightforwardly referential manner. If a theory that says that spacetime is curved is taken as fully equivalent to one that says that spacetime is flat, then clearly both theories are only using reference to spacetime as an instrumental device to generate their real content, the lawlike order among the observables they predict. One really ought not, then, to take such talk of spacetime as really talking about some object and attributing some feature to it. To see this, one need only consider the fact that if any two theory expressions that have the same observational content are fully equivalent, then the mere summary of the observational consequences the theories have in common is equivalent to both of them. And this third "theory" doesn't refer to the theoretical entities and structures (like spacetime and its curvature) at all. The fact that such a summary of observational consequences might be an infinite collection of assertions doesn't seem, from this radical positivist perspective, relevant to the irrealist claim.

But, then, taking observational equivalence as sufficient for full equivalence seems to entail a radical irrealism about the unobservable. All reference, except to that which is directly open to observational inspection, is pseudoreference, and all description of the structure of the unobservable becomes mere manner of speaking and not a serious description of an alleged real part of the world. If such reference to spacetime and its structure is wholly fictional, is reference to electrons equally fictitious? And if we follow the familiar philosophical route of taking the immediately observable to consist only of sense data of direct perception and not of physical features of physical things at all, are we not led to a view of the entire physical world as a fiction? Surely such a radical irrealism about the physical is too high a price to pay to avoid the skeptical challenge to our knowledge of the real geometric structure of the world.

Further Realist Responses

Many realists, in response to these consequences of the positivist approach I have just outlined, have argued that the core error of positivism is in its notion that observational equivalence of theories is sufficient for full equivalence. These realists would want to admit that sometimes apparently incompatible theories really "say the same thing." But they would deny that having observational consequences in common is sufficient for full equivalence. If, they say, the theories have the same structure at the theoretical level, so that one theory can be obtained from the other by a term-by-term interchange (like the switching of "positive" and "negative" in the theory of electricity noted earlier), then it is appropriate to say the theories are equivalent. But when they have the same observational consequences but differ in their structure at the theoretical level, then they should not be counted as equivalent. This is the situation, it is alleged, in our familiar spacetime cases. Special relativity is structurally unlike the aether-compensatory theories, as is revealed by the fact that an infinite number of distinct aether theories correspond to the one Minkowski spacetime. And general relativity is structurally unlike the "flat spacetime plus forces" alternatives to it because, once again, the single general relativistic spacetime corresponds to an infinite number of possible alternatives to it. This just repeats the assertion that the relativistic theories are preferable to their alternatives on the basis of simplicity of a structural sort. We need not, then, assume that the relativistic theories are simply equivalent to their alternatives, because we need not accept the positivists' claim that observational equivalence implies full equivalence.

Returning to this realist perspective leads us back, of course, to the questions asked earlier about how we can reasonably choose between the now inequivalent but observationally indistinguishable theories. It also leads us into the question of how, for the realist, the theoretical terms of a theory do get their meanings. Most realists do subscribe to the idea that meaning is first acquired by the terms of our discourse associated with elements of observational experience, and that the remaining terms of the theory have their meaning given by some relation they bear to the observational terms (although others would deny even such a limited "semantic precedence" to the observational vocabulary). One familiar realist approach is to argue that the theoretical terms gain whatever meaning they have simply by the role they play in the network of laws in the theory that ultimately leads to observational consequences. The idea here is that whereas the observational terms acquire their meaning outside of the role they are playing in the theory, the theoretical terms gain whatever meaning they have from their role as placeholders in the theoretical structure. Thus "null geodesic" is said to have its meaning fixed entirely by the place that term plays in the laws of, say, general relativity.

It is frequently claimed that such a theory of meaning for theoretical terms is not incompatible with realism about theoretical entities and properties. "Null geodesic," for example, has its meaning fixed by the role of the term in the spacetime theory. But that doesn't mean there aren't any null geodesics. If the theory is correct, then there are. They are whatever the term "null geodesic" refers to. The problem is that it is easy to cook up surrogate references for the terms to make the theories still correct, even if the terms no longer refer to what we think of as the real theoretical entities and features. One could, for example, read all the theoretical terms of the spacetime theory not as referring to what we would intuitively think of as spacetime structures but, instead, as referring to some abstract objects such as the numbers. The theory would then be reinterpreted to be the claim that numbers can be assigned to the observable entities and features in such a way that, following the rules of mathematics, certain lawlike regularities among the observables could be inferred to hold, but just those regularities that follow from the original spacetime theory as realistically understood. Talk about theoretical entities and features, then, becomes talk about how we can embed observable behavior in an abstract structure that has consequences for order and regularity among the observables. Whenever one adopts a "meaning is given solely by role in theory" view of theoretical terms, such "representationalist" reconstructions of the theory will plague the realist.

For this reason, some realists would want to argue that theoretical terms, including those referring to spacetime structures, acquire their meaning in some other way. Analogies of meaning with observable terms are frequently brought into the picture at this point. Molecules, it is said, are described as particles, and we know what "particle" means from observable particles. So we know something about what "molecule" means that assures us that, whatever molecules are, they are not abstract objects like numbers. Perhaps the analogy of a path as a spacetime structure with a path constituted of some material stuff can give us access into the meaning of spacetime terms beyond their role in predicting the local behavior of material objects.

Pragmatist Views

The options we have explored do not exhaust all the possible reactions one could have to puzzles of the sort Poincaré has presented to us. Some philosophers have tried to argue that the debates between realists and antirealists all rest upon confusions. Some of these arguments go back to the skepticism earlier noted about the possibility of making the observable consequences a distinguished class of the consequences of a theory. Others rely on a claim to the effect that worrying about which of the possible alternative theories is the true one is misguided. Perhaps there are a number of alternative accounts, all of which would be, on the basis of some totality of possible observational data, equally meritorious of being called "rational to believe." Suppose we take the accounts to be genuinely incompatible, not just reducing them all to mere linguistic variants, as the positivist would have us do. If we pick one of these theories, we will declare its consequences true and the consequences of its rivals incompatible with it false. Had we picked one of the other alternatives we would have changed our views about which assertions were true and which were false, of course, but we would have been equally rational. But what is truth anyway? Isn't it merely a way of characterizing at the level of talk about sentences that which we would express using the sentences themselves, in the sense that we will declare as true all and only the sentences we are prepared to assert? So perhaps Poincaré was right in saying that the geometry of the world was a matter of convention in the sense that it is up to us to pick one of the rational options available and, having done so, to declare its consequences "true."

But what if the option we choose doesn't really conform to the way the world is? At this point, some become skeptical about the very idea of a theory-independent world to which theories do or do not correspond. Whether such a view, sometimes associated with pragmatism, sometimes called "internal realism," really constitutes a stable position, one that doesn't reduce either to skepticism or to some kind of positivist reductionism remains an open question.

Summary

In any case we can now see how the developments in pure mathematics and in theoretical physics have radically changed our attitudes both toward geometry and toward the place it holds in our body of knowledge. For centuries, geometry stood as the prime example of a theory that seemed to tell us significant facts about the world in which we lived; the geometric truths could be known to us, and known with certainty, since they were derivable by certain logical inference from first principles whose truth was self-evident. Geometry was the paradigm for knowledge in general. If only we were smart enough, we could know all the truths about the world, as we knew the geometric ones. Later, as we have seen, as the empiricist trend led most philosophers to affirm that we could know the world only by means of generalization and inference from the basic data of observation and experiment, geometry seemed to remain the exception to this general rule, an exception whose special nature required an explanation such as that attempted by Kant.

With the discovery of a multiplicity of logically consistent axiomatic geometries, and the later generalization beyond these to the multidimensional curved geometries of Riemann, and beyond these to the geometries envisioned in the study of the topology and differential structure of spaces (which we have not touched upon), the status of geometry as knowable without recourse to observation or experiment came under serious doubt. This doubt was made much more significant by the discovery in the twentieth century first of the new spacetimes essential for the relativistic treatment of the behavior of matter and light, and then of the ability to invoke curved spacetime as a theory of gravity in the general theory of relativity. Didn't it seem, then, that geometry, like all other theories of the world, rested for its knowability on observation and experiment?

But as we have seen, this is too simple. It certainly does seem that geometry becomes, in the modern perspective, much more like the other fundamental, general, but observationally based, physical theories of the world. As we have seen, however, reflection on just how observational results can and cannot determine for us what geometry of the world we ought rationally to believe reveals to us the degree to which geometry, like all fundamental physical theory, outruns the simple generalization from data that a crude empiricism would take as the model of inference to theories.

How to respond to the possibility of reconciling a diversity of geometries with any possible observational data is, as we have seen, a very problematic matter. We might take a realist attitude and simply be skeptical about which geometry really describes the world. Or we might try to find methodological rules for rational belief, rules that would guide us to pick one of the many alternative geometries as uniquely rationally most believable. Or we might try to avoid the skeptical challenge and invoke a reductionist claim to the effect that all the alternative geometries, when supplemented by the physical theories needed to make them—each in its own way—compatible with the observational data, are really equivalent to one another. Finally we might try to undercut the thrust of the "underdetermination of geometry by any possible data" problem by denying some of its premises about the distinction between the "in principle observable" and the "in principle unobservable" or by challenging the implicit assumption of a unique true theory corresponding to a theory-independent real world.

Geometry once again has posed problems for our theory of knowledge in general. These problems of theoretical underdetermination are general ones that must be faced by anyone who wants to understand how one can rationally found a theory of the world in its full generality, including its reference to entities and structures taken as immune from direct observation, on the limited data acquirable from observational experience.

What Kind of Being Does Spacetime Have?

As we have seen, it is impossible to explore problems about our knowledge of space and time without getting into issues of being, so-called metaphysical concerns. A positivistic approach to the meaning of theories, designed to undercut the underdetermination problem by identifying the content of a theory with the content of its observational consequences, will demand an irrealist attitude toward the entities and features apparently posited by the theory at the nonobservable level. But there are many other questions of a metaphysical sort that, though they may eventually raise epistemological concerns, are not initially grounded in questions about knowledge. Many of these questions are quite specific to the study of space and time, although, as we shall see, treating them will often bring to light broader questions of metaphysics.

Time and Being

Consider, for example, the traditional doctrines connecting time and being. For some, it seemed intuitively obvious that only what existed now really existed at all. The future was not yet in existence and the past had ceased to exist. Only entities that existed at the present could be said, properly speaking, really to exist. For others, it was the past and present that were real and the future unreal. Here the intuitive idea was that the past and present, having already come into being or occurred, had a determinate reality. What they were like was a matter of hard fact. According to that idea, the future was a realm of that which had not yet come into being. It had no determinate reality at all. After all, following along the thought, if it was a determinate fact now that some future event had a reality, then how could it still be open as to whether the event would in fact occur? How could there be any room for deciding what our future actions would be, for example, if it was already the case now, and had always been the case, that what we would do tomorrow was already a determinate fact today? The issue here is not that of determinism, of whether or not past and present events fix, by their lawlike connections to other events, what future events will, in fact, occur. The issue is, rather, the claim that if future happenings had present and past reality (if it was a fact now that I would buy ice cream tomorrow), then there could be no sense in which the future was open to possibility at all.

Opposed to such intuitions were the views to the effect that any such alleged connections of time to being were mere illusions of language. Past, present, and future, it was argued, were equally real. We don't take it as grounds for denying reality to things that they are not here, where we are located, so why should we take it as grounds for denying their reality that they are not in existence when we are speaking or having thoughts about them? We would think it silly to claim, for example, that things behind us or at our location were real but that things in front of us lacked true reality, so why should we not think it equally absurd to posit reality to past and present but deny it to future realities?

Tied in with these issues are a number of others to which we will be able to direct only the briefest remarks. It is sometimes alleged that time is radically different from space: Whereas space can be correctly viewed from a kind of "perspectiveless" standpoint, an adequate understanding of the temporality of things requires a perspectival viewpoint. We could, it is argued, describe all of spatial phenomena in two—equally adequate—ways. We could assign all spatial locations some coordinate name and say where things occurred by specifying the locations in terms of this, perspectiveless, naming. Or we could specify where something happened in relation to "here," the place at which we are located.

If we try the same trick with time, we see a puzzle. Does the information provided by saying when things occurred, even in relation to one another, fully convey all the temporal aspects of what happened? Some say no. Suppose we give the date on which Julius Caesar died and the date it is now. Suppose we add the fact that the date of Caesar's death is earlier than now, taking "is earlier than" as a primitive relation among times. When we have said all of that, have we said all there is to be said, temporally, about Caesar's death? The claim that we have not rests upon the idea that when we say "Caesar died" or otherwise specify that Caesar's death is past, we are doing more than specifying that it occurred before 1989, say. That latter fact is "timelessly true," but the fact that Caesar *died* was not true before he did, even if the fact Caesar's death is (timelessly) earlier than 1989 is, in a sense, always true.

Couldn't we, though, capture the "pastness" of Caesar's death by saying that it occurred earlier than *now*? To be sure, it is replied, but now is the name of the *present* and in putting things that way we have reintroduced essential tensedness into our temporal description of things. Those who deny that there is anything essentially different between time and space in this regard reply that "now" is a word just like "here." The reference of such words, sometimes called token reflexives or indexicals, varies with their use. Each use of "here" refers to the place at which the speaker is located. Similarly each use of "now" refers to the time the utterance is made. Is there anything more mysterious to "Caesar died," beyond the fact that Caesar's death is (timelessly) earlier than 1989 and that it is *now* 1989, than there is to the fact that the supernova occurred some distance from the earth and *here* is on the earth?

Yes, responds the proponent of the view that there is something radically different about time that distinguishes it from space. Whereas things that exist in space elsewhere than here exist, things that don't exist now don't really exist at all. "Now" isn't a mere indexical, they insist; it is the term that picks out (at any time) that moment of time that is the moment at which things exist, which is of course, the present moment! So this debate about the essential tensedness of time reverts, once again, to the Augustinian intuition that only that which exists now exists at all, properly speaking.

Relativistic Considerations

It is clear that the radical restructuring of space and time into spacetime posited by the special theory of relativity must have a strong impact on this debate. What becomes of the claim that "only that which exists now truly exists," given that events that are simultaneous for one observer occur at different times for an observer in motion with respect to the first even if the two observers are momentarily coinciding? The very meaning of "now" has become problematic. At least it has become a relative matter of exactly which events are occurring "now."

Suppose two observers are coincident at event *e* but in motion with respect to one another. There will be events like event *a* that are after *e* for the first observer but simultaneous with *e* for the second. But then, how could we say that *a* is unreal for the first observer if *a* is real to the second observer at the time in question (being simultaneous with *e* for that second observer) and if the second observer is certainly real at event *e* for the first? The situation is even worse than that. An event in relativity can be later than event *e* or "absolutely later" than event *e*. We speak of "absolutely later" when the event, *b*, is after *e* and causally connectable to it by some signal traveling at or below the speed of light. For events like *a* that are not causally connectable to *e*, *a* will appear after *e*, simultaneous with *e*, and before *e* to different observers. But all observers will agree that *b*, which is absolutely after *e*, is after *e*. Yet it can still be the case that there is an observer whose life event *e'* is simultaneous (for him) with *b*, but such that *e'* is simultaneous with *e* for the first observer. So the first observer will declare the second observer's life at *e'* real at *e*, and the second observer will declare *b* real at *e'*. How then could the first observer think of *b*, in his absolute future, as unreal at *e*?

The arguments here are designed to convince the reader that accepting the spacetime of relativity makes a mockery of the traditional view that "only what is present now is real." It is argued that relativity is clearly compatible only with the alternative view that takes all events, past, present, and future, as equally real, just as we traditionally take all that goes on in space, wherever it is happening, as equally entitled to be called real. If past, present, and future are as relative to states of motion as the special theory of relativity takes them to be, how could we think of reality as varying with the temporal place of an event relative to the present event in the life of the agent concerned?

But, of course, it isn't that easy. The attempt to read off a metaphysical conclusion from a scientific theory requires more care than we have given it so far. One could, formally, hold to the old doctrines of the unreality of all but the present, even in the face of accepting relativity, simply by denying that "is real" is a fully transitive notion. If "is simultaneous" has the feature in relativity that *e'* can be simultaneous with *e* for observer one, *b* simultaneous with *e'* for observer two, but *b* *not* simultaneous with *e* for any observer (which feature it certainly does have), than why should we not relativize "is real to" in just the same way, so that although *e'* is real to *e* for observer one and *b* real to *e'* for observer two, *b* isn't real to *e* for anyone? So no observer at event *e* will ever declare *b* to be a real event no matter what his state of motion when he is coincident with *e*.

A more interesting response proceeds by seeking for the sources of the intuition that past and future are unreal in the first place. One motivation for that view, although by no means the only one, is the epistemic remoteness of past and future to the present. It is a common idea that the present is "presented" to us immediately in experience, but that what happened in past and future can only be known by inference from present experience (including such experience as "having the memory that such-and-such an event occurred"). As we saw in "How Do We Know the True Geometry of the World?" the ontological status of the inferred is frequently one that is placed in doubt. There are arguments designed to cast skeptical doubt on the adequacy of any claim to know the truth of a proposition whose truth can only be known indirectly and by means of an inferential process. *If* one bases the claim to unreality of past and future on their remoteness from the kind of knowability that the present has for us, then a way of holding on to the intuition that past and future are unreal in the relativistic context becomes evident.

When we looked at the foundations of relativity theory, we saw that it is based on a critical examination of our knowledge of events remote from us in space. It is on that critical argument that Einstein's original critique of the intuitive notion of simultaneity for distant events rested. Following out what is suggested by the remarks above suggests a metaphysical reading appropriate to relativity for someone who wants to hold to the view that past and future are unreal. It is to deny the reality of the else*where* as much as to the else*when*, taking as that which has genuine reality only that which is coincident with one's place-time as an observer. Now, to be sure, such a reduction of the real to a point in spacetime is even worse than retaining reality only for the infinitely thin moment of time that is the now. Needless to say, I am not advocating such a radical diminution in what we view as real. The claim being made, however, is that the impetus and the intuitions that lay behind the earlier irrealist attitude toward past and future can't be dismissed out of hand simply by pointing out the relativity of the notions of past and future to the state of motion of the observer in a relativistic spacetime. The reader interested in the questions of why anyone would hold to such dramatic irrealism about past and future in the first place and why, in the relativistic context, apparently sane people might be tempted to the even more radical irrealism about the elsewhere will have to seek out the more detailed works on these issues.

Substantivalism Versus Relationism

A topic with rather more substantial possibilities is the impact of relativistic theories on the debate between substantivalists and relationists that I introduced earlier. As we shall see, the issues here are multiple, subtle, and complex. But as we shall also see, it turns out, once again, that one must be wary of the tendency to infer a metaphysical view from the results of science prematurely. Trying to arrive at some philosophical conclusion concerning the existence and nature of space and time by examining what our best available scientific theories tell us about space and time is a worthwhile task. But it is one that requires a healthy dose of philosophical caution and prudence.

The relationists denied that one should posit space and time as entities in their own right, arguing that all that could be posited were the spatial relations material objects bore to one another and the temporal relations material events bore to one another. After the development of the special theory of relativity, it was commonly asserted that Einstein had finally fulfilled the Leibnizian relationist program. But these claims were very misleading. Although the special theory does tell us that some features of the world we once took to be absolute are really relative, this is not at all the same thing as saying that relationism is correct. In Newton's account of space and time, there is a definite, non-relative, spatial, and temporal separation between any two events. In the theory of relativity, such separations are only relative to a choice of inertial reference frame and differ depending on the frame chosen. But such relativity has nothing to do with whether in order to account for observable phenomena, we must posit space and time or, now, spacetime, as structures over and above the material things and features of the world. It should also be noted in passing here that although special relativity turns some previously nonrelative notions into relative ones, it introduces new, nonrelative, features of its own. The spacetime interval separation between events is, in the special theory, an absolute relation between the events and is independent of any observer, as is the proper time elapsed along a specific path in spacetime from event to event.

If Newton's argument for a substantival view of spacetime, which he used with such great effect against Leibniz, was correct, then special relativity would seem to be a theory that posits a substantival spacetime as well. As we have noted, the distinction, so important in the Newtonian argument, between genuinely uniformly moving, inertial systems and absolutely accelerated systems holds up in the special theory of relativity. In the newer theory, the inertial frames are, as they were in the Newtonian theory, those in which no inertial forces are experienced. But they are also now distinguished by being the states of motion in which the optical round-trip experiments give their famous null results. The distinction between being really in accelerated motion or not, which is at the core of Newton's argument against relationism, remains in the special theory of relativity.

Does this mean that if we accept the special theory, we must accept the metaphysical position of the Newtonian antirelationist (with, of course, Minkowski spacetime, rather than Newton's absolute space, as the substantival spacetime structure)? Do we still need a "spacetime itself" relative to which absolute acceleration is acceleration and whose existence is posited as part of the explanation of the existence of inertial forces and the optical effects that reveal absolute acceleration? Maybe, but once again it would be hasty to leap without further thought from a scientific theory to a metaphysical conclusion. Could we not find some way of reconciling special relativity with a relationist account of spacetime?

Perhaps. But the philosophical issues involved are complex, subtle, and problematic. There are arguments designed to show that the substantivalist's program of positing spacetime as an entity needed to explain the distinction between absolutely accelerated motions and those absolutely nonaccelerated is flawed and that the explanations offered are spurious. Inertial forces and the optical effects of acceleration are explained by reference to the acceleration of the laboratory with respect to the "inertial reference frames" of spacetime itself, these taking the place in special relativity of Newton's "space itself." But the spacetime structures themselves remain, in some sense, immune to direct observability, showing up only indirectly in terms of the causal effects of motion with respect to them. Can't we explain all that there is to explain without positing spacetime itself?

Now we can explain the differences in felt inertial effects in two laboratories by reference to their relative acceleration to one another. "But," says the substantivalist, "you can't explain why in one set of these frames no inertial effects are felt at all, the effects being felt only in the laboratories in acceleration with respect to these preferred laboratories. I," he says, "can explain why these frames are preferred. They are the ones unaccelerated with respect to spacetime itself." The relationist can counterargue by claiming that although he cannot explain why one set of these frames is preferentially inertial, he can simply take that as a "basic brute fact of nature" that simply doesn't ever get explained. After all, he can say, there must be some fundamental brute facts, so why not these? He goes on to argue that the substantivalist requires brute facts in any case. For the substantivalist, it is a brute fact of nature that acceleration with respect to the inertial geodesics of spacetime induces the inertial effects. So, the relationist claims, the substantivalist is no better off in explanatory terms than is the relationist, but the former must posit the mysterious entity "spacetime itself," which does no real explanatory work. And once again following Leibniz, the relationist will produce a series of arguments to the effect that the substantivalist view posits other facts, such as at which event location in spacetime a particular event occurs, that have no observable consequences whatsoever. So, continues the relationist, the positing of spacetime itself introduces "differences in theory without an observational difference." Such differences in theory were a puzzling feature of Newton's space itself.

There remain many other puzzling features on both sides of the argument. Indeed, as in any metaphysical debate in philosophy, the very terms in which the debate is being argued are highly problematic. Do we really understand what the substantivalist is claiming we must postulate in order to explain the observable phenomena? Do we really understand what the relationist is denying and what he is putting in its place? In particular, can we really fully understand on what the two approaches differ? I shall say just a little about these issues later.

Mach's Proposal and General Relativity

For the moment, though, let us return to the proposal of Mach that an alternative, relationistically acceptable, explanation of the famous inertial effects might be possible after all. Could we not assume that the inertial forces, and now the inertial optical effects as well, were the result of acceleration of the test apparatus not with respect to space itself or, in the relativistic case, with respect to the inertial geodesic structure of Minkowski spacetime but, rather, with respect to the cosmic matter of the universe? After all, in the theory of electromagnetism, we are familiar with magnetic forces that depend upon the velocities charged particles have with respect to one another. Could there not also be acceleration-dependent forces among bits of ordinary matter? If these forces depended very little on the separation of things from one another, but were highly dependent on the amounts of matter involved, couldn't it be possible to explain the inertial effects as the result of the acceleration of the test object with respect to what Mach called the "fixed stars," and what we would now speak of as the distant matter of the superclusters of galaxies that make up the cosmic matter of the universe?

Whereas special relativity doesn't provide a context suitable for Machian ideas, perhaps general relativity is more promising in this direction. After all, it deals with gravity, a long-range force. Newtonian gravity certainly couldn't provide the kind of long-distance, acceleration-dependent interaction Mach posited as responsible for the inertial effects, but perhaps when gravity is reconciled with relativity in the manner of the new curved spacetime theory of gravity, a Machian-type theory will result. Indeed, Einstein was certainly motivated by such hopes when he began the research that led to the general theory of relativity.

If Mach were right in positing that inertial effects are the result of the interaction of the test system with the remaining matter of the universe, what would be some consequences of this? First consider Newton's early remarks about what would happen in an empty universe. From the Newtonian point of view, a distinction between a spinning object and one not spinning should exist even if the test object were the only object in the universe. The spin would be revealed by the inertial effects on the test object generated by the absolute motion. Mach doubts that we should even think about empty universes. The universe is, he says, given to us only once, "complete with fixed stars intact." This might mean that we have no way of inferring from what we do observe to what would be the case in a radically different universe, or it might be the stronger claim that because the laws of nature are merely summaries of what does in fact occur in the world as it is, it is meaningless to talk about what would occur in a universe radically unlike the actual one. Be that as it may, we can certainly ask of a theory like general relativity, which can describe gravity in many different kinds of possible worlds, if its predictions for an empty universe would, like Newton's, still make a distinction between absolutely rotating objects and objects not rotating, or whether that distinction would disappear in this world—without Mach's cosmic matter as the reference frame for absolute motion.

We would expect that in a Machian world the inertial effects generated on a test object would vary if the matter of the universe surrounding the object were radically modified, as the inertial effects are the result of interaction of test system and surrounding matter. Does the general theory of relativity predict that? It should make no difference if we spoke of an object in a Machian world rotating and the surrounding matter not or, instead, spoke of the matter rotating about the test laboratory, for, according to Mach, it is only the relative acceleration of test system and matter that determines the inertial forces detected. Is this what general relativity predicts? Finally, if Mach is right, it should be absurd to speak of the matter of the universe as itself in absolute rotation. If the effects of rotation in the test system are due to its motion relative to the cosmic matter, then it should be impossible for there to be effects owing to the cosmic matter itself's being in absolute rotation, for that would mean rotation of this matter with respect to itself, which is absurd. What does the general theory have to say about this?

Some early work with general relativity indicated Machian aspects of the theory. It is certainly true that what a test object in accelerated motion experiences will be dependent on the general distribution of matter in the universe, for in general relativity, absolute acceleration is deviation of motion from the local, curved, timelike geodesics of the spacetime. And because the overall curvature of the spacetime is correlated with the distribution of matter in the spacetime, radically changing the amount or distribution of cosmic matter will have an effect on inertial forces generated by local motion. Again, it can be shown in general relativity that an object that is itself at rest, but that is surrounded by matter in high rotation, will experience forces similar to those the test object would have experienced had it been put into rotation and the surrounding matter been at rest.

But if one looks further, the theory seems less and less one that Mach would have desired. Although inertial effects are modified by the changing distribution of external matter in the world, it is as though there was a basic inertial effect due to absolute rotation to which the new, modifying effects were added. In other words, even in a universe devoid of external matter, general relativity predicts a distinction between being in absolute rotation and not. To determine what spacetime is like in a general relativistic world requires the specification of boundary conditions for the spacetime, just as finding what an electrical field is like requires more than knowing what charges are present. The usual assumption made in general relativity, at least in open universes, is that spacetime far from matter is flat, Minkowski spacetime. A reasonable spacetime for an empty universe, then, would be just this flat, Minkowski spacetime of special relativity. But then, in such a world the old Newtonian distinction between the absolutely rotating and the not rotating would still hold up. Indeed, general relativity allows for even stranger empty spacetimes. Spacetime curvature has its own gravitational self-energy. So it is possible to have nonzero curvature in an empty universe, or for there to be regions of curved spacetime whose deviation from flatness is supported by no matter at all but simply by the self-energy of the curved spacetime region. Therefore, Mach's idea that in an empty world there would be no inertial effects doesn't hold up in general relativity.

Again, although matter spinning around an object generates inertial effects, the situation can be seen to deviate from what Mach would expect. If a test object is surrounded by two cylinders rotating with respect to each other and with respect to the test object, what one experiences in the laboratory will depend not only on the relative rotations involved but also on which cylinder is "really rotating," directly contrary to Machian expectations. Most dramatic of all was the discovery by K. Gödel that there are possible worlds consistent with general relativity in which all the matter of the universe is in rotation. It is not as if that matter were some gigantic, cosmic, spinning rigid sphere. That would be relativistically impossible. But in this world, an observer at any point whose laboratory was at rest with respect to the cosmic matter could perform an experiment to show himself that he was rotating along with all that matter. For each observer, there is a special plane. If the observer shoots out free particles or light rays along that plane, they follow spiral paths in the reference frame fixed in the cosmic matter. This indicates that this matter is in rotation, just as the path of a particle moving in a straight line out from the center over a phonograph record spinning on a turntable will mark a spiral groove on the record. So it is as if each observer could count himself as central to the spinning of the cosmic matter. For a Machian this seems absurd, but it is a possibility consistent with general relativity, once more revealing that theory's non-Machian aspects. (See Figure 2.10.)

Attempts to make general relativity more Machian exist. Some of the objections to a Machian interpretation of general relativity rest on the fact that the distribution of matter is not always sufficient to determine fully the structure of spacetime, hence, not adequate to determine fully what inertial effects of motion will exist. In universes that are always spatially closed, however, there is a tighter bond between the distribution of matter and spacetime structure, so that only one spacetime structure is compatible with the full distribution of matter. So, it has been proposed, the Machian version of general relativity is one where the spacetime has the appropriate closure. But this is a long way from Mach's hard-nosed relationism.

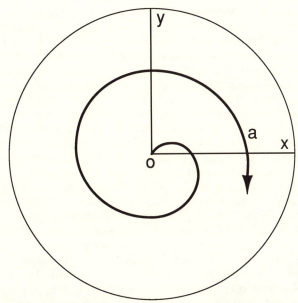

Figure 2.10   The absolute rotation of matter in the Gödel universe. In a solution
to the equations of general relativity found by K. Gödel it is plausible to speak of
the smoothed-out matter of the universe as being in "absolute rotation." What does
this mean? At any point there is a plane with the following feature: Fix x and y
coordinates in the plane so as to be at rest relative to the smoothed-out matter of
the universe. Now send out from point o a free particle or light ray, a. In the coordinates at rest in the matter, the particle or light ray will trace out a spiral path
as the particle or light ray moves away from o. If we think of the free particles and
light rays as in straight-line motion relative to some "absolute" reference frame, it
is "as if" the smoothed-out matter is rotating relative to that frame.

More on General Relativity and the Debate
Between Substantivalists and Relationists

In fact there are aspects to the theory of spacetime in general relativity
that make us begin to wonder whether the distinction between relationism and substantivalism, as they were traditionally understood, is
coherent. We have noted that, in general relativity, the spacetime itself
has mass-energy. But mass-energy is the characteristic basic aspect of
matter as usually understood. Can we then talk about "relations among
matter" versus "spacetime itself" if the distinction between matter and
spacetime is itself problematic?

Even before the theory of general relativity presented the issues just
discussed, it was clear that the distinction between substantivalism and
relationism as traditionally understood was under stress. In the late
nineteenth century, the concept of "the field" became essential in physics. In order to deal with the facts of electricity and magnetism, for

example, it became necessary to add to the elements of nature items quite different from the material particles familiar from earlier physics. Entities such as the electric field are thought of as being extended over all space, with differing intensities at different spatial points. They have a dynamic evolution over time. Such physical "objects" as fields are essential to standard physical theory. But they are clearly a very different sort of thing from the localized material objects presupposed by the relationist. In many ways, they are more like the substantivalist's "space itself" than like ordinary material particles. When one considers how much one's view of what there is must change when fields are admitted into the physicist's picture of the world, it seems clear that the breakdown of the terms of the substantivalist-relationist debate had already begun with the introduction of field quantities into physics.

If we focus on a different aspect of general relativity, we see another way in which the existence of our fundamental theory of spacetime affects the traditional debate between substantivalists and relationists. The problem of determinism in physics is an enormously complex one. The eighteenth-century scientist P. S. de Laplace is famous for asserting that given the truth of the Newtonian mechanical picture of the world, a specification of the state of the world at one time determined its state at all future times, because the laws of nature generated from that state all the necessarily following states at later times. But everything about the issue of whether he was right, whether the world is really deterministic, becomes complex and problematic.

To begin with, there are some philosophical problems. As B. Russell pointed out, if we let the notion of "state of the world" be broad enough and the notion of "law of nature" be flexible enough, then determinism becomes a trivial doctrine, for no matter what the world was like, we could simply take the laws to be the statements saying which actual states followed which others. Let us suppose we have some way of avoiding such trivializations by demanding that genuine laws meet some stricter constraints. Many scientific problems come next. Even in Newtonian mechanics, there are problems with determinism. If we deal with point particles whose strength of interaction gets unlimited as the particles approach a zero separation, it becomes impossible to follow states deterministically through collisions of the particles. Again if we specify the world at a given time, the future may be influenced by a particle that "comes in from infinity" after that time, blocking the determination of the future by the full state at the time in question.

When we move first to special and then to general relativity with their new spacetimes, many more-complex issues arise. States of the world "at a time" are a relative matter in special relativity. In general relativity, it may not even be possible to slice up the spacetime of the world into "spaces at a time," so that the very notion of the state of the world everywhere at one time may no longer make sense. The pattern of possible causal influence in these theories is, of course, more complex than it was in the Newtonian theories, and the complexity of the causal structure leads to important and interesting mathematical problems of trying to characterize which worlds are deterministic in which senses one can give to the term. In general relativity, another problem arises because of the possibility (and, often, inevitability) of singularities in the spacetime. The Big Bang at which our spacetime universe started (if it exists) is one such singularity, as would be those at the center of so-called black holes. These singularities are points of spacetime where curvature becomes infinite. Their presence in a space-time blocks the ability to predict through them from earlier to later states of the world. Thus they introduce a form of indeterminism into the picture.

The very connection between determinism and predictability, as-sumed to mean much the same thing by Laplace, is also problematic. Does saying that the world is deterministic imply that it is predictable, at least in principle? Many have argued that such an implication doesn't hold. After all, determinism says that the state of the world at one time fixes, by the laws of nature, states at other times. But if we can't know the full state of the world at a given time, as a matter of fundamental principle, then the world might be deterministic but not predictable. Minkowski spacetime has this nature. The full state of the world on a space (relative to an inertial frame) may very well fix the state of the world on later spaces. But for any given observer, it may be the case that he will never be able to accumulate the information about the state of the world on any entire space-at-a-time, because the information he gets is what can causally reach him from the past, and this is restricted to what falls inside his backward light cone. That is, he can only gain information about events in the past that can be connected to him at the present by causal signals from the past. For this reason and, we shall see, for others as well, too immediate an identification of deter-minism with predictability is naive. However, if determinism and pre-dictability are unconnected entirely, it becomes hard to solve the prob-lem Russell posed for us of finding a way of restricting what can count as state and law so that the issue of determinism doesn't reduce to triviality.

In Chapter 3 we will return to the subject of determinism. There we will look at how the sensitivity of the development of a system to its exact initial conditions has led some to deny determinism in the world. What kind of deterministic world is it if even an infinitesimal change in the initial state of a system can lead to vast changes in its future development? In Chapter 4 we will explore some of the issues of de-terminism and indeterminism that arise in the even more radical con-text of quantum mechanics. There we will see why some have alleged that if quantum mechanics truly describes the world, determinism must be radically false.

But for the moment, I want to focus on an argument concerning determinism in the general theory of relativity, an argument designed to support a kind of Leibnizian relationism by claiming that if we interpret general relativity in a fully substantivalist way, we must take it to be an indeterministic theory—whose indeterminism is strikingly peculiar. Some of Leibniz's most telling arguments against substantivalism relied upon the supposition that each point of space was just like every other and each direction in space like any other. So the material world displaced in space from where it actually was would be qualitatively identical with the world the way it is. There would be no sufficient reason for it to be in one place in space rather than another. And the world would appear exactly the same to any observer, no matter where the material world was in space.

This is no longer true in general relativity, for spacetime can now have a structure that varies from place and time to place and time. Shifting the ordinary matter through spacetime would make a big difference in a world where curvature (the gravitational field) varied from spacetime location to spacetime location. But something like a Leibnizian argument can be reconstructed in which the shift of matter through spacetime is accompanied by a compensating shift in the spacetime structure itself.

A consequence of this is a problem noted by Einstein and called the "hole" problem. Let a small region of spacetime be empty of matter. Let the matter distribution and spacetime structure outside the region be anything you like. Then spacetime structures that appear to be distinct from each other in the hole are equally compatible, according to the laws of general relativity, with the nonexistence of matter in the hole and the distribution of matter and spacetime outside it. There is a way of reading this result that tries to explain it away as just saying that the structure in the hole can be described in terms of alternative coordinate systems. But if we take spacetime point locations seriously, surely part of the substantivalist reading of the theory, there is a way of reading this result that says that no matter how small the hole is, there are genuinely different spacetime structures in it compatible with the surrounding spacetime and matter structure. This is the new kind of indeterminism that, it is alleged, gets thrust upon one if one sticks to the substantivalist reading of the new theory of spacetime.

Clearly the discussion is not at an end. We have a long way to go before we have sorted out what the many distinct issues are between relationists and substantivalists of various sorts. And there are many aspects of the current physical theories of spacetime that must also be better understood. Until both the philosophical and the physical sides of the issues are made clearer and more precise, it will be impossible to say just what metaphysical reading best fits what current physics tells us about the space and time of the world. The issues here are important, for the theoretical arguments that underlie the critique of substantivalism and the advocacy of relationism, and the opposition to these arguments on the part of the substantivalist, are used in similar forms in other philosophical debates.

Spacetime Relations and Causal Relations

We have been exploring the debate between those who take spacetime as a fundamental entity of the world and those who take only spatio-temporal relations among material things and events as constituting the world's spatiotemporal reality. Another group of important issues concerning the nature of spatiotemporal reality is centered around the relationship between spatiotemporal and causal features of the world. There is a causal structure among the events of the world. Some events cause others or, at least, are partial causes of others, needing other events along with them to be sufficient to cause the event effected. There are deep and important relationships between what we take the spatiotemporal structure of the world to be like and what we take the causal structure among events to be like. These relationships were noted long before the discovery of the relativistic theories but became quite important when the philosopher's attention was directed toward the questions concerning what relativistic theories tell us about the nature of our world. Of particular importance are a group of claims to the effect that the causal structure among events is the real structure among them, the most fundamental physical structure constituting reality. From the perspective of these claims, spatiotemporal relations are real only to the extent that they can be reduced to or defined in terms of causal relations. But such claims turn out to be complex and subtle.

Perhaps the earliest connection between causal and spatiotemporal notions of this sort was made by Leibniz. Suppose events cause other events by means of signals sent along a continuous spacetime path from earlier to later event. Suppose, as we did before relativity, that these signals can travel at any velocity we like, as long as the speed is finite. Then any event is possibly connected to any other event by some causal signal, unless the two events occur at exactly the same time. Couldn't we then "define" the notion "x is simultaneous with y" by the notion "x is not causally connectable to y"? Indeed, might we not say that what it means for one event to be simultaneous with another is for the events to be not causally connectable to one another?

Now look at what happens in relativity theory. Because there is a maximal speed of the propagation of a causal signal, the speed of light in a vacuum, there will be many events that are causally connectable to one another (and, therefore, clearly not simultaneous with one another), all of which are in the realm of not being causally connectable to a given event. It seems then that in this case we could not define "x is simultaneous with y" as "x is not causally connectable to y" and must use some other method, say, that chosen by Einstein, using reflected light signals and clocks. It is an easy step from this to assertions that because simultaneity can't be causally defined as "not being causal connectable," simultaneity isn't a real relationship in relativity but is a matter of mere convention or stipulation.

To see how problematic such a claim might be, we must look at some discoveries made by the mathematician A. Robb soon after Einstein's discovery of relativity. Robb was able to show that there is a relation, definable using only the notion of causal connectability, that holds between events in the spacetime of special relativity if and only if those events are simultaneous according to Einstein's definition of simultaneity. So "at the same time" is causally definable, although the causal relation that defines simultaneity is a more complex one, not the simple intuitive notion used by Leibniz of not being causally connectable. Indeed, Robb was able to go much further and show that such notions as spatial separation and temporal separation (relative to an observer) can also be defined in terms of the single notion of causal connectability. (Actually Robb used the notion of "after" to do the defining, where this meant "absolutely after" in the relativistic sense, but his work can be reconstructed using the time-symmetrical notion of causal connectability.)

Does this mean that simultaneity and the other metric notions of relativity are real and nonconventional because they are reducible to causal notions? Once again, things are not so simple. Suppose we move to the general relativistic context, where a variety of different spacetimes are possible—not just the spacetime of special relativity. In some of these worlds, various postulates that Robb used about the structure of the causal relations among events no longer hold true. In such worlds, it is clear that Robb's definitions of the metric spacetime relationships in terms of causal relationships can't hold. Even when Robb's postulates still hold, there can be a failure of his definitions. There are spacetimes allowed by general relativity in which all Robb's postulates about causal connectability hold, but are such that if one used Robb's definitions for the metric quantities (like simultaneity and spatial and temporal separation), one would assign values to these quantities that differed from those assigned by the general relativistic theory. The values assigned by using Robb's definitions would differ from the values one would get using, say, measuring tapes, clocks, and reflected light signals in the usual relativistic way.

It seems that what is really going on here is the following: It is true that in the spacetime of the special theory of relativity, various metric notions coincide with notions definable using causal connectability alone. But it seems much more dubious to claim that this fact shows that the spatiotemporal metric notions in any way, shape, or form reduce to or are definable by the causal notions. An analogy might make this clearer. Imagine a world in which it happens (perhaps by accident, perhaps as the result of a law of nature) that all blue things are square and all square things are blue. This, by itself, doesn't imply that blueness reduces to squareness, or is definable in its terms, or vice versa.

Yet there does seem to be something to the claim that whereas events being causally connectable or not is a hard fact of nature, the choice of which events are simultaneous with one another in relativity theory seems to have an element of arbitrariness or conventionality built into it. Can we get any more insight into the intuitions behind this?

What we have so far is this: In prerelativistic physics, there is a natural association of a causal notion (mutual noncausal connectability) with the spatiotemporal notion of simultaneity. Some are led to maintain that the real relation in the world is the causal relation, and that simultaneity is reducible to or definable in terms of the causal relation. When we move to the special theory of relativity, this natural association of causal and spatiotemporal relations breaks down, leading some to assert that relativity shows simultaneity to be merely conventional or stipulative. Robb's results show that not only simultaneity but also all the spacetime metric notions of special relativity can be defined in causal terms. This leads some to claim they are nonconventional. But further thought shows that Robb's causal definitions are peculiar. The associations they utilize are not so natural as those of the Leibnizian sort. In the general relativistic context, these associations generally break down. Robb's axioms usually fail to hold, and even when they do hold, the metric relations, as Robb defines them, are frequently in disagreement with the standard metric relations. What can we infer from all of this?

Topology and Causal Structure

Before answering that question, let us explore how in the general relativist context a very similar series of arguments takes place; the series once again deals with the degree to which a spatiotemporal relation can be given a causal definition and with alleged philosophical consequences of the existence or nonexistence of such causal definitions. It was realized early in the study of general relativity that two metrically distinct general relativistic spacetimes could have the same causal structure. That is, although the metric spacetime relations among the events in the worlds had quite a different structure, the structure of the causal relations among the events could be the same. So any hope of a casual definition of the metric was defeated. In order to determine fully the metric structure of a spacetime, one must add something to the causal structure. This could be spatial metric structure as determined by measuring tapes or temporal metric structure as determined by ideal clocks. Later it was realized that specifying both the causal structure and the paths traveled by ideal free material particles (that is, particles acted upon only by gravity) fully determined the metric structure. But causal relations alone would not do.

Now the *topology* of a spacetime constitutes a much weaker structure than its metric. Two spacetimes can be topologically alike, i.e., alike in respect to all matters of continuity in the spacetime, yet metrically quite distinct. The topological features of a space can be thought of intuitively as those features preserved under any deformation of the space that keeps continuity properties intact. The space can be deformed in any way and its topology will remain the same as long as no "cuts" separate points originally "right next to one another" and no "tapings"

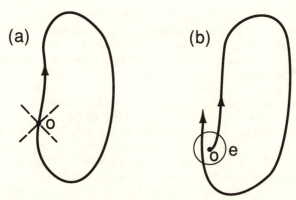

Figure 2.11 Causally pathological spacetimes. In spacetime with closed causal loops—illustrated in (a)—a causal signal can leave an event *o* and progress into the future. Following the signal, always into the "local future," we trace a path that returns to the originating event *o*. Even without such a closed loop a spacetime can be causally quite "pathological." This is illustrated in (b). Although no signal from *o* can "get back" to *o* itself, it can still be the case for every spacetime region around *o*, no matter how small, that a signal from *o* that leaves a region, *e*, may eventually return to it and thus return "arbitrarily close" to the originating event *o*.

bring next to one another previously separated points. Can the primitive continuity structures of the spacetime, those described by topology, perhaps be causally definable, even if the full metric structure cannot? The answer is a fascinating, if somewhat complex, one. If we take as our basic causal notion "event *x* is causally connectable to event *y*," then it turns out that the topology can sometimes be defined by causal connectability, but only in "causally well-behaved" spacetimes. In "causally pathological" spacetimes it cannot. What is a causally pathological spacetime? Basically, it is any spacetime where there is a closed causal curve or where an infinitesimal change in the spacetime might generate such a curve. Such paths constitute sequences of causally connected events that "loop around time" to come back to, or almost to, the initial event one starts with. Only in worlds of a specified degree of good causal behavior can causal connectability be sufficient to specify the topology. This is brought out particularly pungently in certain pathological spacetimes where the topology is nontrivial (some events are "near" other events and some are not), but where every event is causally connectable to every other event. (See Figures 2.11 and 2.12.)

So the situation is not too unlike the one we looked at earlier. Only in certain cases will the specified causal notion be adequate to define the desired spacetime relations. In other cases the definition can't be found. But the situation is more complicated still. We have been taking as our causal notion—to which the spacetime notions are to be reduced—the relation one event has to another when they are causally connectable. A richer causal notion is that of a *path* in spacetime being

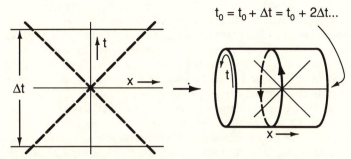

Figure 2.12   A universe "closed up in time." Take ordinary Minkowski spacetime of special relativity and "slice" it at two simultaneity lines relative to some observer, one such line at time t_0 and the other at a time $t_0 + \Delta t$. On the diagram t represents the direction of time and x that of space. Then "identify" the two edges of the sliced-out piece of Minkowski spacetime and so roll up that piece into a cylinder. The result is a spacetime "closed up in time" but extending to spatial infinity. Naturally such a spacetime is highly artificial. No one takes it to be a possible model of the actual spacetime of the world. But its consistency with the defining equations of the theory of spacetime suggests that more-realistic models of the universe might very well contain closed causal loops, as does this pathological spacetime.

a continuous causal path. If we imagine a pointlike particle (or light particle) traveling from one spacetime point to another, the path followed is such a continuous causal path. The result is important and may be stated as follows: If two spacetimes are exactly alike in their structure of continuous causal paths, they are exactly alike in their topology, at least if only the standard kinds of topologies (so-called manifold topologies) are considered. The notion of causal connectability says only that two events are connectable by some continuous causal path or other. This new causal notion requires specifying just what path fragments in the spacetime are genuinely the continuous causal paths. What the result says is that all the topological facts about the spacetime are fully determined once it is determined which collections of events in the spacetime constitute continuous paths of causal propagation or, rather, that this is true if the standard topologies alone are considered. So here we have a positive result in general relativity about the definability of at least the topology by causal facts alone.

Are Spacetime Features Reducible to Causal Features?

But how are all of these results relevant to our initial idea that the causal facts relating events to one another are the real or hard facts about the structure of the world? Remember that the claim the causal theorist wanted to support was that insofar as spacetime facts were hard facts, they were reducible to causal facts, and that insofar as spacetime facts were not so reducible, they were not real facts at all but merely the result of conventional choice or stipulation on our part.

The issues here are controversial, but let me outline one response to these claims. One approach to understanding the intuitive motivation behind causal theories of spacetime features focuses on the epistemological question of how we come to know the spacetime of the world. Here, as we discussed earlier, it is sometimes argued that features available to us by some direct process of inspection are the ones that we must take as the genuine facts about the spacetime world. Other features, attributable to spacetime only by choosing some not directly testable hypothesis about the spacetime structure, are taken in this view to be a matter of convention, as no directly inspectable observational facts pick the correct hypothesis out for us. In both the earlier Leibnizian version and the modern relativistic versions of causal theories of spacetime, it is assumed that causal influence propagates along continuous paths in spacetime, traversable by some material thing like a particle. Of course, in Leibniz any spacetime path directed to the future is so traversable; in the relativistic versions only those paths that represent a speed less than or equal to that of light can be traveled. But if a particle can travel such a path, so, in principle, can an observer.

Someone might, then, argue like this: Features of spacetime determinable at a single spacetime point, like simultaneity for events at the same place, are directly observationally determinable by us. Therefore, these constitute hard facts about spacetime. Also observationally available to us, in principle, are facts about continuity of paths that are causal, that is, that are such that an observer can move along the path and directly check its continuity properties. It is for this reason that we ought to take simultaneity at a point in special relativity as a hard fact but simultaneity for separated events and other nonpointlike metric features as matters of convention. Again, continuity along causal paths ought to be taken as a matter of hard fact. Any other topological fact must either reduce to these facts or be taken as conventional. That is why it is important to show that the continuity of causal paths fully determines the topology in general relativity. Only then can we be assured that the topological facts are all (because they are determined fully by directly accessible topological facts) hard facts.

If causal theories of spacetime features are interpreted this way, we see that calling these theories causal theories is somewhat misleading. For Robb, causal connectability (in the form of the "after" relationship) was the only legitimate relationship on which to found the metric features of a special relativistic spacetime. For causal theorists of spacetime topology, continuity along causal paths is the only legitimate feature of the spacetime on which to ground all topological facts. But these basic causal features are privileged in this way not because they are facts about causal relationships, i.e., about how events in the world determine, bring about, or make happen other events in the world. Rather, they are privileged because they are the spacetime features that we can determine to be the case without reliance upon hypotheses that, not being checkable by some direct inspection procedure, are infected with an arbitrariness that can be resolved only by making an arbitrary or conventional decision.

From this perspective, it is not causal facts that are fundamental, but a limited subset of the spacetime facts. Spacetime order is not to be reduced to causal order or defined in terms of causal order. Instead, all of spacetime structure is to be reduced to, or defined in terms of, the limited subset of spacetime facts that are genuinely open to our epistemic access. Indeed, at this point, one is likely to think of attempts to analyze the notion of causation that are familiar from philosophy. Usually causation is thought of as having a spacetime aspect itself. Hume, for example, when trying to say what causation amounted to, insisted that spacetime continuity was an element required in defining the causal process. A cause and effect had to be, he said, "contiguous in space and time." Naturally there has to be more to the causal relation. There has to be whatever it is that constitutes the determining of effect by cause. But from this perspective the spacetime features, at least some of them, are primitive and not reducible to causation properly so-called. Instead, causation has as part of its analysis a fundamental spacetime relation among events.

The problem of the interconnections between causation and spacetime features of the world is hardly solved by the brief remarks above. Our conception of the world as existing in space and time and our conception of the world as governed by a process of events determining other events, that is, by causation, are two of the very deepest, and broadest, conceptualizations of the world we have. How these two fundamental aspects of the world are related, and how they depend upon each other for their meaning and intelligibility, are ongoing matters for thoughtful philosophical exploration.

In Chapter 3 we will touch on an issue related to the ones we have just discussed. There we will see how a special feature of time, its asymmetry, in the sense that past and future seem radically different from each other in many ways, is related by some scientists and philosophers to another fundamental asymmetry in the world, the tendency of physical systems to go from ordered to disordered states. The view that the increasing disorder of the world is fundamental to our ideas of asymmetry of time and of systems in time is also sometimes, misleadingly, lumped into the general category of "causal theories of spacetime structure." The theory in question really isn't a causal theory at all; it is an additional claim to the effect that some spacetime structure can be reduced to a different kind of structure, a claim we will look at closely in Chapter 3.

Summary

We have now seen that the problem of the kind of "being" to attribute to space and time has a rich history and a rich future. The basic metaphysical issues themselves have a complex and long-developing structure. Whether we are to view space, for example, as a substance existing over and above the material contents of the world, a set of relations among the material objects of the world, or something else entirely remains an open question. We have also seen that the issue of whether there is any sense in which spatiality or temporality is reducible to some other aspect of the world, such as a causal aspect, is also unanswered. Most important, we have seen that each revolutionary scientific advance in our understanding of space and time brings with it a new context in which the philosophical debates take place. Although the scientific achievements cannot by themselves fully resolve the metaphysical issues, any adequate philosophical treatment of the nature of space and time must do full justice to these scientific accomplishments.

Further Readings

Some books covering the topics treated in this chapter in greater detail and depth are Reichenbach (1956), which is historically very important, and Grünbaum (1973), which is encyclopedic in its coverage. Van Fraassen (1970) is very useful because it presents the historical background of many of the important issues. Sklar (1974) is a systematic introduction to the major issues, and Sklar (1985) follows up a number of the problems. Friedman (1983) introduces the reader to the technical vocabulary of modern mathematical physics of space and time and also delves deeply into the philosophical controversy.

Smart (1964) contains important, brief extracts from the major historical texts. Jammer (1954) is a brief historical survey of philosophical views about space. Alexander (1956) contains the original debate between Leibniz and the Newtonian Clarke on the nature of space and time. Barbour (1989) is a compendious survey of the history of ideas about space, time, and motion, from the ancient Greeks through Galileo, Huyghens, Descartes, Leibniz, and Newton. Kant's theory of space can be found in Part 1 of Kant (1950) and in the "Transcendental Aesthetic" of Kant (1929).

Introductions to the special theory of relativity and its spacetime abound. Taylor and Wheeler (1963) is excellent, as is Bohm (1989). Møller (1952), Synge (1956), and Rindler (1977) are all useful. Toretti (1983) and Lucas and Hodgson (1990) have a historical and philosophical orientation, as does Anderson (1967).

There are also numerous introductions to the general theory of relativity. Geroch (1978) gives the basics. Møller (1952), Rindler (1977), Anderson (1967), and Wald (1984) are all classics. Misner, Thorne, and Wheeler (1973) is encylopedic. Toretti (1983) is historical and philosophical. Einstein et al. (1923) contains the original papers in the field, translated into English.

For the history of the epistemology of geometry see Toretti (1978). Poincaré's original papers are in Poincaré (1952). Eddington (1920) contains a stimulating early discussion. Reichenbach (1956) is a classic of conventionalism. Recent general discussions can be found in Sklar (1974) and Friedman (1983).

A useful survey of philosophical issues about time is in Newton-Smith (1980). A good introduction to the issues of time and tense is Mellor (1981). For some discussion of tense in the context of special relativity see Rietdijk (1966), Putnam (1967), Chapter 11 of Sklar (1985), and Stein (1991).

The issue of substantivalism versus relationism in spacetime theories is exhaustively examined in Earman (1989). The history of the subject is treated at great length in Barbour (1989). Friedman (1983) and Nerlich (1976) offer arguments for substantivalism. A general discussion of the issues is presented in Chapter 3 of Sklar (1974). "Geometrodynamics" is discussed at length from a philosophical perspective in Graves (1971).

A full discussion of determinism is in Earman (1986). The role of determinism in the "hole" argument in general relativity is treated in Earman (1989). The structure of causation in general relativity is treated (from a very advanced standpoint) in Hawking and Ellis (1973). Some philosophical reflections on causal theories of spacetime are in van Fraassen (1970) and in Chapters 9 and 10 of Sklar (1985). Regarding Robb's causal theory of spacetime, see Winnie (1977) for an exposition and Chapter 3 of Sklar (1985) for a critique.

3

The Introduction of
Probability into Physics

Philosophers on Probability and
Statistical Explanation

Probability: The Formal Theory

It is to our great advantage to be able to predict reliably what will happen in the future. In certain, very exceptional, cases we can predict that the future will have one and only one outcome, say, when we predict the future position of one of the planets from its present condition and the dynamical laws of motion. In many cases, we have only the vaguest idea of what the future will bring. There is a special set of cases where we cannot tell with assurance which of a number of possible outcomes will occur, but where we can have reliable knowledge of the proportion in which the outcomes will occur in a large number of repeated trials of a similar kind. The craps shooter doesn't know what the next roll of the dice will bring, but he does know that in a long series of rolls, the total of seven will come up on the dice about one-sixth of the time. The exploration of such situations, beginning with the typical gambling situation, resulted in the development of the theory of probability. The probability of an outcome was taken to be something closely related to the frequency with which that outcome could be expected to occur in a large number of identical repeated trials of some specified kind.

A formal mathematical theory of probability has been constructed. It is of surpassing simplicity and elegance. Surprisingly, it was not formalized until the 1930s despite the fact that the basic ideas had been known for hundreds of years. A collection of basic outcomes is given, such as the number that comes up on the face of a die. Numbers from zero through one are assigned to subcollections of the collection of basic outcomes. Thus we assign to the collection consisting of just "the number one comes up" the number—that is, probability—of one-sixth. To the collection characterized by "some even number comes up," we assign the number one-half. The empty outcome (none of the possible outcomes occurs) is given probability zero, and the trivial outcome (some one of the possible outcomes occurs) is given probability one. The most important postulate is that of additivity. Suppose that if an outcome is in collection A, it cannot be in collection B, and vice versa. Then the probability assigned to the outcome "either A or B" is taken as the sum of the probabilities assigned to A and to B. Thus if one cannot be simultaneously a citizen of New York and of California, the probability that one is a citizen of one of the two states is the sum of the probabilities that one is a New Yorker and that one is a Californian.

In ordinary circumstances, we are familiar with the situation where the number of possible basic outcomes is finite: the die with six faces, the roulette wheel with thirty-seven slots, and so on. The mathematician, however, and, as we shall see, the physicist must deal with cases where the number of basic outcomes is infinite. For example, a basic outcome might be a point particle having any one of the infinite number of possible positions in a box. A generalization of the additivity postulate is usually assumed. This is called countable additivity. It is a natural assumption but has some peculiar consequences. One consequence is that probability zero is no longer assigned just to the empty set of no basic consequence occurring but is assigned to nonempty sets as well. For example, if one is engaged in the gamble of picking some number out of all the real numbers between zero and one, countable additivity implies that the probability of getting a number that is rational, that is, that can be represented as a fraction of two integers, is zero. Yet, of course, there are an infinite number of such rational numbers in the collection. The idea is that there are "many more" nonfraction real numbers than fractions. In these contexts, then, the impossible event has zero probability, but not all zero probability events are impossibilities. And having probability one doesn't mean an event must necessarily occur.

An important notion in probability theory is that of conditional probability. Suppose we know that a seven has come up on the toss of two dice. What is the probability, given that outcome, that one of the dice shows a one on its face? Well, seven can come up in six ways, and in only two of the cases does one of the dice have a one showing. So the probability is one-third. Crudely, the expected frequency of a kind of outcome, B, given that a kind of outcome, A, has occurred, is the probability of B conditional on A or the conditional probability of B given A. If the probability of B given A is just the unconditional probability of B (and the probability of A given B just the probability of A), then A and B are said to be probabilistically independent of each other. Two successive tosses of a coin are usually taken to be so independent. The chance of heads on the second toss remains one-half, the result of the first toss being irrelevant to this probability. However, being a Californian and being a Westerner are certainly not independent. Our probability that someone comes from California given that he comes from the West is certainly higher than our probability that he is a Californian given only that he lives somewhere in the United States.

From the basic postulates of probability theory, a group of important theorems, called Laws of Large Numbers, can be proven. Do we expect heads to come up half the time in a small number of tosses of a coin? If the number of tosses is odd, it can't. Even if the number of tosses is even, we expect the actual outcome to deviate from the exact one-half proportion in any given sequence of tosses. But as the number of tosses gets very large, we expect that there will be some kind of convergence of the frequency of heads observed to the posited probability of one-half. What the Laws of Large Numbers tell us is that the probability of such convergence (in various senses of convergence, which can be of different strengths) goes to one ("probabilistic certainty") as the number of trials goes to infinity. This holds if the trials are probabilistically independent of one another. So although we certainly couldn't prove that in any sequence of trials going to infinity, the frequency would converge to the probability, we can prove, given independence of the trials, that such an outcome is a probabilistic certainty.

Objectivist Interpretations of Probability

It is one thing to have a set of formal axioms of probability. There are some variations in these, but they are well understood. It is quite another thing to get agreement about just what probability *is*. What are we talking about when we talk about probabilities? Given the close connection between frequencies of outcomes in the world and attributions of probability, wouldn't it be simpler to identify probabilities with actual relative frequencies of occurrences? To take account of those cases where the number of basic outcomes is infinite rather than finite, we might want to generalize and speak of actual proportions rather than actual frequencies, but the basic idea would be the same. This simple view, though, encounters the familiar objection that in any actual class of experiments, we don't expect the actual frequencies or proportions to be the exact probabilities. We expect a kind of "centering" of the actual outcomes about the probability values, not their identity.

To get around this, it is often suggested that we ought to identify the probabilities with the relevant frequencies or proportions "in the long run," that is, as the number of trials goes to infinity. One problem with this is, of course, that the actual number of trials is always finite. What is this peculiar idealized "sequence of trials going to infinity" within which the frequencies are to be determined? Is it supposed to be something actual or, rather, some kind of idealization? And if it is the latter, what has happened to the original view of probabilities as actual frequencies or proportions? Another difficulty with this view is that even in the long run, the connection between probabilities and frequencies is only a probabilistic connection. The Laws of Large Numbers hold only when the trials are independent of one another, and that is a probabilistic notion. Worse yet, the identity of frequency and probability, even in the long run, is only assured "with probability one," and as we have noted, that doesn't mean that in any actual infinite sequence of trials, limit of relative frequency and probability must be identical.

Often a looser connection between probabilities and actual frequencies or proportions is suggested. Take "probability" as an undefined term and probabilities as some primitive feature attributed to physical systems. Which feature this is, is fixed by the role that probability plays in our schematism for predicting, controlling, and explaining events. We have, for example, "upward" rules, which tell us how to infer from observed frequencies and proportions to attributed probabilities, and "downward" rules, which tell us, given an attribution of probability to a phenomenon, what kinds of frequencies and proportions to expect in finite trials. So rather than identifying probability with some actual proportion or frequency, perhaps we ought to take it that such actual frequencies and proportions specify what probability is only by means of their connection to probabilities through these upward and downward rules of inference, rules that connect actual frequencies and proportions to attributed probabilities.

Other suggestions include looking at the entire schema of statistical and lawlike attributions we make of the world. We have a broad and deep hierarchical structure of generalizations, some lawlike and exceptionless, some statistical and utilizing probability attributions. All of these generalizations are about the order of connections between phenomena in the world. Maybe we should think of probabilities as those idealized attributions of frequency and proportion that appear in the posits that play a fundamental role in this structure of generalizations. It would then be a mistake to think of probability as frequency in a simple-minded sense: Probability is a kind of idealized simple proportion taken as representing the general structure of the world at the level of fundamental generalizations. A variety of different schemes can be proposed to try to make this notion of "idealized proportion" somewhat less vague.

The point of all of these interpretations is to assign probability to some outcome in a class of trials, either the frequency or proportion of that outcome or some projection or idealization of that. Another objectivist interpretation of probability looks, rather, at the process by which the required frequencies would be generated. Probability, according to this view, is a feature of the object, or of the process involving an object, by which an outcome may or may not be produced. Just as a window can be fragile even if not broken, so, on this view, a coin tossing has a disposition or tendency to produce heads or tails, even if this tendency is not realized in certain cases. To describe the probability of heads on a coin toss as one-half is to attribute to the tossing apparatus or situation a "propensity" to produce heads half the time were a large number of trials to be attempted. So probability, on this view, is the attribute of a single toss, its dispositional magnitude to produce an outcome of a specified kind.

As we shall see later in this chapter and in Chapter 4, determining the degree to which probability inheres in a single event, rather than merely being some measure of a class of outcomes over a class of events, will involve more than purely philosophical questions. By these I mean questions such as whether the dispositional view presupposes a frequentist underpinning and whether that view can solve the difficulties encountered in the earlier views. Questions of physics will arise as well. For the issue of whether the proportions we observe in the world inhere in some irreducible sense in single events is intimately related to the question of whether, in every event, there are sufficient conditions to determine fully that only one of the possible outcomes will actually occur. Can there be cases where a muliplicity of outcomes remains even if all the conditions (known, unknown, or even unknowable) governing the event are specified? This is an important question in quantum mechanics, as we shall see, where the issue of "hidden" determining parameters is important.

There is another problem area that must be explored by anyone who wishes to understand probability as some objective feature of the world. This is the problem of randomness. Suppose a sequence of coin tosses looks like this: $H,T,H,T,H,T, \ldots$, and so on. Should we say that in such a sequence the probability of heads on a given toss is one-half? That is, after all, the limiting frequency with which heads occurs. Yet the orderliness of the sequence, an orderliness that allows us to tell whether a head or a tail will result on the next toss, given the result of our last toss, leads many to say that it would be misleading to think of the probability of heads on a given toss as being one-half. If probabilities are to be assigned at all, shouldn't we assign heads probability one on odd tosses and probability zero on even tosses? Only, they say, in a *random* sequence does probability equal limiting relative frequency. But what, exactly, is a random sequence?

The study of randomness from the objectivist viewpoint has led to interesting, if not fully conclusive, results. Researchers such as L. von Mises and A. Church have tried to define randomness as a property that holds when the frequencies of outcomes in the sequence are the same in any subsequence derived from the original by any "mechanical" process. Thus the sequence above is not random, for the subsequence of odd tosses can be mechanically selected by a suitably programmed automatic computer. And the frequency of heads in that sequence is one, not one-half. The concept of a mechanically selectable subsequence can be made mathematically precise. But there are sequences that are random in this sense but that are, intuitively, nonrandom in the sense that some gambling strategies can be adopted against them that are "unfair."

A different proposal for giving an account of objective randomness relies upon the intuition that "almost all" sequences ought to be random. The orderly sequences ought to be sparse in the collection of all sequences, a notion we might make formal by demanding that a sequence be random "with probability one." So one looks for definitions of nonrandomness that will select out from all sequences a collection of probability size zero. The basic problems with the definitions that arise when this intuition is followed out is that they lose the close connection with the intuitive notion of randomness with which one started. Still another definition of randomness devises a "universal" effective procedure for testing for nonrandomness and declares a sequence random if it passes this test.

A fourth alternative adopts a highly intuitive strategy. Consider a computer programmed to generate as its output the sequence of experimental results that actually occurs. How long must the shortest program be that will do the job? Obviously one program will always work, the instruction that just says "Print . . . " where the " . . . " is the sequence in question. But "nonrandom" sequences have, intuitively, shorter programs. For example the sequence $H,T,H,T, . . .$ can be given as just "Print H and T alternately." So a sequence is less random, the shorter its generating program can be. All of this can be made formally respectable. But it doesn't quite give what the objectivist wanted, because it turns out that a satisfactory definition once again seems to presuppose that the sequence is already understood as being generated by some probabilistic process. This makes it hard to use a notion of objective randomness defined in this way to serve, along with the notion of limiting relative frequency, as a means of saying what probability is in the first place.

Subjectivist Interpretations of Probability

An understanding of the nature of probability that is radically different from all the objectivist accounts we have been looking at so far focuses not on what is in the world but, instead, on what is in us. We use probability as a guide to action in the face of risk, betting on a given outcome only if we take the odds to be sufficiently high to overcome our doubts that the outcome will actually occur. Perhaps we should think, then, of probability as some measure of *our* degree of confidence that an outcome will occur, a measure of "partial belief" on our part, if you will.

Suppose probabilities are measures of partial belief, in the sense that they are indicators of the minimum odds relative to which we will bet on an outcome. Why, then, should our probabilities obey the standard laws of probability theory? That they should obey these laws is a rather trivial result from the frequentist standpoint, but the subjectivist needs an argument that they should. Some arguments are designed to show that only if our probabilities obey the standard rules will we be immune to getting ourselves into a situation where a bookie offers us odds that we accept, even though they guarantee a loss on our part no matter how things turn out. Another approach tries to show that if one's preferences among "lottery tickets" (you get A if x occurs and B if x doesn't occur), as revealed by one's choosing one ticket over another, are rational in the sense that if ticket 1 is preferred to ticket 2 and 2 to 3, then 1 is preferred to 3, then there will always be a way of representing our partial beliefs in the outcomes that will obey the standard probability axioms.

Therefore, for the objectivist, probabilities are features of the world waiting to be discovered. For the "subjectivist," they are degrees of partial belief by the agent that guide his actions and beliefs in an uncertain world. But which probabilities should the rational agent attribute to events? The arguments just outlined are designed to show that whatever probabilities are chosen, they must jointly satisfy the standard probability axioms. But is there any further constraint on probabilistic rationality?

One set of arguments is designed to describe and justify a procedure for modifying one's subjective probabilities in the light of new evidence. A fundamental theorem of probability theory, Bayes' Theorem, relates the probability of a hypothesis on the basis of evidence (a conditional probability) to the conditional probability of the evidence, given the truth of the hypothesis and the initial probability that the hypothesis is true. Suppose we take it that after the evidence is in, we ought to adopt for our new probability for the truth of the hypothesis its old probability conditional on the evidence. We then have a way of changing our probabilities in the light of new evidence that is "conservative." It makes the minimal changes imaginable in our antecedent probabilities. And the new probabilities will, like the old ones, conform to the axioms of probability theory. This process of probability modification in the light of evidence is known as conditionalization. It can be generalized to cover cases where the new evidence is not known for certain but is only assigned some probability. Someone following this procedure might, for example, start with the assumption that a coin, which might be biased, has a probablity of heads of one-half. As new coin tossings come in, the agent will then modify that probability in the light of the observed outcomes. A run dominated by heads will, for example, lead the agent to raise his estimate of the probability that the coin has for generating heads. Once again, arguments can be given that modifying one's probabilities by conditionalization is the rational thing to do. Some of these arguments are like the arguments that were used to try to convince one that having one's probabilities conform to the usual axioms was rational.

I noted above that in getting new probabilities for hypotheses in the light of evidence, one relied upon initial probabilities for the truth of the hypotheses in question. So mustn't one start with some "intrinsic" plausibility for the hypotheses, their so-called a priori probabilities? Where could these come from? Some have advocated that we should accept probabilistic hypotheses in our body of accepted beliefs only on the basis of observed frequencies as evidence. More often it is alleged that hypotheses can have intrinsic probabilities generated without reliance on observed frequencies. Indeed, such a priori probabilities were the object of study of the earliest work in probability theory in the seventeenth and eighteenth centuries. If we toss a coin, there are two "symmetric" possible outcomes, heads and tails. Doesn't it seem reasonable, then, to assume initially that the probability of each is one-half? If we toss a die, there are six symmetric faces. Shouldn't we then, in the absence of evidence of bias, attribute a probability of one-sixth to each outcome of a specific face coming up on top? So we can try to arrive at a priori probabilities by dividing up the outcomes into symmetric cases and attributing equal probability to each. This is the famous Principle of Indifference.

Later philosophers formalized these notions and generalized upon them. If we choose a language in which to describe the world, we can find various means for sorting the possibilities for the world as described in this language into symmetric possibilities. Initial probability is then distributed over the possibilities in an intuitive and symmetrical fashion. Then, having so obtained one's "rational" a priori probabilities, one could modify them in the face of experimental evidence (especially evidence about actual observed frequencies of outcomes) by using the process of conditionalization described above. The methods invented seemed to some a generalization of the formal theory of deduction, because they allowed for the definition of a kind of "partial logical entailment" among propositions, i.e., of a notion of one proposition's logically supporting another to a degree. So the formal systems received the name of inductive logics.

It was realized long ago that these techniques suffer from difficulties when the Principle of Indifference is subjected to analysis and criticism. They all rely on a division of the possible outcomes into symmetric cases. But the rationale behind such a division is not always clear. Yes, we can say that the die can come up with a one, a two, and so on, making for six cases. But we can also say that the die can come up either with a one or without a one on the top, making for two cases. So why not give "comes up with a one" a probability of one-half? In other cases, the need for some principled way of choosing *how* to be "indifferent" becomes clearer. Imagine a vase so constructed that the volume filled is not proportional to the surface area of the interior of the vase wetted (easy to do with curved sides for the vase). Knowing nothing about how filled the vase is, should we guess, using the Principle of Indifference, that it is half full? Or should we guess, with equal justification, that half of its interior is wet? The two guesses are incompatible with one another, but both seem equally justified, a priori, by pure symmetry considerations.

Later in this chapter we will explore how probability is utilized in statistical mechanics, the first area of physics in which it played a fundamental role. We shall see that the disputes among philosophers concerning the nature of probability and disputes about the origin and justification of initial probability assignments are crucial when one is trying to understand just how probability ought to enter into physics. As we shall see, various physical discoveries not only throw light on the philosophical issues but also reveal additional questions that complicate the philosophical problem situation even more.

Statistical Explanation: Explanation, Law, and Cause

We wish not only to describe the world as we find it but also to explain what happens in the world. To explain, we feel, is to answer the question *why* what occurs occurs, and not just to describe *what*, in fact, does occur. But what is it to answer a why question? And what is it to provide an explanation for a phenomenon?

The intuitive notion of a cause has played a role in attempts to analyze the notion of explanations in science ever since the question of providing such an analysis first occurred to a philosopher. To explain an event is to give its cause and to explain a class of events is to provide the kind or type of cause that generates them.

In an early analysis of causation, Aristotle distinguished among the stuff in which a change occurred; the nature of the change; the end, or purpose, of the change; and the immediate generator of the change as four different kinds of causes. He labeled these the material, formal, final, and efficient causes. The matter and properties involved are not now thought of as causes of a process but as constituents of the change to be explained. The issue of final causes—ends, or purposes—is one that still provokes much discussion. In the intentional activity of an agent, perhaps in biology (in the form of functional explanations of an organ, for example), and in the social sciences something like the Aristotelian idea that giving an end, or purpose, is explanatory still seems appealing. Even in physics, it isn't clear that there is absolutely no room for "final causes." Explanations of the path of light as being that which takes the least time are sometimes alleged to be final in nature. And in thermodynamics (presented later in this chapter), explaining a process in terms of a system heading toward an equilibrium state as a "goal" has been alleged to be an explanation using the notion of "final cause."

But when a contemporary scientist thinks of causes he or she usually thinks about efficient causes, the events that "bring about" the occurrence of the event to be explained. But what is it to explain an event by demonstrating its efficient cause? The intuitive idea seems to be that an event is explained when an antecedent event is discovered that "necessitates" the occurrence of the event in question. Closing the switch causes the light to go on, pushing the object causes it to accelerate, and so on. But what is the nature of this necessitation, or "making," that makes it appropriate to describe the cause as making the explained effect or event happen?

In a justly famous critical examination of the notion of causality, David Hume argued that it would be a mistake to view causal relations as resting on some special "causal nexus" or "necessary connection" between events in the world. Rather, he argued, what we find in the world when we look at events related as cause and effect is, first of all, a spatiotemporal relation among the events, with the events being in spatiotemporal contact but with the cause event preceding the effect event in time. We also find the events being contained in a class of pairs of events of the same kind that are constantly accompanied by each other. That is, event 1 causes event 2 if and only if they have the right spatiotemporal relationship and if and only if events of kind 1 are always followed by those of kind 2 and those of kind 2 are always preceded by those of kind 1. Whereas we think we can explain this "constant conjunction" of the kinds of events by saying that events of kind 1 "cause" events of kind 2, we are really only redescribing that constant conjunction when we speak of causation, according to Hume.

It isn't quite that simple for Hume, for he asks where we get the idea that the cause event "necessitates" the effect event. His understanding of this is that the necessitation is not a reflection of some real relationship between the events in the world but, rather, a projection onto the world of a psychological phenomenon. Seeing events of kind 1 always accompanied by those of kind 2, we become accustomed to events of the first kind always being followed by events of the second kind. So when we experience an event of the first kind, our mind immediately leaps to the expectation that an event of the second kind will occur. It is this expectation, grounded on "custom or habit," that constitutes the origin of our notion of the first kind of event's necessitating the second kind of event. But, Hume claims, this is a matter of our psychology. All there is in the world of the events themselves are the spatiotemporal relations of "contiguity and precedence" and the constant conjunction of the events of the kinds in question.

Closely associated with this Humean analysis of causation is a model of scientific explanation called the deductive-nomological model (although one might espouse that model without being a Humean). There it is argued that to explain an event is to show that a statement of the occurrence of the event in question could be logically deduced from the statements of the occurrence of other, usually antecedent, events if in addition to the description of those explaining events, one used assertions of the "laws of nature" connecting the kinds of events. For a Humean, these laws are just the general statements of the constant conjunctions of the relevant kinds of events.

The proponents of this model of scientific explanation draw one's attention to the close connection between explanation as they construe it and the goals of prediction and control shared by most human agents.

If we are able to explain events of a certain kind, then we have available to us the lawlike generalizations connecting events of one kind to the other kinds of events used in the explanation. So if, in other circumstances, we know what kinds of "cause" events have occurred, we can, using the generalizations we discovered in our search for deductive-nomological explanations, predict what events will occur. Or we could, by manipulating the occurrence of the right kind of "causing" events, control the world by determining which kinds of manipulable events will bring about (or prevent) events of the kind we wish to occur. Once more, the connections between the appropriate kinds of events is revealed in the lawlike general statements discovered in the search for explanations.

As we shall see, some people object that the model of deducing a description of an event from descriptions of other events and general statements of laws demands too much from an explanation. Others say it demands too little. One important problem is connected, once again, with the notion of causation. If the explaining and explained events don't have the right causal relationship, it is argued, then the connections between their descriptions don't constitute explanations, even if the conditions of the deductive model of explanation are satisfied. We might derive the position of a planet yesterday from the laws of dynamics and its position and velocity today, but that doesn't explain *why* it had the position it had yesterday, it is said, because the past explains the future and not vice versa. And the reason for this, it is said, is that causation goes in the direction from past to future. To explain, it is claimed, is to reveal causes. Again, two events might be correlated in a lawlike way because they are the common effect of some third event that is their common cause. The two events don't, then, explain each other, although both are explained by the common cause. If a bacterial infection results in both a rash and a swelling, it is said, the rash doesn't explain the swelling or the swelling the rash. Rather, both are explained by their cause, the bacterial infection. But what is the additional causal element necessary for explanation over and above constant conjunction?

Explanations Invoking Probability

Many of those who think the deductive model of explanation demands too much refer to historical explanations. Here we seem to accept explanatory accounts that make no use of lawlike generalizations. After all, what are the laws governing historical events? Of more interest to us are those explanations where events are connected by generalizations, but where the generalizations are not full-fledged laws of nature but probabilistic or statistical connections between events. Smoking doesn't always cause lung cancer, but it certainly raises its probability. Haven't we offered at least some explanation of someone's lung cancer, then, if we point to his heavy smoking, even if the smoking doesn't necessitate getting the disease? What sort of probabilistic relation between explaining and explained event is sufficient for the former to be said to explain the latter?

A first natural thought is that an event is explained if we can find other events such that the occurrence of the event in question follows from the occurrence of the explaining events with high probability. The "follows from" is mediated by the existence of lawlike statistical generalizations that take the place of the exceptionless laws used in deductive-nomological explanations. We immediately notice that such a "statistical explanation" of an event would be rather different from the explanation when pure laws are used. For example, in the deductive case, if we can explain event 1 and explain event 2, we can generate, automatically, an explanation of "event 1 occurred *and* event 2 occurred" simply by conjoining the explanatory resources used to explain each individual event. But if event 1 follows from some explanatory base with "high probability," i.e., with a probability greater than some specified amount, and event 2 follows from its explanatory base with a similar high probability, that is no guarantee that "event 1 and event 2" will follow from the conjoined explanatory bases with a probability above the minimal value.

Further, if an event has high probability relative to its explanatory base, it may have low probability relative to that base supplemented with further information. Although we may say that it is highly probable that someone raised in a dreadful environment has criminal tendencies, when we are told, in addition, that he is the child of a healthy family, and so on, we lower this probability in our estimate. This can't happen with deductive–nomologically explained events.

We soon think of cases where we feel that an event can be given a probabilistic explanation even if it doesn't have high probability relative to that which is brought forward as the explanation. Something that bursts into spontaneous combustion has its combustion explained when we say that sometimes, although rarely, such a phenomenon takes place in the relevant situation. How can we have explained an event by reference to facts relative to which it has low probability? It is pointed out that without the explaining facts, the event in question had even lower probability. So we can explain why something happens by referring to facts that make it *more* probable than it would otherwise be, even if after the addition of the explanatory facts, its probability still remains low.

Then it is noticed that there are many cases where we explain an event by referring to another event, even if given the new information, we *lower* the probability of the event relative to our background knowledge. A physician explains the death of a patient known to be suffering from a dread disease by pointing out that in this particular case it was the very improbable side effect of a drug that killed the patient, not the disease. The cause of death can be the drug even though death from the disease, treated or untreated, is much more probable than such a death from the drug's side effect.

We can combine these observations with others similar to the ones deployed when those discussing a deductive-nomological explanation argue that the causal element is missing from the theory of explanation that takes explaining to be subsuming under a generality. We get a theory saying that to explain, probabilistically as well as in terms of exceptionless laws, is to give the causal origin of an event. But now causality is taken to be a relation that allows a probabilistic connection. Here the idea is that one event might cause a number of different outcomes, each one with a specified probability of being caused. Although one cause may result in a multiplicity of effects, it is still a causal relation that generates the effect event as a consequence of the cause event. Looking at things this way may do justice to the cases noted above. It will also serve to distinguish correlations that are not explanatory, being not causal, from those that are explanatory, being genuinely causal even if probabilistic.

But other interesting issues now arise. If we give a probabilistic explanation that is causal, are we then forced to maintain that there are irreducibly probabilistic causal relations in the world? Must we assert that the world has, at its base, a genuine "tychistic," or chancelike, nature, not underpinned by fully deterministic causal relations? Not necessarily. Some have argued that there may be causal-probabilistic explanations that explain an event as the "pure chance" outcome (although a causal outcome) of some antecedent events that have causal dispositions to generate outcomes of the kind to be explained. In other cases, the probabilistic explanation, once again revealing causal structure, may be explanatory because the probabilistic causal relation is grounded on some underlying fully deterministic causal relations. We shall see some advocacy of this viewpoint later in this chapter. In this second kind of explanation, the later state of a system is fully determined by its earlier dynamical state. But, it is argued, many initial dynamical states are possible consistent with the initial description of the system. Each such initial state has a different future outcome. Each evolution is fully deterministic. Probability comes into the explanatory picture here when we begin to talk about the "probability of a given initial dynamical state" consistent with the initial description of the system. So we will have probabilistic elements in our explanatory structure. The explanatory structure will rest on a basis of revealing the underlying causal processes that generate the events to be explained. But the probability will come in, not because the causal relation is "intrinsically random," but because many different possible causal evolutions are being simultaneously explored. Later, when we discuss quantum mechanics in Chapter 4, we will see why there is some plausibility to the claim that in that context, genuinely "chancy" causality must be postulated.

From this perspective, then, the requirements of high or increased probability seem misguided. What we are trying to do when we probabilistically explain an event is to place that event in a structure of causal relations, where the structure revealed is probabilistic either because the causal relations are intrinsically indeterministic or because a number of alternative causal evolutions are being considered simultaneously. Even if the event in question has low probability, or reduced probability, on the chain of causation leading up to it, we can still provide an explanation of it. Of course that doesn't mean to deny that alleviating surprise by showing that an event is highly probable, or by showing it more probable than we would otherwise have expected, has any value. We do these things and we do think of them as, in some sense, providing explanations.

Does all the importance of the revealing of causal relation in explanation mean that we are turning our backs on a Humean theory of what it is for one thing to be a cause of another? Not necessarily. Some would claim that because explanations require reference to causal relations among events, we must presuppose the notion of a causal relation as a primitive element in our understanding of the nature of the world. Others look for some understanding of what the causal relation is in terms of other relations that events bear to one another. One approach, already present in Hume in a few places, is to try to understand causality in terms of "what would happen" in the world were things other than they are. Thus, a cause might be thought of as that event such that had it not occurred, the effect event would not have occurred. Actually it isn't that simple. Such phenomena as overdetermination (one effect being multiply caused) and preemption (something being caused by an event that, had it not occurred, would have allowed a second event to have brought about the effect; and the first event was such that it blocked the second event from occurring) require a more sophisticated analysis of the relation between "what would have occurred if" and what it is for one event to cause another. Additional problems arise because of noncausal connections that are also associated with such "what would have beens." On top of this, we want some understanding of just what such talk about what would have happened had things been otherwise means, an understanding that itself doesn't rely on presupposing an understood causal relation.

Other analyzing approaches to causation rely upon combining Hume's constant conjunction with other actual elements in the world. It is often emphasized, for example, that the structure of the world is such that we identify a constant conjunction as a causal relation only if the events in question are joined to one another by appropriately continuous paths of constantly conjoined events. There must be, then, paths of "causal influence" or "causal propagation."

Finally, it is very important to reflect upon the fact that the fully lawlike or only probabilistic regularities that we use in our scientific explanations form a unified hierarchy of propositions in a theoretical structure. Some generalizations are much broader, deeper, and more fundamental than others. It can be argued that the difference between mere correlations and causal correlations suitable for explanation is that the latter fit the correlation of the events in question into the deeper levels of correlation of the more fundamental theories. So, it is argued, reference to the fact that we have causation and, therefore, explanation only when the *mechanism* of the correlation of the events is laid bare may be taken as indicating, not that some mysterious causal relation over and above correlation must be produced, but that a correlation is explanatory only when it fits the relation of the events in question into the fundamental correlations of our appropriate basic theory. Wouldn't something like this make sense of the debate between those who think that the known correlations between smoking and getting cancer are enough to argue that smoking causes cancer, and those who deny this? Aren't the latter demanding causation for explanation in the sense of fitting the correlation between the smoking and the disease into a much broader and deeper framework? Biology, chemistry, and physics are all used to fill in the overt correlation with much finer correlations founded on the much deeper laws of science. Such details as the correlations between inhaling chemicals, the chemicals' presence being correlated with genetic changes, these changes being followed up in detail in terms of the deepest correlations of all of physics—which show what is going on at the molecular level—are given by these sciences. From this perspective, then, the demand for causation in explanation is warranted, but on basically Humean grounds.

This last aspect of the role of causation in explanation is particularly relevant to our purposes here. As we get into the details of the role of probability in the theory of statistical mechanics, we will see that what goes on there is that a "surface level" theory of macroscopic behavior, thermodynamics, is related in an explanatory way to a "deep level" dynamical theory. This deep-level theory is the theory of the behavior of systems founded on the basic laws of dynamics of the macroscopic system's microscopic components (such as the molecules of a gas). The probabilistic considerations arise when we try to fit the two levels of description together, using the deep-level theory to explain the surface theory. It is, then, presupposed that we can give a causal account of the evolution of the system in terms of the dynamics of its microscopic constituents. This is the broad, deep, fundamental level of scientific description noted above. Probability plays its role in fitting the description of the system formulated in the upper-level terms into this overall causal picture. As we shall see, the relation of correlation and causation here introduces its own special puzzles.

Explanation and Reduction

Our discussion has proceeded as if individual happenings were the primary objects of scientific understanding, that is, as if what we wished to explain were particular events. More often in science, however, it is the understanding of generalizations, laws or probabilistic correlations, that we are looking for. How can we increase our understanding of lawlike generalizations? How can we explain them?

The main idea is that lawlike generalizations, either fully lawlike or statistical, are explained by being placed under broader, deeper, or more fundamental generalizations. Our laws form a hierarchy, ranging from narrow, surface generalizations (such as Snell's Law of refraction in optics, or Ohm's Law in electricity) to the extremely general and deep laws of our fundamental physical theories. We explain lower-order laws by showing that they follow from the higher-order laws. The lower-level laws may hold only in certain well-definable special circumstances (i.e., when the situation possesses the appropriate special conditions). We explain geometrical optics by showing that it follows from physical (wave) optics, explain physical optics as a consequence of electromagnetic theory, explain electromagnetism as a component of the electroweak field described by quantum field theory, and so on.

Generally the idea is that the more superficial laws are explained by their being derived from laws of the more general and fundamental sort. But things are, actually, much more complicated than that. One familiar assertion is that the more superficial laws are usually found, on being explained, to be not really true. Often they are only good approximations to the truth and then only in certain circumstances. Thus, once the wave theory of light is understood, we realize that geometric optics applies only when the wavelength of the light is small compared to the dimensions of the physical objects in the light path. Making the notion of approximation rigorous here is no easy task.

More problematic are the issues that arise when the less deep laws and statistical generalizations to be explained are framed in different concepts from those used to frame the deeper principles. This will be the case where a less deep theory is reduced to a deeper theory, requiring that some connection be made between the sometimes quite different concepts of the two theories. Whereas biology talks of organisms and cells, for example, molecular chemistry talks of molecules, concentration gradients, and so forth. How are cells, for example, related to their microscopic constituents? Here the answer seems clear, that the cells are constructed out of the molecules, but this needs to be made fully clear.

In the case with which we will be dealing in this chapter, this intertheoretic connection is rather more problematic. The reduced theory I will be describing, thermodynamics, deals with such features of the world as temperature, quantity of heat, and entropy. But the explanatory—reducing—theory deals with systems in terms of their construction out of microscopic constituents such as molecules. Although the macroscopic objects are constructed out of the microscopic components, relating the properties of systems used to characterize them on the explained level (temperature and entropy, for example) to the properties of the systems (their number of microscopic constituents and the space to which these are restricted, for example) and the properties of the microscopic constituents themselves (their momentum, energy, mass, and size, for example) is a subtle and complex matter.

This is made doubly difficult by the curious interworking of full laws and statistical generalizations in the explanatory scheme. The laws to be explained seem, initially, to have the status of exceptionless laws. But the very act of explaining them throws doubt on this assumption. At the deepest explanatory level are the fundamental laws of the dynamics of the microscopic constituents. These are, again, full-fledged laws, although in the version of statistical mechanics that takes quantum dynamics as its fundamental dynamical theory, these laws have latent in them, as we shall see in Chapter 4, a fundamentally statistical element. What is important for the present is to note that in between the fundamental dynamical laws of the microconstituents, and the explained laws of the theory to be reduced, we find generalizations that introduce probabilistic or statistical elements into the explanatory picture. Thus, as we shall see, it is often alleged that the fundamental dynamics explains the thermal behavior at the macroscopic level only by presenting it as the overwhelmingly most probable behavior or, in other cases, as the average behavior to be expected.

When one attempts to understand statistical mechanics, the most important and interesting questions arise at just this point. How are the statistical generalizations that form the core postulates of the theory related, on the one hand, to the fundamental dynamical laws governing the microscopic constituents of the system in question and, on the other hand, to the laws governing the macroscopic behavior of the systems as characterized by the concepts of traditional thermal physics? The explanation of the behavior at the macroscopic level is to be done in terms of understanding it as a consequence of the constitution of the large system out of its microscopic parts and of the fundamental laws governing the dynamics of those parts. What kind of explanation is this going to be? As we shall see, it is an explanatory scheme that introduces, at the intermediate level, fundamentally probabilistic and statistical notions.

But what *grounds* the introduction of these additional probabilistic posits and assumptions? Can they be derived from the fundamental dynamics by itself? Or are additional fundamental postulates necessary to introduce them into physics? That question is very difficult and complex. And it is very important. For how that question is answered will determine just what kind of explanation of the macroscopic phenomena physics is providing. Although there are cases where a lower-level generalization can be said to be explained by the more fundamental theory by means of a derivation of the former from the latter, with, possibly, some notions of approximation thrown in, in the case of statistical mechanics, important elements play a role in the derivation; these are quite unlike the usual elements of the standard philosophical models of the statistical explanation of generalizations.

From Thermodynamics
to Statistical Mechanics

Thermodynamics

The phenomenon of heat is available to us from our everyday experience, so it is not surprising that physics would try to understand it. Early efforts included the development of devices such as the thermometer to assign precise numerical measures to replace the subjective feelings of hotness and coldness that we experience. With some intellectual effort, the distinction was made between degree of temperature and quantity of heat, the former as an "intensive" and the latter as an "extensive" quantity. This is analogous to the distinction between the density and the quantity of matter respectively. Thus a smaller amount of water at a higher temperature when mixed with a quantity of cold water would result in the same ultimate temperature for the mixture as a larger quantity of water at a lower temperature being added, so that one could claim the quantity of heat added in the two cases was the same although the temperatures differed.

Early attempts to understand these results viewed heat as a kind of substance or stuff called caloric and temperature as a kind of measure of the density of caloric in matter. The more caloric in a given portion of ordinary matter, the higher the temperature would be. Such a substantival view does justice to many experimental results when a principle of "conservation of caloric" is introduced. But other results, in particular, the generation of new heat by mechanical action or the conversion of heat into mechanical action (as in a heat-powered steam engine), do not fit neatly into the caloric view. Even at a very early stage, some thinkers had the idea of heat as a kind of motion of tiny components of the system too small to be detected in the usual way.

A great deal of progress was made in formalizing a theory of heat even before the theory of heat as inner motion was victorious. Reflection on the experience of those working with heat engines led S. Carnot to the important observation that the amount of heat that could be converted to mechanical work, even in a perfectly efficient engine, was limited by the temperature difference between the heat put into the engine and the heat removed at its exhaust. This immediately led to the idea of an absolute zero of temperature, the temperature of the heat exhaust of an engine that could transform all its input heat into usable mechanical work. R. Clausius and others developed a formal theory of heat out of Carnot's ideas.

First it was noted that whereas mechanical work and heat can be converted into each other, their total quantity is invariant. This is the so-called First Law of Thermodynamics. Next the fact that getting useful work out of heat requires that the heat be put into the engine at a higher temperature than the heat is exhausted led, after brilliant reflection, to the general principle of irreversibility, the so-called Second

Law of Thermodynamics. There are many subtle formulations of this law. One says basically this: Take an energetically isolated system. Let some heat in it be transformed into mechanical work. Let the system start in a given state. Then, at the end of the process, it cannot be in its initial state. At the end of the process, we might have transformed the work obtained back into heat, but the net result of the entire process will be that although total heat is the same as when we started, it will now be at a lower temperature and, hence, less "available" to be converted into work.

The notion of an equilibrium state of a system becomes crucial. Let a system be energetically isolated from the rest of the world. Sooner or later it settles down to a macroscopically unchanging state, its equilibrium state. Thus an iron bar hot at one end and cold at the other settles down to a state of uniform intermediate temperature. A gas initially in one side of a box settles down to a condition of uniform density throughout the box. A "Zeroth" law of thermodynamics asks us to consider three systems, *A, B, C*, each in its equilibrium state, and where *A* and *B* are such that when brought into energetic contact, they remain in the same equilibrium state. Suppose the same thing is true of *B* and *C* when they are brought into contact. Then *A* and *C* will remain in their original equilibrium states when they are brought into contact. We can label the equilibrium "commonality" of the systems by their common temperature. Finally, it is necessary to introduce the new concept of entropy. Entropy keeps track of the "usefulness" of heat for conversion into mechanical work. Whereas the *amount* of heat at a high and at a low temperature may be the same, the former has more usefulness as a source of mechanical work. It is then, said to have a *lower* entropy. If we take a system from one equilibrium state to another, the amount of heat transferred and the amount of mechanical work done may differ from one process to another with the same end states. But the entropy change from one state to the other will be the same. So equilibrium states of system have a definite absolute temperature and they have a definite entropy (up to an arbitrary constant). These, along with various mechanical (or electrical, and so forth) features (such as the pressure and volume of a piece of gas in equilibrium), completely characterize the nature of the equilibrium states.

We end up, then with an elegant formal theory of heat. Systems have equilibrium states. In a transformation from one of these to another, mechanical work can be generated or absorbed. Energy can also be transferred without such work being done. This is called heat flow. Equilibrium states are characterized by their temperatures, so that heat flows only between systems whose temperatures differ from one another. The amount of work that can be obtained in a transition from one equilibrium state to another depends on the temperature of the states. Only if the final state has an absolute zero of temperature will all the heat available have been transformed into mechanical work. The transformation of heat into work is, in nonideal engines, irreversible:

That is, you can't transform heat into work in an isolated system and then do something more so that you end up where you started with all the heat as available as before to do still more work. You can get work out of heat and then transform the work back into heat. You will end up with the same amount of energy in the form of heat with which you started, but it will no longer be so available for conversion to mechanical work. Equilibrium states have not only mechanical features such as pressure and volume; they also have a definite temperature and a definite entropy (or at least a definite entropy relative to one state's getting an arbitrarily assigned value). The entropy of a state indicates how available for conversion to work its internal heat energy is, low entropy indicating high availability. The basic laws of the theory are the transitivity of equilibrium (Zeroth Law), the Conservation of Energy (First Law), and the Law of Irreversibility (Second Law). Sometimes a Third Law, the unachievability of absolute zero, is added.

The Kinetic Theory of Heat

To some physicists, the theory of thermal phenomena just outlined was perfectly satisfactory as an autonomous fundamental theory of physics. They saw no reason to reduce it in any way to some deeper theory nor any need to provide explanations as to why its basic propositions held true. But for others, the theory cried out for a deeper explanation. What, ultimately, *was* heat, this something convertible to and from mechanical energy? What was the feature of systems that constituted their having a specific temperature? Why did equilibrium states of systems exist, and why, given that they existed, did they have the particular structures they were observed to have? And, most important of all, what was the source of the strange asymmetry in time of the world, the asymmetry revealed in the fact that systems not in equilibrium, if left by themselves, moved uniformly toward the equilibrium condition, always in the future direction of time, and having obtained equilibrium, stayed there?

Although the idea that heat was a kind of energy of motion of small components of the macroscopic system, components so small that their individual motions were undetectable directly on the large scale, was speculated upon by F. Bacon, J. Bernoulli, and others, it was only in the nineteenth century that this idea became dominant. Even if heat was motion, what kind of motion was it? Systems might, after all, have a very complex and subtle microscopic structure. Two British thinkers, J. Herepath and J. Waterston, both suggested that for gases the situation was very simple. They were, these thinkers said, made up of tiny particles that spent most of their time in free motion, interacting only by colliding with one another and with the walls of the container. The heat content of a system was merely the energy of this motion of microscopic parts. But their suggestions were ignored. Finally when the ideas were presented by German physicists A. Krönig and Clausius, they got the attention they deserved.

Suppose a gas in a box is composed of small particles in mostly free motion. If we make simple assumptions about the heat's being the total energy of this motion and about its being evenly distributed among the molecules, such results as the Ideal Gas Law, giving the relation among pressure, volume, and temperature of the gas at equilibrium, can easily be derived. Pressure is a result of the particles' bouncing off the walls of the container, and temperature is a measure of their individual energy of motion. Assuming the molecules collide with one another, we can solve such puzzles as why, if the particles (i.e., molecules) are in such fast, almost free, motion, diffusion of gas from one side of a room to another is as slow as it is measured to be.

The next important advance was J. C. Maxwell's realization that the assumption that at equilibrium each molecule had the same speed was implausible. By use of an ingenious, if not totally persuasive, argument, he derived a curve giving a distribution of speeds for the molecules in the equilibrium gas. Some would be moving very slowly and others more quickly, with a clustering around a mean value. Could this result be given a better, more convincing, justification? Here L. Boltzmann made his greatest contribution. Boltzmann asked how a gas not in equilibrium would be expected to evolve. The evolution would take place because the molecules moved, and especially because they would trade energy with one another upon collision. Could one show that if the gas started with any velocity distribution other than Maxwell's, it would by this process of energy exchange approach the Maxwell distribution and then stay there?

By making plausible assumptions, one of which we will look at in detail shortly, Boltzmann was able to derive an equation for the evolution of the velocity distribution function. He showed that the Maxwell distribution was a stationary solution of the equation, and once having been obtained, it would not change. He was able to define a function of the velocity distribution and show that as long as this function had not obtained its minimal value (obtained for the Maxwell distribution), the velocity distribution would not be stationary. Therefore the Maxwell distribution was the *only* stationary solution to the equation. Taken together, this seemed to show why a gas not in equilibrium would evolve toward equilibrium and why once in equilibrium, it would stay there.

But now the troubles began. First critics noted that the systems were supposed to be composed of molecules obeying classical dynamics. But as long as any such system is confined and energy is conserved, which is true in this case, it should evince the finding of H. Poincaré: The system started in a given dynamical state will return infinitely often to states very close to the original state. But, then, how could Boltzmann be right in claiming that the system starting in nonequilibrium evolved to the equilibrium state and then stayed there? Another result of classical dynamics tells us that if a system evolves from state S1 to state S2, it will evolve from the state like that of S2, except with all directions

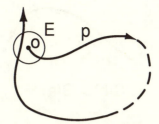

Figure 3.1 Poincaré recurrence. We work in phase space where a single point represents the exact microscopic state of a system at a given time, say, the position and velocity of every molecule in a gas. Poincaré shows that for certain systems (a gas confined in a box and energetically isolated from the outside world is one such system), if such a system starts in a certain microscopic state, *o*, then, except for a "vanishingly small" number of such initial states, when the system's evolution is followed out along a curve, *p*, the system will be found, for any small region of microstates around the original microstate, *o*, to "return" to a microstate in that small region, *E*. Thus "almost all" such systems started in a given state will eventually return to a microscopic state "very close" to that initial state.

of motion reversed, to the "time reverse" of state *S1*. Call the time reverse states *S1'* and *S2'*. The evolution from *S2'* to *S1'*, if *S2'* like *S2* describes an equilibrium state and *S1'* like *S1* a nonequilibrium state, would violate Boltzmann's equation, which always describes evolution toward equilibrium. How can Boltzmann's equation, then, be consistent with classical dynamics? (See Figures 3.1 and 3.2.)

It is at this point that probabilistic ideas begin to play a role in versions of the theory. Can it be that the Boltzmann equation describes not how every system must behave but only how systems *probably* behave? Although we would, then, expect evolution toward equilibrium with overwhelming probability, we would also expect rare cases where a nonequilibrium system evolves further from equilibrium or where an equilibrium system evolves to a nonequilibrium state. But one still must be very careful here. The recurrence theorem of Poincaré tells us that we can be probabilistically certain that systems started in a given nonequilibrium condition will eventually recur to an nonequilibrium condition as close as one likes to that in which they started. So how can a monotonic approach to equilibrium be probable? And for every evolution from nonequilibrium to equilibrium, there is one possible reverse evolution. So shouldn't the evolutions in both directions be equally probable?

The response of Boltzmann, clarified by P. and T. Ehrenfest, has a number of important components. First there is Boltzmann's discovery of a new way of deriving the equilibrium velocity distribution. Think of all the ways molecules can be put into small "boxes" in an abstract space corresponding to small regions of position and of momentum. Momentum is crucial here—if we use velocity or energy we would get the wrong results. We obtain a new arrangement by moving a molecule

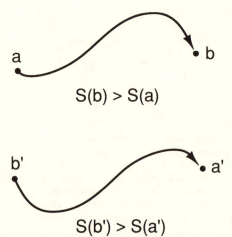

$$S(b) > S(a)$$

$$S(b') > S(a')$$

Figure 3.2 Loschmidt's "reversibility" argument. Let a system be started in microstate a and evolve to microstate b. Suppose, as is expected, the entropy of state b, $S(b)$, is higher than that of state a, $S(a)$. Then, given the time-reversal invariance of the underlying dynamical laws that govern the evolution of the system, there must be a microstate, b', that evolves to a microstate, a', and such that the entropy of b' equals that of b and the entropy of a' equals that of a (as Boltzmann defines statistical entropy). So for each "thermodynamic" evolution in which entropy increases, there must be a corresponding "antithermodynamic" evolution possible in which entropy decreases.

from one box to another. Many permutations of the molecules, however, may correspond to one "combination" state, i.e., a state characterized by numbers of molecules in each box, irrespective of which particular molecule is in a given box. The equilibrium distribution is a combination state corresponding to the combination obtainable by the overwhelmingly greatest number of permutations of the molecules in the boxes. In general, combinations near equilibrium are obtainable by a vast number of permutations. Combinations corresponding to macroscopic states far from equilibrium are obtainable only by vastly fewer permutations. If we look at each permutation as equally probable, then using a kind of principle of indifference or symmetry, can't we think of equilibrium as the "overwhelmingly most probable" state of the system?

We should then think of the situation like this: A given system, viewed over all of time and perpetually isolated, will spend almost all its time at or near equilibrium. Deviations from equilibrium will occur, but the further the deviation is, the rarer will be its occurrence. The situation will be time symmetric, with transitions occurring from nonequilibrium to equilibrium and the reverse equally often. It will still be the case, however, that almost every state far from equilibrium will be followed by states much closer to equilibrium, as described by the Boltzmann equation. (See Figure 3.3.)

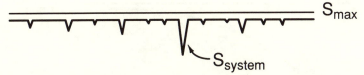

Figure 3.3 "Time-symmetric" Boltzmann picture. In this picture of the world, it is proposed that an isolated system whose entropy is S_{system} "over infinite time" spends nearly all the time in states whose entropy is close to the maximum value, S_{max}, that is, in the equilibrium state. There are random fluctuations of the system away from equilibrium. The greater the fluctuation of a system from equilibrium, the less frequently it occurs. The picture is symmetric in time. If we find a system far from equilibrium, we ought to expect that in the future it will be closer to equilibrium. But we ought also to infer that in the past it was also closer to equilibrium.

The Boltzmann equation cannot be thought of as giving the most probable evolution of a system over infinite time, however, because this would conflict with recurrence. Rather, the situation should be viewed as follows: Take a big collection of systems, all starting in non-equilibrium at a given time. Look at them at discrete time intervals, noting at each time interval the state of the system that is obtained by the dominating majority of systems. Draw a curve through those "most probable" evolved states. *That* curve, the "concentration curve" of the collection's evolution, will obey the Boltzmann equation. Nearly every system will eventually move away from equilibrium, but these excursions will be incoherent, happening for different systems at different times. After a long time, almost all of the systems will, at any given specified time, be near equilibrium, just as the Boltzmann equation, interpreted in this way, demands. So this probabilistic interpretation of the Boltzmann equation is consistent with the recurrence results. (See Figure 3.4.)

But we need to reflect still further. If, as this new interpretation suggests, equilibrium is the "overwhelmingly most probable" condition of a system, why is the world we live in so grossly far from equilibrium? Boltzmann offers a series of arguments to get around this. First, he says, the universe is very large in space and in time. We may postulate that the region available to our observation is very small. Remember that this work is being done in the 1890s and that the existence of galaxies outside of the Milky Way was not established until some time later. Now we expect small portions of large systems to be, for short times, in states far from equilibrium. Thus we can understand the pervasive nonequilibrium that we experience as a "local fluctuation" away from a pervasive equilibrium situation.

Next we might ask why it is that we find ourselves in such an unusual portion of the universe instead of in the dominating equilibrium spatiotemporal region. Here the answer is in terms of a special kind of observational bias. In order for there to be sustained, complex organisms (like ourselves) that could perform observations, there must be

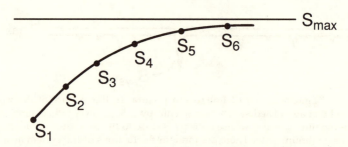

Figure 3.4 The "concentration curve" of a collection of systems. A collection of systems is considered, each member of which at time 1 has entropy S_1. The systems evolve according to their particular microstate starting at the initial time. At later times, 2, 3, 4, 5, 6, . . . , the collection is reexamined. At each time the overwhelming majority of systems have entropies at or near values S_2, S_3, S_4, S_5, S_6, . . . , which are plotted on the "concentration curve." This curve can monotonically approach the equilibrium value S_{max} even if almost all the systems, individually, approach and recede from the equilibrium condition in the manner depicted in Figure 3.3.

energy flows. Only these can counteract the normal process of equilibration and keep a highly structured active organism, like a life-form, in operation. But such energy flows presuppose a nonequilibrium situation. So if there are to be observers at all, they must be found in the small, deviant, nonequilibrium portions of the universe.

Now it is overwhelmingly probable that such a nonequilibrium part of the universe will be one that is even further from equilibrium in one time direction and closer in the other. These are much more common than the rare extremal cases of portions of the universe that are turning points where the region is closer to equilibrium in both time directions, and even more relatively probable than the extraordinarily rare cases of a state far from equilibrium bracketed in both time directions by states even further from equilibrium.

But why should we find that the states closer to equilibrium are, in our portion of the universe, in the *future* time direction rather than in the past time direction? Isn't either option equally probable? At this point, Boltzmann argues that what we *mean* by the future direction of time is the time direction in which the local entropy is increasing, i.e., the direction of time in which the local portion of the universe is getting closer to equilibrium. He argues that the direction of time that counts as future will, possibly, be opposite in separated regions of the universe in which the process toward equilibrium is in opposite time directions. This is just like "down" for someone antipodal to us on the earth, which is in the opposite spatial direction from our "down." And, he says, in the pervasive equilibrium portion of the universe, there will be no distinction between past and future, although there will still be, of course, two opposite directions of time. The analogy is with empty space, where all spatial directions still exist, but where no one of them is "down" in the absence of a local direction of the gravitational force. We will critically examine these brilliant Boltzmannian ideas shortly.

The Ergodic Approach to Statistical Mechanics

Maxwell and Boltzmann occasionally offer a somewhat different treatment of the equilibrium situation. Here the idea is to consider an infinite collection of systems just like the system in whose specified macroscopic aspects one is interested. One might, for example, consider a gas with a specified internal energy of its molecules and confined to a stipulated size container. One imagines a collection, each of whose members has the same internal energy as the given gas and is confined to the same size container, but each of whose members has a different microscopic condition of its microcomponents. Thus one considers samples of the gas with constant macroscopic features but with every possible position and individual momentum for its molecules being realized.

Next a certain natural probability distribution is placed over these microscopic conditions, so that the microscopic state of the case being in a specified range of such states has a definite probability. The distribution chosen is almost inevitable. It is derived, once again, by an application of a principle of indifference or symmetry. But, as we noted in the section on probability, applying that principle means already having chosen a preferred characterization of the system, which must itself be justified. One can prove that the specified probability distribution will not change in time. That is, as each gas in the collection has its microscopic state change, the total number of systems with their states in a given range will stay constant, even though some systems have their state leave this range and others have their state enter the range. So this probability seems natural for describing equilibrium, an unchanging macroscopic state.

Next we identify the macroscopic observables (like pressure) with averages over a function of the microstates of the system, where the averages are computed using the probability distribution in question. It is easy to show that when this is done, the quantities calculated will be related to one another just as we find them to be in systems in equilibrium in the world.

This method of calculating equilibrium values, by identifying them as "phase averages" over a collection (or "ensemble") of systems all subject to the identical macroscopic constraints, becomes formalized and generalized by J. Gibbs. He develops ensembles (i.e., probability distributions over microstates of systems) appropriate not only for energetically isolated systems but also for the important cases of systems kept in energetic contact with a constant-temperature heat bath and for systems that can interchange molecules with an external supply.

Notice that there are some subtle differences between this method and Boltzmann's other approach. Before, we thought of the equilibrium state as being the "overwhelmingly most probable" microscopic state of the system. Now equilibrium quantities are thought of, not as those that hold in the overwhelmingly probable microstates, but as averages over quantities over *all* possible microscopic states, including the less probable ones. Only if the probability distribution over microscopic states has the feature of being both symmetrical about and highly peaked about the most probable state will the two quantities (in general) be equal. It can be shown for the probability distributions used in statistical mechanics and for the quantities calculated with them that the two ways of calculating the equilibrium values will agree with each other.

Although the picture presented by Boltzmann and the clarifiers of his work has some plausibility, and although this new account avoids the obvious contradictions with the underlying dynamics present in the earlier understanding of the theory, many problems remain. It is one thing to posit such a picture of the behavior of systems; it is quite another to justify the claims that systems will behave as they have now been described; and still another to explain *why* systems behave in this Boltzmannian fashion, if, indeed, they do.

One early attempt at justifying a portion of the standard procedures of what can now be called statistical mechanics was an early suggestion by Boltzmann that would, if it could be made to work out, justify both the choice of the standard probability distribution used in the equilibrium ensemble for an energetically isolated system and provide part of the justification of his picture of a system over infinite time as spending almost all the time near equilibrium. Suppose, Boltzmann says, that any individual system will eventually have its microscopic dynamical state go through every possible microscopic dynamical state compatible with the constraints on the system. These constraints might be given, for example, by the system's fixed total energy and the volume of the box to which it is confined. Call this assumption the Ergodic Hypothesis. (See Figure 3.5.)

Many things would follow from the Ergodic Hypothesis if it were true. From it, one could show that the standard probability distribution is not just *a* stationary distribution under dynamic evolution but that it is the only such distribution. One could not only show that a system will, over infinite time, spend almost all of its time at or near equilibrium; one can even show that the time spent by the system with its microstate in a particular region of microstates will be just that proportion of time that the region has as a proportion of the set of all the available microstates according to the standard probability measure. This would allow the identification of the "probability" of a microstate (as determined by the standard probability distribution) with a more physical kind of probability, to wit, the proportion of time spent by the system with the microstate having a specified feature. All this will hold, however, only in the limit of infinite time. If one then used the large number of degrees of freedom of a system (its vast number of molecules) and the special natures of the functions used to calculate ob-

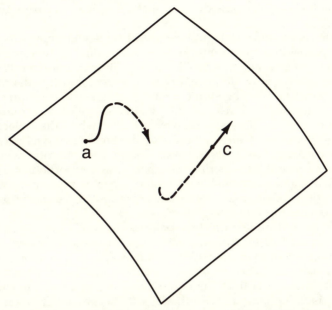

Figure 3.5 The Ergodic Hypothesis. Let a system be started in any microstate, represented by point *a* in the phase space. Let *c* represent any other microstate possible for the system. The Ergodic Hypothesis posits that at some future time or other the system started in state *a* will, eventually, pass through state *c*. But the posit is, in fact, provably false.

servable macroscopic features, a pretty complete rationalization of the identification of averages calculated by means of the standard probability measure with "overwhelmingly probable values" would be available. Then if we think of equilibrium as the overwhelmingly probable state, a justification of taking ensemble averages as representative of equilibrium would be available.

Alas, Boltzmann could not show the Ergodic Hypothesis to be true. Indeed, it is false and demonstrably so on very general topological (or measure-theoretic) grounds. But as we shall see, a modification of the Boltzmannian idea has proven enormously fruitful.

Justifying the claims of the nonequilibrium theory that describes the approach to equilibrium of systems started out of that state is even more problematic. The new Boltzmann picture suggests this: If we start with a collection of all possible systems in a given nonequilibrium state, follow their evolution over time, and then keep track of the dominant state of the systems at each time, the curve through those dominant states will be the curve generated as the solution of the Boltzmann equation. But will it? And if so, *why* will it? How the systems will actually behave will depend on two things: the microscopic dynamical state in which they were started and the laws of dynamics that determine how their microscopic dynamical states will evolve from that initial state.

So a thoroughgoing statistical theory of nonequilibrium should tell us what probability to attribute to a class of initial microscopic states of systems prepared in a given initial nonequilibrium condition. It should explain to us also why we have a right to expect that this distribution of initial microstates will genuinely represent in some appropriate way how the initial states of real systems will be distributed in the world. Next the theory should show us why it is that when the collection of systems evolves over time, each individual system having its microstate change according to the given dynamical laws, the collection of systems will have its probability distribution, that is, its proportion of systems in specified regions of possible microstates, evolve in such a way that the later collections come to resemble more and more the probability distribution appropriate to equilibrium.

It was realized quite early that Boltzmann, in his derivation of his famous equation of evolution, relied on a crucial assumption. In describing the evolution of the molecules of a single gas, he assumed that the frequencies of collisions of the molecules of a given speed would be proportional to the fractions of the molecules in the gas having that speed. This is his famous Hypothesis with Regard to Collision Numbers. It assumes that there is no special correlation among the molecules prior to collision. The evolution of the collection of gases toward the equilibrium collection in the statistical version of the theory depends upon a similar assumption, the Postulate of Molecular Chaos. It is assumed that not just at the beginning of the evolution but also at each following moment, a posit of "randomization" of the collisions of molecules is applicable. But the evolution of the ensemble is fixed by the initial ensemble and by the deterministic dynamical evolution of each gas in the collection. Is it, then, *consistent* with the appropriate initial collection and these laws to posit that Molecular Chaos holds? Surely, if the evolution is fully determined by the initial state and the laws, one must justify the legitimacy of making such a rerandomization assumption. We will explore some of this shortly.

It is important to note that it is just such a rerandomization assumption, applied to molecules *before* they collide, but not after they collide, that provides the source of the time asymmetry of the Boltzmann equation and its solution describing the time-asymmetric approach to equilibrium in the future but not in the past. But the laws of dynamics show no such time asymmetry. Where, physically, does it come in? Are there hidden asymmetries in the laws of dynamics? Is our idealization of the system as isolated from the rest of the world a misidealization? Or is the source of the asymmetry something about the physical nature of the world that makes an appropriate *initial* ensemble—one that generates the asymmetry in time of the probabilistic ensemble description of the world and that then captures in our theory the observed asymmetry of the world as summed up in the Second Law of Thermodynamics—the right one to choose? Such questions, as we shall see, continue to haunt the foundations of this subject.

The Problem of Irreversibility and Attempts to Solve It

The years following this pioneering work in statistical mechanics have seen enormous progress. One great advance was the expansion of the early work to apply to systems more general than the rarefied gases of the early studies. The theory of systems in equilibrium has been generalized to cover such systems as dense gases and systems of radically different sorts such as radiation in interaction with matter. There has been less success in generalizing the theory of nonequilibrium to nondense gases because the methods of approximate solution, which work well in the equilibrium problem, usually break down when one is trying to generalize the nonequilibrium equations. But even here some significant progress has been made.

A major revision in the theory occurred when the classical dynamics used to describe the behavior of the microscopic constituents in the original theory was replaced by a new fundamental dynamical theory, quantum mechanics. As we shall see in Chapter 4, quantum mechanics brings with it its own probabilistic description of the evolution of systems over time. But the standard view is that the probabilistic elements of statistical mechanics remain ineliminable elements. They describe a probabilistic aspect of the world beyond any such probabilistic aspect described at the quantum mechanical level. The problem of reconciling the statistical, or probabilistic, theory that grounds thermodynamics with the underlying dynamical theory remains, then, an open one, even when the underlying dynamical theory is quantum mechanics. Indeed, for certain technical reasons, some of the rationalizing and explaining arguments we will be discussing in this section, arguments that presuppose that classical dynamics is the underlying dynamical theory, break down in the new dynamical context. The grounds of the probabilistic posits in statistical mechanics become somewhat more difficult to explain, rather than easier, in the new dynamical framework.

Apart from generalizing the theory and reconstructing it on the new dynamical basis, much work has been done to supply the foundational justification for the theory, the need for which we discussed earlier. The general program is to see how much of the probabilistic postulation embedded in the theory of statistical mechanics can be shown to be nonautonomous. That is, we wish to find out to what extent the probabilistic assumptions (and their use in calculating observable quantities) can be given an explanatory foundation in nonprobabilistic sources. In particular, what we have to work with are the facts about the structure of the systems in question (that the gas is made of molecules and is confined in a box, for example) and the facts about the underlying dynamical theory (that the molecules move in a manner specified by classical dynamics, that their exchange of energy upon collision is also described by that theory, and so forth). To what extent can we derive the needed posits of statistical mechanics from the fundamental dynamical features of the system? Some of the elements of statistical mechanics that we would like to derive are the standard probability distribution used in equilibrium theory, the identification of observable equilibrium quantities with averages derived from this probability distribution, the Postulate of Molecular Chaos used in the nonequilibrium theory, and so on. And if some of the basic probabilistic assumptions of statistical mechanics are thus not derivable from the structure of the system and its underlying dynamics, what room for them can be found in the world described by physics? If they are autonomous postulates, what is the physical reason why they are true?

Because the remainder of this section on the problem of irreversibility is rather dense, let me outline the structure it will take. We will first look at some efforts to understand the equilibrium state. Next, we will discuss the general problem of the approach to equilibrium. Following this, we will distinguish some "nonorthodox" approaches to the nonequilibrium problem from the more standard approaches. Then we will look at some variations of the standard approach to the issues. Next, we will look at the problem of characterizing the initial probability distribution that is to be assumed. Finally, we will look at some attempts to account for the fundamental problem of the irreversibility of systems that bring facts about the overall structure of the cosmos into the argument.

Characterizing Equilibrium

Let us look first at the case of equilibrium theory. As we previously noted, the standard procedure for calculating the equilibrium values of observable quantities was to identify these quantities with averages of specified functions of the microscopic state of the system. The average is calculated using the standard probability distribution. Boltzmann's "picture" of the reasonableness of this procedure was that the isolated system would spend almost all of its time at or near equilibrium. Because the standard probability measure could be interpreted as giving the proportion of time spent by a system with its microstate in a given range of conditions, and because, in addition, the overwhelmingly most probable states completely dominated the others so that average values could be identified with most-probable values, the average of a quantity calculated using the standard probability measure would be equal to its overwhelmingly most probable value. This would then be its equilibrium value. As we noted, a justification for these claims was made using the Ergodic Hypothesis—that each system would, eventually, have its microstate evolve through all the possible microstates. But the Ergodic Hypothesis was provably false. Could something be found to take its place?

A theorem was proven to the effect that if a system met a certain specified constraint (essentially, the absence of any "global" constants of motion other than those used to specify the system), phase averages of quantities calculated using the standard measure would equal time averages of those quantities, at least for almost all systems. That is, except for a set of systems whose size had probability zero in the standard measure, the infinite time average of a quantity for a given system as the systems evolved would equal the average of that quantity taken over all systems at one time, using the standard probability measure to specify how many systems had their microstate in a given range of such microstates. If this condition were met, one could prove that for "almost all" systems, the time spent by the system in a given region of microstates (in the limit as time went to infinity) would be equal to the probability of that region of microstates in the standard probability measure. Thus a kind of "law of large numbers," that in the limit of infinite time, *time* proportions were equal to probabilities, could be derived, even though, in this case, we are dealing *not* with probabilistically independent trials but, rather, with deterministic evolution. And one could prove if the condition were met, that the only probability measure that (1) was invariant in time and that (2) gave probability zero to classes of microstates that had probability zero in the standard measure was the standard measure itself. These results are close to those obtainable by using the false Ergodic Hypothesis. (See Figure 3.6.)

But do interesting systems ever meet the condition in question? First a dynamical condition for being a so-called ergodic system (i.e., for meeting the condition of the theorem outlined) is found. It is a condition on the instability of the paths of evolution of the systems in their microstate descriptions and, essentially, demands that for each microstate there be nearby microstates such that the evolution of systems from them diverges from the evolution of the given state very quickly. Then certain model systems are shown to meet this dynamical condition and, hence, to be ergodic systems. In particular, the system consisting in "hard spheres in a box" is such an ergodic system. The particles must interact only instantaneously by collisions with each other and with the walls of the box, and the collisions must be perfectly elastic. Perfectly elastic means that no energy is absorbed or emitted in collisions. As this model is a standard one adopted for the ideal gas, it looks as though a kind of rationalization for the equilibrium theory has been found using only the structure of the system and the laws of dynamics governing the microcomponents.

These results are impressive. But we should be cautious. First, there is the "set of measure zero" problem. With the help of the ergodic results, we can show that except for a set of initial conditions of probability zero in the standard probability measure, every system will have its time averages of quantities equal to its averages computed using the standard probability. But why assume that just because a set has probability zero in the standard measure, it is unlikely that a system in the

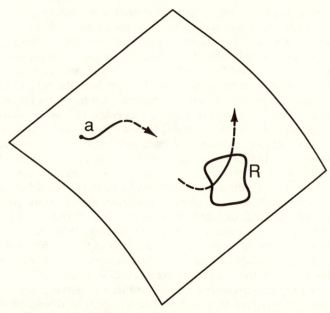

Figure 3.6   The Ergodic Theorem. Let a system be started in some microstate, *a*. Let *R* be any region of microstates possible for the system given its constraints. Such constraints might be a specification, for example, of the total energy of the gas. Let *R* have a definite, nonzero, size in the phase space. Then, when a system is ergodic, it will be the case that, except possibly for a set of initial microstates of size zero, the trajectory from the initial microstate *a* will eventually pass through the region *R*.

world will have such an initial condition? Again, we can show that of all the probability distributions that assign zero probability to those sets given zero probability by the standard probability distribution, only the standard probability distribution is constant in time. But why restrict our attention to just those probability distributions that "ignore" (i.e., give probability zero to) the sets that have zero probability in the standard measure? It is as if we have replaced our original probabilistic postulate that the standard probability measure gives the correct probabilities with a weaker, but still nontrivial, autonomous probability assumption, i.e., that members of the set of initial conditions that has zero probability in the standard measure can be ignored. We are assuming that they can be expected with "probabilistic certainty" not to occur.

Another important problem stems from the fact that although the conditions necessary for the Ergodic Theorem to hold are provably true of such idealized systems as that of hard spheres in a box, they are probably not true of more realistic systems. The molecules in a gas are not perfect hard spheres that have no interaction with each other or

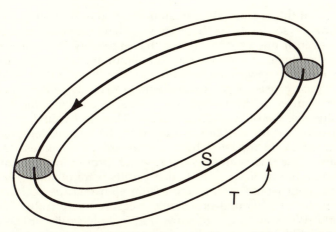

Figure 3.7   The KAM Theorem. The closed curve, *S*, represents a system that passes from a given initial state through a series of intermediate states and then returns to its exact initial state and repeats the process, ad infinitum. An example might be a planet that, unperturbed, repeats forever a closed orbit. The KAM Theorem states that for systems satisfying its demands, a small enough perturbation of the system (say, of the planet by the gravitational tug of another planet) will result in an orbit that, although it will not any longer be closed, will be confined to a finite region (indicated by the tube *T*) surrounding (in phase space) the initial curve *S*. Such a system cannot then be ergodic and "wander" over the available phase space.

with the walls of the container until collisions occur. Instead, there is a smooth and gradual interaction between molecules and between molecules and walls, an interaction that varies with the separation of the interacting components. In mechanics there is another theorem, the Kolmogorov-Arnold-Moser (or KAM) Theorem, which tells us that in certain specified cases there will be regions in phase space that are of nonzero measure and that are such that all systems whose initial conditions are in such a region have their state remain in the region for all times. These systems have a stability that prevents them from wandering all over the possible microstate region as ergodicity demands. Although we can't (in general) prove that realistic systems have the condition necessary for the KAM Theorem to hold, it seems very plausible that they do. So the more realistic idealizations of a system would not satisfy the conditions for ergodicity. (See Figure 3.7.)

What one would like to show in these cases would be something more modest than ergodicity. One would use the fact that the real systems with which we deal are composed of a vast number of microcomponents such as molecules. This is not brought into play at all in the ergodic results. Then one would try to show that for such systems the region of stable trajectories, demanded by the KAM Theorem, becomes very small in the natural probability measure as the number of components in the system becomes vast. Indeed, computer modeling seems to show that this is true. The remaining region of instability would not necessarily be so chaotic as the ergodic system's unstable region would be. But even if one couldn't prove that ergodicity held for the phase region as a whole, or even for the dominating region of instability, perhaps one could show that a *kind* of instability held in this region. This region would consist of the overwhelming majority of the initial states when measured in the natural way. This would be sufficient to get something like the Boltzmannian results. That is, it would be sufficient to assure us that for trajectories started in this region, long-term time behavior could be modeled by the standard probabilities. Exploring possibilities like this is an ongoing research project in the foundations of statistical mechanics. Even if such results were obtained, however, applying them would require the assumption that the regions of stability, small in the natural probability measure, were really "small" in the world. We would need to show that it is physically unlikely that a system would be found with its microstate in such a region of stability. This would not be derivable from the underlying dynamics.

Finally, we should notice the structure of the statistical explanations offered by this equilibrium theory. How are equilibrium features of systems *explained* probabilistically by this theory? They are not shown to be the features of systems we are overwhelmingly likely to find in the world. Indeed, if that were shown, we would have a problem, because, as we know, we are overwhelmingly likely to find systems in the world *not* to be in equilibrium. Nor does the theory in some way show that equilibrium features are more likely to be the case than we would have expected on the background evidence. And the theory does not provide a kind of statistical-causal account of equilibrium. It does not derive equilibrium from some causal tychistic propensities or derive its probability from some probabilistic distribution over causal initial conditions. Such a probabilistic-causal account, if it can be given at all, will be in the provenance of the statistical-mechanical theory of nonequilibrium and of the approach to equilibrium. We will turn to this soon.

Instead, the equilibrium features of systems are made understandable by the theory by virtue of its demonstration that under the appropriate conditions the features that hold of systems when they are observed to be in equilibrium are just those features that dominate the behavior of a system over the long run of an idealized infinite time. Once again, as we have noted, even getting this established requires substantial idealization. The legitimacy of the idealization is a matter of debate. But the pattern of explanation is certainly interesting. A macroscopic feature is identified with an average of the microscopic quantity appropriate to it using a natural probability distribution. The probability distribution is rationalized by showing that it is the uniquely stationary one that gives probability zero to regions given probability zero in that very natural measure. Time spent in regions of microscopic states in the infinite limit is shown to be equal to the size of the region given that natural measure. And with the large number of microscopic components introduced, average values of quantities can be shown to be equal to overwhelmingly highly probable values, and these to be equal to the standard equilibrium values. Finally, and of greatest importance, is the degree to which the naturalness of the probability measure can be given a firm grounding. It can be shown, relative to all the qualifications we have noted, to be the "right" probability measure. The demonstration uses only the structure of the system and the laws of dynamics. To some extent, at least, the need for positing the natural probability measure as a fundamental and autonomous part of the theory has been reduced. As we shall see, however, things are not so simple when it is nonequilibrium that is at issue.

The Approach to Equilibrium

What kind of theory should we look for to provide us with a general statistical description of the approach to equilibrium and with an explanation of the nonequilibrium phenomena? We expect our description to involve probabilistic elements, because we know from the structure of the basic dynamics that individual systems can, in fact, behave in the "counterthermodynamic" fashion. They can fail to move smoothly from initial nonequilibrium to an equilibrium state. It will be in the behavior of a collection of systems, each started in the same nonequilibrium condition, that we will find our description of the approach to equilibrium. It is something about the evolution of the ensemble of systems, or, more rigorously, something about the evolution of an initial probability distribution over possible microstates of systems compatible with the original nonequilibrium condition of the system, that will represent for us the approach to equilibrium.

There is a nice way of characterizing the kind of behavior we are looking for that would do justice to the ideas of Boltzmann and the Ehrenfests discussed earlier. This was made clear by Gibbs. Look at an initial nonequilibrium probability distribution. Follow its evolution as determined by the dynamical laws that tell us how each system in the collection, characterized by its specific initial microcondition, will evolve. Could this probability distribution itself approach, in time, the equilibrium probability distribution for the specified constraints? For example, suppose we have in a box gas started in the left-hand side and allowed to spread out to fill the box. Initially the probability is all concentrated on states corresponding to the gas's being on the left-hand side of the box. Will this initial probability distribution approach the one corresponding to the equilibrium distribution for a gas spread out smoothly throughout the whole box?

The answer is, provably, no. A fundamental theorem tells us that the original probability distribution can't spread out in this way. But it can "spread out." The initially compact and regularly bounded probability distribution can become a wildly fibrillated distribution that occupies the whole of the region of possible microstates in a "coarse

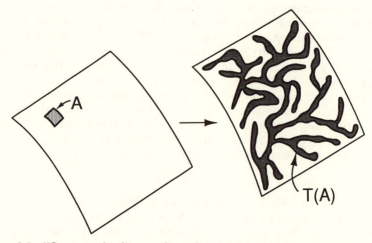

Figure 3.8 **"Coarse-grained" spreading of an initial ensemble.** The region *A* represents the collection of points in phase space corresponding to a collection of systems all prepared in a nonequilibrium condition that is macroscopically identical but that allows a variety of microscopic initial states. As the systems evolve following the dynamics governing the change of microscopic state, *A* develops into *T(A)*. The size of *T(A)* must be equal to that of *A* by a law of dynamics, but whereas *A* is a simple region confined to a small portion of the available phase space, *T(A)* is a complex, fibrillated region that is spread all over the available phase space "in a coarse-grained sense." A uniform distribution over the available phase space is what corresponds to equilibrium in the theory. *T(A)* is not really uniformly spread over the phase space but may nonetheless be considered to represent a spreading of the initial ensemble that represents approach to equilibrium.

grained" sense. As time goes on, each microstate will be either one occupied by one of the original systems or one not so occupied. The fraction of microstates occupied will remain constant. But the situation will change from one where all the occupied points are in a compact region of the available states to one where, for any small region of possible microstates, the same proportion of that region will consist of occupied states. The analogy Gibbs draws is with mixing insoluble ink into water. Although each part of the fluid is, if looked at closely enough, always either ink or water, the ink, which started floating on top of the water, eventually becomes mixed evenly throughout the allowed volume. Such a coarse-grained approach to equilibrium of the initial nonequilibrium probability distribution will nicely correspond, as a formal notion, with the ideas of approach to equilibrium summed up by the Ehrenfests in their solution of the Boltzmann equation representing the "concentration curve" of the evolving probability distribution for the collection. (See Figure 3.8.)

But can we show that an initial probability corresponding to a nonequilibrium situation will, in fact, evolve, in the coarse-grained sense, toward the probability distribution associated with equilibrium? We can get that result if we impose some general version of a Postulate of Molecular Chaos on the theory. This can take different forms, depending upon how we choose to model mathematically the evolution of the probability distribution. But in each case the posit, the descendant of Boltzmann's Hypothesis with Regard to Collision Numbers, must be added to the underlying assertions about the structure of the system and to the underlying dynamical laws. How can we have any assurance that the evolution so determined will, in fact, have the kind of permanently "rerandomizing" nature used to derive the approach to equilibrium when Molecular Chaos is assumed? There are deep problems of the consistency of the postulate with the underlying dynamics here.

Some Nonstandard Approaches to the Problem

Before tackling this problem, let us explore some of the views regarding the physical origin of the approach to equilibrium of systems. The orthodox theory assumes that the systems whose evolution we are interested in can be viewed as genuinely isolated from the outside world. But is this assumption legitimate? The standard theory assumes underlying dynamical laws of nature that are "time reversal invariant," and it seeks for the time asymmetry of thermodynamics and statistical mechanics in some source other than an underlying asymmetry of the basic dynamical laws. Is this assumption correct? The orthodox approach assumes that asymmetry in time is grounded in some matter of fact about the world that requires an explanation similar to the physical explanations offered other discovered phenomena. But is this correct, or can we find the justification for the probabilistic assumptions of the theory in some general features of inductive and probabilistic inference, rather than seeking for their grounding in some facts about the physical world?

The standard methods of statistical mechanics treat systems as if they could genuinely be energetically isolated from the outside world. But such perfect isolation is, of course, impossible. If nothing else, there is the gravitational interaction between the system and the external environment, an interaction that can never be shielded away. The forces exerted by the interaction may, however, be very small indeed. Consider a gas started on the left-hand side of a box. Let it spread throughout the whole box. The pure-isolation view maintains that implicit in the positions and momenta of the molecule at the later time is the information about the original state of the gas. But, the interventionist argues, even the infinitesimal changes in the microstate induced by the weak interactions with the outside world will so modify the microstate of the gas that the real microstate at the later time will lose any correlations indicating the initial macroscopic state of the gas. The time reversal of this real as opposed to ideal microstate will not be a microstate that would evolve back to the gas's being on the left side of the box but, rather, one of the overwhelmingly large number of microstates corresponding to the gas's staying spread out. Can the paradoxes of reversibility be eliminated in this way?

Most think not. There are special cases where isolation is sufficient for a genuine kind of reversal of a state to be constructed. We can construct a microstate that leads the system to show antithermodynamic behavior. The spin-echo experiment is one of these. Nuclei with magnetic moments evolve from a macroscopically ordered to an apparently disordered, equilibrium, state. A radio pulse can "flip" the nuclei over, so that the system appears to evolve back spontaneously to its original ordered, nonequilibrium, condition. Here the isolation is sufficient for the later microstate of the equilibrium system to retain the information about the original nonequilibrium state. The experiment can even be carried out when the nuclei magnetically interact with one another. Yet the system does seem, until the "flip," to show the usual macroscopic approach to equilibrium, indicating that we must account for such behavior even when isolation is "perfect." Most physicists are still convinced that even systems perfectly isolated from the external environment would show the time asymmetry characterized by the Second Law. (See Figure 3.9.)

The standard puzzles concerning reversibility also assume that the underlying dynamical laws have the property of time-reversal invariance. This would imply that the reversed microstate of a system that has evolved from nonequilibrium would be one that would evolve into the time reversal of the original, nonequilibrium, microstate. This would be an evolution back to a nonequilibrium situation. Could this assumption of time symmetry for the underlying dynamical laws be wrong, so that time asymmetry at this level of fundamental dynamics is really the source of the thermodynamic asymmetry? Most think not. The laws of classical dynamics and, it is usually claimed, the laws of quantum dynamics as well are symmetric in time in the sense usually assumed. Actually, for quantum mechanics, this is an issue that might be controversial. As we shall see in Chapter 4, in the quantum mechanical view of the world, there is a process called measurement that has a special kind of time asymmetry built into it. The nature and origin of that asymmetry is itself controversial, some crediting it to the thermodynamic asymmetry taken as the fundamental asymmetry. But the general opinion is that the familiar asymmetries of thermodynamics don't have their origin in any such quantum mechanical measurement asymmetry, and that the source of asymmetry in statistical mechanics must be sought elsewhere.

Interestingly, there are phenomena in nature that do seem to require time-asymmetric fundamental laws. These become evident in the study of certain interactions in the realm of quantum field theory. Here, it seems, we do find processes that are possible according to the fundamental laws, but whose natural time reversals are impossible. More exactly, the probabilities of the process are not invariant under time

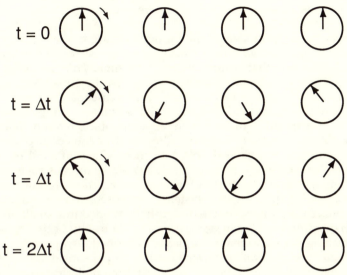

Figure 3.9 The spin-echo experiment. The top row of the figure represents a collection of spinning nuclei whose spins are all lined up in the same direction in a plane that is perpendicular to a magnetic field imposed on the crystal whose atoms have the nuclei in question. In the second row a period of time has elapsed. The directions of the spins have precessed, at different rates, around the imposed magnetic field, so that at this point the spins, although still in the same plane, now point in all directions "at random." In the third row, the spins have been "flipped" by a radio frequency pulse. The spins "farthest ahead" in the "precession race" are now "farthest behind." The result is shown in the bottom row. The time is now twice that elapsed from the top row to the second row. The spins have now all "caught up" with one another, leading to their all once again pointing in the same direction. From the third to the bottom row there is the appearance of an equilibrium condition (randomized spins) spontaneously evolving into a nonequilibrium condition (spins all aligned).

reversal. Some work has been done that purports to show that no explanation for the familiar asymmetries we are concerned with here could be forthcoming from these phenomena, even if they do reveal a genuinely lawlike time-reversal noninvariance in the world.

Finally, there is the school that seeks the rationalization of the applications of probability in statistical mechanics, not in the discovery of actual proportions in the world or in some special feature of the laws and structures of systems like ergodicity, but in general principles of inductive reasoning. In the equilibrium case, it is argued, the justification for the usual probability measure is the Principle of Indifference. This tells us, in the absence of further evidence, to treat alike in terms of probabilistic weight all symmetric cases allowed by the evidence we have. But, as we have noted, the Principle of Indifference is empty until a definitive way of characterizing the systems is provided. Where, if not in features of dynamics and structure, do the "inductivists" find this?

In the nonequilibrium case, the inductivists argue that as long as a situation is "reproducible experimentally" on the macroscopic level, one can justify the view that entropy increases in time. The idea is this: We can expect that systems identically prepared in their macroscopic features will evolve to systems alike in their macroscopic features only if many more microstates correspond to the ultimate macroscopic situation than corresponded to the original macroscopic situation. But such an increase in microstates corresponding to an evolved macrostate is just the statistical mechanical notion of increasing statistical entropy. Well, yes. But what we wanted explained was *why* there is such a thing as experimental reproducibility of systems when they are macroscopically described. Why is it that systems composed of vast numbers of components can be given simple descriptions framed in a small number of parameters that evolve in a lawlike way? And why is the evolution of the systems when so macroscopically described always in the same time direction when motion toward equilibrium is considered? Why is it, if you wish, that experiments are all experimentally reproducible in the same time direction and not some in the reverse direction? And why is it that this time direction is the one we think of as the future?

If we see a system in a nonequilibrium state, we are able to infer its states at different times in one time direction only. We know that a system heated at one end and cold at the other will later be warm all over, although given a warm bar we are not able to infer the nonequilibrium state from which it came, since many nonequilibrium conditions evolve to the same equilibrium state. But *why* do such macroscopic characterizations and their lawlike behavior exist? Why do the systems evolve parallel to one another in time? Why is the direction of approach to equilibrium the future direction? These are the facts that we wanted explained. The inductivist line seems just to presuppose that the phenomena in question exist and then point out the consequences of this existence and what this existence and nature presupposes about the microscopic evolution of systems. But just *why* the phenomena exist in this way is what we wanted explained in the first place.

Some Standard Approaches to the Problem

Let us return to the orthodox school of thought. Consider a system energetically isolated from the rest of the world and in a nonequilibrium condition. How should we represent its approach to equilibrium in statistical mechanics? Well, we consider every possible condition of its microscopic components compatible with the original, nonequilibrium, state of the system. We imagine a vast (in fact, infinite) collection of systems having all the possible initial microstates, and we impose a probability distribution over those microstates. We now imagine each individual system in the collection evolving, according to its structure and the dynamical laws governing the dynamics of the microcomponents. We want to show that given the original probability distribution and given those laws, an evolution of probability distributions takes place that goes, in some sense or other, toward the equilibrium probability distribution corresponding to the constraints imposed on the system.

A first question to ask is what the initial probability distributions should be like. Only a limited number of cases are well understood. One case is where the system, although not in equilibrium, is close to equilibrium to begin with. Another, more general, case is where the system, although not in equilibrium, can be considered as having sufficiently small regions sufficiently close to equilibrium for sufficiently small times. Thus, in the latter case, although we can't attribute a density, pressure, temperature, or entropy to the system, we can view it as starting with a certain density, pressure, entropy density, and temperature *distribution*. The gas started on the left-hand side of the box has a uniform high density for half of the allowed physical space and a density of zero for the other half. The iron bar started hot at one end and cold at the other doesn't have a temperature; it has a distribution of temperature over the length of the bar. For these cases, rules that generalize the way in which the Principle of Indifference was applied to get the equilibrium probability distribution can plausibly be applied to get the initial nonequilibrium probability distributions. In the cases where even "local temporary equilibrium" can't be assumed, it isn't clear what our initial probability distribution would be like. But, then again, in that case there really isn't a macroscopic theory describing the approach to equilibrium to be derived and explained either.

Can we show, using structure of system and dynamics of microconstituents alone, without resort to a perpetual rerandomization postulate of the Molecular Chaos sort, that this initial probability distribution will approach the equilibrium distribution, at least in the coarse-grained fashion suggested by Gibbs? In some cases we can—sort of. In the cases for which ergodicity could be proved in the equilibrium theory, like those of hard spheres in a box, stronger results can sometimes be proved as well.

Ergodicity is not enough for our purposes. Imagine a vast collection of systems, all prepared in a given nonequilibrium condition. They might all be ergodic, evolving so that over infinite time they were usually at or near equilibrium. Yet the collection might not, as a whole, approach equilibrium. There might be a regular, uniform, approach to and from equilibrium of the systems in a synchronized manner, so that the probability distribution over all the systems failed to show a uniform approach to equilibrium even in the coarse-grained sense. That is, there might be times in the future when the probability distribution was evolving away from the equilibrium distribution, even though individual systems each spent most of their time at or near individual system equilibrium.

However, a stronger result than ergodicity, "mixing," can be proved for such idealized systems as hard spheres in a box. Crudely, what mixing says is that if we start with any "nonpathological" initial probability distribution, it will, at least in the limit as time goes to infinity, approach, in the coarse-grained sense, the equilibrium probability distribution. "Nonpathological" means, essentially, that the initial probability distribution will give probability zero to any region of microconditions that have zero probability in the familiar, standard measure.

One can, in fact, prove results stronger than that of mixing for such systems. One can prove that they are *K*-systems. To be a *K*-system is to have a kind of coarse-grained "probabilistic indeterminacy." Suppose we think of the microstates of systems as grouped into small collections of microstates. If a system is a *K*-system, we will not be able to determine with probability one or zero in which subcollection the microstate of a system will be at a time even if we know which subcollection the system's microstate was in at all previous, discretely separated, times back to the infinite past. The only exception would be if it was trivially true that the system had a probability of one or zero of having its microstate in the designated subcollection.

And, stronger still, one can prove systems to be Bernoulli systems. This means that one can construct sets of subcollections of microstates that are such that the infinite time descriptions of which subcollection the microstate of a system is in at every observation time fully determines the statistical evolution of the probability distribution. But the information about where a system has been in the subcollections over the past gives no probabilistic information whatever as to which subcollection it will be in, in the next moment of time. When it comes to which subcollection the microstate will be in, the system, although evolving deterministically, behaves just like the outcomes of series of probabilistically independent coin tosses. So determinism at the level of the exact microstate is compatible with the most random imaginable behavior at the coarse-grained level. (See Figure 3.10.)

Do such results solve, once and for all, all the puzzles about the approach to equilibrium? Certainly not. First there is the fact that when we apply mixing to model the approach to equilibrium, we must ignore "sets of measure zero." In assuming that we can ignore pathological initial probability distributions in which nonzero probability is concentrated in collections of microstates that have probability zero in the standard measure, we are assuming that such collections of microstates can be ignored. Once again this is a probabilistic assumption not derivable from the structure of the systems or the dynamics.

Next, there is the problem that most realistic systems will not meet the conditions necessary for mixing to hold. This is because they are (probably) within the domain of the KAM Theorem. Once again, this demands the existence of nonzero regions of microstates that generate stable trajectories, trajectories that fail to wander all over the available region of microstates. Just as this made ergodicity impossible for more-

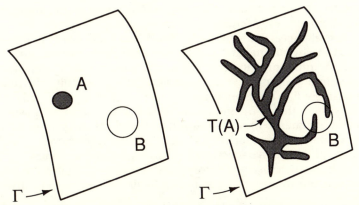

Figure 3.10 A mixing ensemble. Γ is a region of the phase space for the system in which the phase point for the system is located. A and B are two nonzero-sized regions of points in the phase space. B is kept constant. We track the evolution of systems whose initial microstates are in the A region. The result is a series of $T(A)$ regions as time goes on. A "mixing" system is one in which the A region will evolve into a $T(A)$ region in the limit "as time goes to infinity." This $T(A)$ region is evenly distributed over the phase space in the coarse-grained sense. For this to be the case, it must be that in the infinite time limit the proportion of any B region occupied by points that evolved from the A region is equal to the proportion of the phase space originally occupied by points in the A region.

realistic cases in the equilibrium theory, it makes the stronger result of mixing impossible as well. Just as before, some resort will have to be made, at this point, to the large number of constituents in the system and to some argument to the effect that the regions of stability will be very small and that outside of these regions motion will be chaotic enough to generate, if not mixing in the pure sense, some reasonable surrogate for it.

But there is a much greater difficulty than these for someone who wants to found the approach to equilibrium on mixing results alone. If a system is mixing, then any nonpathological initial probability distribution over its microstates will coarsely approach the equilibrium probability distribution in the infinite time limit. But what will happen in the "short run," that is, in time intervals corresponding to those we are interested in, the typical times taken by a nonequilibrium system to get close to equilibrium?

Mixing is compatible with any short-time behavior one can imagine. The nonequilibrium probability distribution can coarsely approach the equilibrium distribution, move away from it, stay a nonequilibrium distribution, or follow any pattern of approaches, retreats, and stayings-the-same that you like and still be the probability distribution for a mixing system. But what we wish to model is the uniform, short-term, approach to equilibrium of real nonequilibrium systems. What needs to be added to the fact that a system is mixing to assure us that our model will have these features?

One can also see that mixing by itself is not enough to answer all our questions by noting that it is a time-symmetric notion. Any non-pathological initial probability distribution for a mixing system will, as time goes into past infinity, also evolve into a probability distribution that is coarsely like the equilibrium distribution. It is hardly surprising that any system that is mixing to the future is mixing to the past. After all, the "mixingness" of a system follows from its structure and from the time-symmetric underlying dynamical laws. Naturally the time asymmetry of thermodynamics, and of the statistical mechanics we want to underpin the macroscopic theory, can't be derived from the elements of structure and microdynamics alone. Again, something else must be added.

We will discuss the needed additional element momentarily, but let us first note that the approach to nonequilibrium statistical mechanics we have just been discussing is not the only way of trying to rationalize the nonequilibrium theory. There is an important and quite a distinct approach; its contrast with the approach we have just been discussing is illuminating. Certain results tell us that if we idealize a system in an appropriate way, in particular, by letting the number of molecules in the gas go to infinity, the density of the gas go to zero, and the size of the gas molecules go to zero compared with the size of the box (the so-called Boltzmann-Grad Limit), then we can show that for sufficiently short time periods, "almost all" systems (i.e., all systems except a set of probability zero) will evolve according to the manner described by the Boltzmann equation. This is the "rigorous derivation of the Boltzmann equation."

Now these results can be proved to hold only for times that are a fraction of the time expected between a molecule's colliding with one molecule and then with another. But there is some reason to think that they are true results, even if unprovable, for longer times. This result, unlike that of mixing, does provide a justification for taking the usual statistical description as holding even in the short run and for taking the evolution to have the unidirectional nature we expect.

But the results cited here are puzzling indeed. Suppose we take the result to hold for all time, even as time goes to infinity. Then we will have a contradiction with the Recurrence Theorem. This new result says that almost all the systems will evolve toward equilibrium and stay there, but the Recurrence Theorem tells us that almost all systems will recur to their original nonequilibrium condition infinitely often. And the result is incompatible with mixing as well. There is no mathematical contradiction, of course, for the results here are only proved to hold for short, finite times. More important, they only hold in the limit noted. In that limit you can no longer represent the behavior of the system as a flow of trajectories from initial microstates, so that the conditions necessary for recurrence and mixing to be demonstrated are no longer valid.

But it is not the absence of a mathematical contradiction that is most interesting. The main point is that this model for approach to equilibrium, a model that tries to show that in an appropriate idealization it is highly probable that a system will evolve from nonequilibrium to equilibrium and will then stay in equilibrium, is conceptually quite at variance with the idealization familiar since the Ehrenfests' clarification of the Boltzmann program. In this more familiar idealization, recurrence is accepted and mixing is the idealization of nonequilibrium behavior sought for. The solution of the Boltzmann equation is not supposed to represent what almost every system will do but, instead, to represent the "concentration curve" of the evolution of the probability distribution. It is not "most probable evolution" but "evolution of most probable conditions" that is to represent the approach to equilibrium.

What the existence of these two approaches shows is that there is as yet no real agreement about which idealization is the correct one to use in trying to represent thermodynamic behavior in terms of microscopic dynamical behavior and probabilities. A genuine conflict about how the final statistical mechanical theory ought to be constructed and how that construct ought to be taken to represent the world still splits the community of theorists. We should note that the problems of introducing time asymmetry for the mixing approach, to which we will soon return, appear in this alternative "rigorous derivation of the Boltzmann approach" as well. And we should note how different the roles of the large size of the system are in the two approaches. For the mixing approach, the vast number of microcomponents comes in only at the end of the argument when we want to get from average values of quantities to overwhelmingly most probable values of quantities. For the other approach, though, the fact that the system is a very dilute one of innumerable small components is crucial to the idealization from the very beginning. Even a system of two hard spheres in a box is mixing, but the Boltzmann-Grad Limit is crucial for the rigorous derivation of the Boltzmann equation.

The Problem of Initial Probability Distributions

Let us, for the time being, work in the context of the idealization that relies upon the mixing of the initial ensemble to represent the approach to equilibrium. As we noted, even if the system is a mixing system, initial ensembles, that is, initial probability distributions over the microstates compatible with the original nonequilibrium macroscopic condition, can be found that will show the appropriate short-term, uniform, coarse-grained approach to an equilibrium probability distribution. But initial ensembles can also be found that will show any other kind of short-term behavior. Consider, for example, the probability distribution over microstates that arises when an even more nonequilibrium distribution evolves in the expected way into one compatible with the given nonequilibrium condition of the gas. The time reverse of that

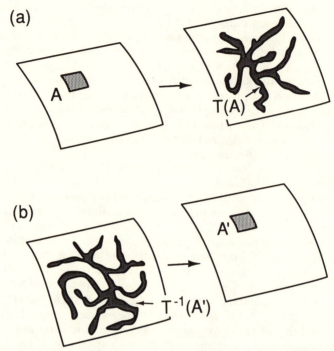

Figure 3.11 Reversibility at the ensemble level. Suppose, as in (a), A is a region of phase space that evolves over time into the fibrillated region, $T(A)$. One can then show, as in (b), that there must be a fibrillated region of phase points, $T^{-1}(A')$ that evolves as time goes into the future into a compact, simple region like A'. Furthermore, both A' and the region from which it comes will be equal in size to A and its fibrillated successor.

latter probability distribution will be a probability distribution over microstates compatible with the nonequilibrium condition of our system that will evolve to an even-less-equilibrium condition. (See Figure 3.11.)

So to get the right short-term, uniform, coarse-grained approach to equilibrium, we need to start with an "appropriate" initial probability distribution. Essentially, we want the probability to be distributed uniformly (relative to the standard measure) over a region of microstates that is not too small and that has a regular shape. The demand for a sufficient size is to ensure that the initial distribution will coarsely spread out fast enough to represent the actual "relaxation time" taken by real systems to get to equilibrium. The demand for regular shape is to exclude the regions that can be constructed so as to represent antithermodynamic behavior.

But *why* should such initial probability distributions be chosen? What is it about the nature of the world that makes them the *correct* initial ensembles to choose to get the results that represent the world as it is?

One account was offered by the physicist N. Krylov. He starts with a critique of those who would offer as an explanation of the special nature of these initial probability distributions just the remark that this is how probability seems to be distributed over initial states in the world. These theorists would deny that any deeper explanation is possible. (Philosophers sometimes speak of the "mere de facto" nature of the Second Law, meaning the "it just happens that the initial states are so distributed" line.) Krylov insists that this approach will not do justice to the lawlike, even if only statistically lawlike, nature of the Second Law. He also argues that it can't do justice to the fact that for systems that are intermediate in the process of evolution from an initial non-equilibrium to an equilibrium condition, such a uniform probability distribution relative to their intermediate macroscopic description can't be true of them, as we know they came from a specified initial state even further from equilibrium. But such systems will still obey the Second Law.

Krylov, whose positive theory never received an adequate exposition because of his premature death, explains the special nature of the initial probability distribution by relying on an argument taken from early attempts to understand quantum mechanics. In Chapter 4 we will discuss the so-called Uncertainty Principle in quantum mechanics. This principle tells us that it is impossible to specify simultaneously the position and the velocity of a particle to within arbitrary degrees of accuracy. An early interpretation of this principle, now no longer accepted by most who think about the issues, was that the attempt on our part to measure one of the two quantities physically interfered with the system in such a way as to "disturb" the existing value of the other quantity. It was this physical interaction of observer with observed system that generated the "uncertainty." Krylov argues that the sensitivity of a system to a small perturbation in its initial state, so that a slight variation in the position or velocity of a single molecule will wildly change the future microevolution of the system, gives us an Uncertainly Principle of a "higher level" in dealing with the systems of thermodynamics. It is this interference with the system when the system is prepared in its nonequilibrium condition that causes the probability distribution over microstates to have its appropriate large size and regularity.

How this would be made to work in its details isn't clear. But there is a deeper problem as well. What constitutes the "preparation" of a system? Suppose we look at a system that is in nonequilibrium when it is created (i.e., separated off from the rest of the universe energetically). We also look at it when it is destroyed (i.e., reintegrated with the outside world). It is appropriate to assume that from the initial non-equilibrium condition it will move closer to equilibrium. So the appropriate probability distribution over the microstates at the initial time is the standard one. But if we made the same assumption regarding the final state of the system, we would be led to infer, falsely, that this state was a spontaneous fluctuation from states closer to equilibrium.

What makes it appropriate to attribute the standard probability distribution over microstates at the beginning of a systems evolution but not at the end?

Well, the initial state is the way the system is "prepared." The final state is the result not of preparation but of evolution. But what constitutes preparation, and why should it and it alone have the feature of demanding the correct, thermodynamic, probability distribution over microstates associated with macrostates obtained by it? Essentially, the time asymmetry of statistical mechanics is being built in by the assumption that it is always the earlier states of isolated systems that are "prepared" and never their final states. Intuitively, we think that is true, but making coherent sense of what that intuition captures, aside from its repeating the asymmetry we wanted to explain in the first place, is a puzzling matter.

A distinct, and more radical, solution to the puzzle has been offered by I. Prigogine. His solution has a number of elements. First he adopts the very radical view that individual systems do not have exact microstates. He maintains, instead, that the radical instability of the dynamics means that the exact microstate of a system as posited in the usual underlying dynamics is a false idealization. He considers that the probability distribution over microstates used in statistical mechanics ought to be taken as characterizing the individual system. This probability distribution, he maintains, does not characterize an imagined collective composed of many systems each of which has some exact microstate. Once again quantum mechanics and its interpretation are relevant here. As we shall see, there exist "no hidden variable proofs" in quantum theory. These, it is sometimes alleged, show us that the "uncertainty" characteristic of systems in quantum mechanics ought to be taken as irreducible. There are, it is claimed, no underlying parameters, even unknowable ones, that determine exactly the system's future course.

Now such proofs of the nonexistence of a fully deterministic microstate are certainly lacking in the statistical mechanical case. Indeed, the possibility of exact reversals of behavior as are illustrated by the spin-echo results referred to earlier make the denial of the exact microstate a pretty dubious claim. But the remaining portions of Prigogine's view don't really depend for their support on this radically new ontological view.

Prigogine outlines methods whereby the original probability distribution whose evolution followed the time-reversal invariant laws derived from the time symmetric laws of the underlying dynamics can be transformed into a new "representation" whose time asymmetry of evolution is manifest. This works in cases where a suitably strong "chaos" condition holds, such as the system's being a K-system. What is going on here is nothing too mysterious. If a system has the proper mixing features, then it will show coarse-grained time approach to equilibrium, even if its evolution is time reversible on the microlevel. The techniques used in going to the new representation here essentially show how this coarse-grained behavior of the original probability distribution can be reflected into a new way of representing the statistics of the ensemble so that the time asymmetry represented only in the coarse-grained sense in the original representation is now built in to the new way of characterizing the probability distribution. This new probability distribution is uniquely specified given the original one and uniquely specifies it. It generates the same average values for all quantities the original probability distribution generated and is, therefore, "statistically equivalent" to the original representation.

Does the existence of such a new representation of probability solve the time-asymmetry problem? No. One reason for the negative answer is that there is also a new representation of the original probability distribution that is manifestly antithermodynamic. Just as the original distribution coarse-grainedly approached equilibrium going to time minus infinity as well as to time plus infinity, so there are two transformations of it to a new representation—one making manifest thermodynamic behavior and the other antithermodynamic.

So where does time asymmetry come from? Prigogine thinks that one can't capture it using any nonpathological initial probability distribution, for any such distribution will coarse-grainedly go to equilibrium in the infinite time limit both in the future and in the past. Instead, he suggests, we ought to look at certain "singular" initial distributions, ones that concentrate all of probability on a region of probability zero in the standard measure. Now in the original representation such a singular initial distribution could not approach the equilibrium distribution even in the coarse-grained sense, as it would always evolve into a new distribution whose size is zero in the standard measure. But, Prigogine points out, it can be the case that although the new representation of the original distribution is also singular and of size zero, the new representations of the distributions it evolves into may not be singular. They may, in fact, evolve into the equilibrium distribution. And if the initial singular distribution is picked properly, this is just what happens. So maybe the solution to time asymmetry is found in the rule that physical systems started in nonequilibrium are always properly represented in statistical mechanics by these kinds of singular initial probability distributions.

Is that the answer? I don't think so. First, it is important to note that there will also be initial singular probability distributions that are intrinsically antithermodynamic. They, of course, can't represent real systems. But weren't we seeking the *physical* reason why one kind of behavior is possible and the other not? We were not just looking for one more way of "plugging in" an asymmetrical feature to our representation of the world. Worse yet, the use of such singular initial probabilities seems inappropriate to some real physical cases. A situation that fits the Prigogine model would be, for example, a perfectly parallel beam of particles. This is a "probability zero" initial state. Such a beam would, of course, lose its original astonishing coherence and order, this loss being represented by the spreading out of the transformed representation of the originally singular probability distribution picked to represent the system. But now consider gas confined to the left-hand side of a box. Let the partition be removed. The appropriate initial probability distribution for this case will not be one of probability confined to a region of zero size or even an approximation of such a singular distribution. Instead, the right way of representing the physics here would be for a coarse-grained spreading to equilibrium of an initial distribution that is not, originally, coarse-grainedly spread over the available totality of microstate, but that also is not, originally, confined to a zero-size region either.

The point is that the right initial ensembles will show spreading toward equilibrium even in the short run. They can correctly represent physics even if in the infinite time limit they spread to equilibrium (in the coarse sense) in both time directions. Prigogine's singular initial ensembles seem both to be unnecessary and sometimes to misrepresent the real physical situations of interest.

Cosmology and Irreversibility

What, then, is the physical ground for time asymmetry? Let us look at one popular approach. This one is founded on the facts of cosmology. As we noted earlier, Boltzmann had already invoked speculative posits about the global structure of the universe in order to reconcile his final views about equilibrium with the observable facts about the dominance of nonequilibrium in the world as we find it. Let us review the structure of the Boltzmannian claims: First, the universe is large in space and time. It is in most regions of space and for most periods of time near equilibrium. But there are small regions that for short times deviate from equilibrium. Second, we can expect to find ourselves in such a fluctuation region, for only in such a region could observers evolve and survive. Third, entropy increases in the future time direction in our region because what we *mean* by the future direction of time is the time direction in which systems are having their entropy increase, i.e., in which they locally move in parallel with one another toward equilibrium.

Now we do find ourselves in a universe far from equilibrium. And we do find that temporarily isolated systems have their entropy increase in the same time direction, the direction we call the future. Can what is now known about the overall, cosmological, structure of the universe explain this for us?

The picture of the cosmos presented to us by contemporary cosmology is quite different from Boltzmann's overall quiescent universe. The universe, or at least that part available to our observational inspection, seems to have been concentrated in a singular point of mass-energy some ten billion years ago. Since that time, the universe has been in expansion. Whether that expansion will continue forever or whether, instead, it will sometime recontract and become a singularity again is not known. That depends upon the density of mass-energy in the universe. The universe as a whole seems to obey the Second Law, with entropy increasing in the future time direction.

This entropy increase needs accounting for. Here the thermodynamic state of the original singular condition is crucial. It is usually posited that matter was originally in a uniform, equilibrium condition, the current state of hot stars shining into cold space, a grossly nonequilibrium situation, being a later evolution. But does this mean entropy *decreased* over time? Not necessarily. The entropic decrease in matter was, according to most theorists, "paid for" by a vast increase in the entropy of the gravitational field or, if you wish, of spacetime itself. Originally uniform, spacetime developed "clumpiness" as matter went from its original uniform to its present highly nonuniform condition. For special reasons having to do with gravity's purely attractive nature, this transformation of spacetime from smooth to lumpy corresponds to an increase of its entropy. One could, then, blame the entropic increase of the cosmos on its original highly organized, very low entropy, spacetime condition.

Why should the original condition be one of low entropy? Of all possible original conditions, this is a "highly improbable" one. Here the very limits of scientific explanation are being probed. We will just have to accept it as a fact that this is how things were, although a variety of "explanations" of this fact have been suggested. It is important to note that it is not the expansion of the universe that is responsible for the entropic increase on its own. In a recontracting universe, according to the prevalent view, entropy would continue to increase, leading to a final singularity, intrinsically clumpy in nature. The time reversal of such a recontraction would be compatible with all the laws and would represent a universe expanding with entropy decreasing. It is the special nature of the Big Bang and Big Crunch, with the former low entropy and the latter high entropy, that distinguishes a universe in which expansion followed by contraction is accompanied by increasing rather than decreasing entropy.

Is the Second Law of Thermodynamics as applied to individual small systems founded, then, on the original low-entropy singular state of the universe? There are problems in trying to make this view work out. The usual proposal is to work with the notion of a branch system. A branch system is an individual isolated system once originally in energetic contact with the outside world, later isolated from it for a time, and, finally, rejoined to it at the end of its finite lifetime.

Suppose we have an isolated branch system in a condition far from equilibrium. Because the universe about us is in a state of gross nonequilibrium, it is far more reasonable to suppose that the nonequilibrium of the branch system is the result of its having been "cut off" from the global nonequilibrium system than it is to suppose that the nonequilibrium condition of the branch system is the result of one of the very rare fluctuations from equilibrium expected even of totally isolated systems.

Now imagine a large number of branch systems, each at the beginning of its life and all in a common nonequilibrium condition. We cannot infer a past behavior for the systems, for they had no past life, having just come into existence as branch systems. If we now make the assumption that the probability distribution over the microstates of the systems is a standard one, we can infer that at a short time in the future, the concentration point of states of the system will be closer to equilibrium. This is the familiar Boltzmann model. It does rest upon a probabilistic assumption about the distribution of microstates compatible with a given macroscopic condition. But, it is alleged, this assumption is not itself a time-asymmetric one. So the parallelism of the evolution of branch systems, the fact that the entropy increase of one will be in the same time direction (probably) as the entropy increase of any other, has been derived simply from the cosmological facts, the fact that the systems are branch systems, and a probabilistic assumption about initial microconditions that is not intrinsically time asymmetric.

A formal version of this argument is given by H. Reichenbach. He arranges the states of a collection of branch systems into an array, with later states to the right of earlier ones and the systems arranged in a vertical list. Assuming that the evolution of each system is statistically independent of that of all the others, and assuming that changes in distributions of microstates in vertical columns (i.e., distributions of microstates over the multitude of systems from one time to another) duplicate the expected changes in a single system over time, he is able to show that if the left-hand column of such an array corresponds to nonequilibrium, in the limit as time goes to plus infinity, the right-hand column will represent equilibrium. He calls such an array a "lattice of mixture."

Does this technique really get the explanation of the parallel behavior of entropy change of systems in time into the picture without simply positing it? I don't think so. It is usually assumed that the direction of time in which the branch systems will increase their entropy in parallel with one another is the same time direction in which the universe as a whole is increasing its entropy. But, curiously, the direction of entropy change of the universe is never used in the argument. All that is used is the fact that the universe is far from equilibrium, not the direction of its entropic change. This hints that parallelism of the branch systems with each other may also have been "smuggled in" to the argument.

Indeed I think it has. Suppose we consider a collection of branch systems half of which begin in a nonequilibrium state and half of which end in that same nonequilibrium state. Now arrange them in a Reichenbach-style lattice with their nonequilibrium state on the left. The same kind of postulates as before would lead us to expect the systems states to be at or close to equilibrium on the right. But that would correspond to the systems that had started in nonequilibrium getting closer to equilibrium in the future and would lead to the inference that the systems ending in nonequilibrium had been close to equilibrium in the distant past! This, of course, is the wrong inference. We ought to infer that the systems ending in nonequilibrium came from isolated systems even *further* from equilibrium in the past.

What has gone on here is something familiar to us by now. It is reasonable to impose the standard-probability distribution over the microstates of a system in nonequilibrium, *if* the nonequilibrium state is a genuinely *initial* state relative to the process one is inferring. It is illegitimate—it gives the wrong results—to use such a probability distribution to retrodict the behavior of a system from its nonequilibrium condition if that condition is a final and not initial one relative to the process we are trying to infer. This is just to repeat the fact that systems do show thermodynamic behavior (i.e., approach to equilibrium) in a parallel time direction and, indeed, in the direction of time we call the future. But the arguments we have just been looking at don't provide a physical explanation for that fact. Rather, they once again build it into their description of the world as a posit. Cosmology by itself, including the Big Bang, its low entropy, the expansion of the universe, and the entropic increase of that universe in the time direction in which it is expanding, doesn't seem to provide the explanation of the parallelism in time of the entropic increase of branch systems. Indeed, the Second Law–like behavior of the cosmos seems, from this perspective, just one more instance of the general statistical lawlike behavior of systems, cosmological or branch.

So the origin of the parallelistic behavior of systems in time in their entropic increase still remains something of a mystery. We know how to represent the asymmetry in statistical mechanics, by imposing a probability distribution over the microstates of systems in nonequilibrium only in a time-asymmetric way. We must assume that the usual statistical assumption about how probable is a microstate holds only if we take the macrostate we are considering to be initial, and only if we are then going to use the statistical assumption to infer the future and not the past behavior of the system. But *why* time parallelism of entropic increase holds is still a puzzle.

But let us assume that parallelism does hold. We might still wonder why it is that it is toward the future direction of time, and not the past, that entropy increases. Here we must once again consider Boltzmann's brilliant suggestion that the very meaning of the past-future distinction of the directions of time is itself grounded on parallel entropic increase. According to Boltzmann and those who followed him, what we mean by the "future" direction of time is just the direction of time in which entropy, with overwhelming probability, increases. Is this plausible? We will turn to this question in "The Problem of 'The Direction of Time.'"

Summary

The structure of probabilistic explanations in statistical mechanics is, as we have seen, a very complex one. It would be pleasant to report that a simple resolution of all the difficulties we have just surveyed is available, but this just isn't so. The issues here are ones that remain very controversial, despite the fact that these problems have been explored for over a century.

We have seen that one can give an interesting account of equilibrium features by identifying them with certain aspects of a system that are displayed in the infinite time limit. But the kind of "explanation" of the observed phenomena we obtain is not at all like the sort of explanation involving probabilities that we would be led to expect from the philosophers' accounts of statistical explanation.

When we move to the nonequilibrium case, the explanatory structure seems more like that outlined by the philosophers. But many puzzles remain. Some accounts of the approach to equilibrium invoke the nonisolation of the system or the possibility of laws of nature not symmetric in time. Other explanations rely upon alleged rules for general probabilistic inference. The more standard approaches rely on the instability of the system's microscopic dynamics and on the vast number of microcomponents that make up the system. But even within these standard approaches, as we have seen, there are conflicting ideas on the appropriate model to employ and on the appropriate notion of statistical explanation to invoke.

We have also seen that within the standard approaches the problem of the correct initial ensemble or initial probability distribution is a crucial one. How to choose the right such initial probability distribution and, having chosen it, how to explain why it can legitimately be assumed to hold in the world, remain open questions. The fundamental problem of the asymmetry of systems in time is part of this problem of the initial ensemble.

Finally, we have seen that even if one invokes the overall asymmetry in time of the universe as a whole, the problem of the asymmetry in time of individual systems remains open. The general problem of fitting the thermodynamic behavior of systems into the general account of the dynamics of their microscopic parts remains one that will require more insights not only into the physics of the systems but also into the very structure of what will count as legitimate probabilistic explanations in our theoretical account of the world.

We have seen that the instability of the dynamical trajectories of the system contributes to the stable, predictable behavior of the system at the macroscopic level. Instability can be a feature, however, of the system's macroscopic behavior as well. Beginning with work of Poincaré, physicists have discovered that the behavior of systems is often radically irregular and unpredictable even at the level of their macroscopic descriptions. Many systems can be described by a parameter that characterizes some feature of the system. For some values of this parameter, the system will show regular behavior, but for other values, the behavior of the system will vary so sensitively with its initial state that any hope of predicting the future behavior of the system is blocked. Such deterministic but irregular systems are called chaotic.

The description of chaotic systems has introduced a new realm of behavior into physics, a realm where probabilistic modes of thought become important tools. And with these new modes of description come new philosophical questions. At the present time, philosophers are dealing with some of these questions, such as the definition of a chaotic system, the modes of explanation used in characterizing the behavior of such systems, and the issues generated by the fact that systems can be fully deterministic but have their macroscopic behavior radically unpredictable. Although we will not be able to survey these issues here, some introductory readings in this new and exciting area have been provided in the reading suggestions appended to this chapter.

The Problem of "The Direction of Time"

Discussions of the Boltzmann thesis are often accompanied by debates about whether the entropic asymmetry represents an asymmetry of "time itself" or merely an asymmetry of the behavior of physical systems in time. Defenders of the former thesis usually point to the pervasive and deep nature of the asymmetry. Defenders of the latter claim frequently refer to other facts about the world that are time asymmetric, but where the asymmetry is not generated by underlying time-asymmetric laws of nature. They argue that only lawlike asymmetries could lead us to infer an asymmetry of time itself.

Those who would maintain that the entropic asymmetry does not reflect an asymmetry in the underlying nature of time usually have in mind that we ought to posit asymmetries of spacetime only when they are needed to explain asymmetries of the laws of nature. An example, noted in Chapter 2, would be the positing of an underlying spacetime difference to account for the lawlike distinction in nature between inertial and noninertial motion. Without such a lawlike asymmetry, they argue, no asymmetry of the underlying spacetime itself need be posited. Those who do think the entropic asymmetry requires us to think of time itself as asymmetric would deny that the entropic asymmetry, with its universal and fundamental scope, could be reduced to any "mere" asymmetry of systems. It requires, they argue, a deeper explanation in the asymmetry of time itself.

As we saw in Chapter 2, the very notion of a spacetime structure explaining some structural feature among the things of the world is itself quite problematic. From the point of view of many relationists, it is far from clear that it makes any sense to raise the question whether the asymmetry of entropy increase is merely a universal statistical asymmetry of physical systems in time or, instead, represents an underlying asymmetry of time itself.

In any case, the crucial issues for Boltzmann would not hinge on the answer to these questions. Boltzmann wants to claim that our intuitive distinction between past and future can be "grounded" on the entropic asymmetry. He is at pains to claim that if there are local portions of the universe where entropy "runs backwards," that is, in the opposite time direction from that in which it increases in our region of the universe, people's memories would also be of events in what we call the future time direction, as would be their records. And they would think of causation as going from that direction of time we think of as the future to that direction of time we think of as the past. They would think of events in the time direction we call future as fixed and determinate, and of events in the time direction we call past as open. But, of course, according to the Boltzmann thesis, they, like us, would claim to remember the past and have records of it and would think of causation as going from past to future. They would call the time direction we call future the past time direction, and would call what we call the past time direction the temporal future.

Sometimes people defend the Boltzmann thesis by pointing out that it is only from entropic facts that we can determine if a film is being run in its proper direction or, instead, being run backwards through a projector. Others criticize the Boltzmann thesis by pointing out that for real events we hardly need to check up on entropic features of systems to determine which events are later than which others. Both of these arguments, however, miss the point by misunderstanding what the Boltzmann thesis is.

Sometimes philosophers claim that one conceptual realm reduces to another because the very meaning of statements in the one realm is given by assertions in the other. The argument here is usually that all our means of determining the truth or falsity of statements of the former kind is by reliance on statements of the latter kind. Thus, the phenomenalist argues that talk of material objects reduces to talk of sense data in the mind, and the spatiotemporal relationist argues that all talk of space and time reduces to talk about spatial and temporal relations among material things and events. But I don't think it is reasonable to think that Boltzmann is claiming that all our knowledge of the direction in time that events have with respect to one another is inferred by us from knowledge about the entropic relations of the states of things to one another over time. It is not that kind of philosophical reduction of time asymmetry to entropic asymmetry that he has in mind.

His notion of reduction, rather, is closer to what the scientist has in mind when claiming that the theory of light reduces to the theory of electromagnetism or when claiming that talk about tables reduces to talk about arrays of atoms. Light waves are electromagnetic waves, we have discovered, and tables are arrays of atoms. It is in something like this vein that Boltzmann wants to claim that the future-past asymmetry of time just *is* the time direction fixed by the facts of entropic increase. But what kind of claim is this?

Boltzmann would have us reflect on our notion of the downward direction in space. For Aristotle, the down direction is a primitive notion. He probably believed that at all points of space a downward direction existed, and that all of these "downs" were in the same spatial direction. But now we realize that "down" is just the direction in which the local gravitational force is pointing. We now understand that there are regions of the universe in which no direction is down and none up, and we accept without difficulty that the downward direction for someone in Australia is not parallel to that for someone in New York. That is how it is with the future-past distinction, Boltzmann claims. Where there is no local entropic asymmetry, there is no future-past distinction, although, of course, there are still two opposite directions of time. And where entropy increases are oppositely directed in time, so is the future-past distinction.

What would be needed to justify that claim? Not even a lawlike association of entropy increase with an intuitive time direction would, by itself, suffice to justify Boltzmann's claim. To see that this is so, we need only note that it now seems clear that certain processes among microparticles of matter are not symmetric between right- and left-handed systems. There is a lawlike asymmetry between right and left in nature revealed, for example, by certain decay processes involving spinning particles being possible, whereas the mirror images of these processes are not. But would anyone be inclined to argue that our very distinction between what is a left-handed and what is a right-handed glove, for example, is in any sense dependent upon that lawlike asymmetry in nature being the case? Not for long, I think. Not only do we not tell left from right by utilizing these spatially asymmetric processes, but also nothing about the existence or nonexistence of such processes seems to have anything to do with explaining why there is the familiar left-right distinction in our intuitive conceptual scheme. But it is quite otherwise with gravity and "down." We are inclined to say that even if the asymmetric processes discovered by recent physics did not exist, the left-right distinction still would exist. But if there were no gravitational force, there simply would not be an up-down distinction, either in nature or in our conceptual scheme to deal with nature.

The difference between the two cases is, I believe, this: In the case of gravity and "down," we believe that all the relevant facts about the downward direction—that rocks fall down and helium balloons float up, for example—are explained by the facts about gravity. Even the fact that we can tell, without inference, which direction is the downward direction is explained by the effects of gravity on the fluid in our semicircular canals. But nothing about our intuitive distinctions between right- and left-handed objects receives an explanatory account in terms of the so-called parity conservation violating processes of physics. The crucial question, then, is this one: Is the connection between the future-past distinction and the entropy increase asymmetry more like that between the up-down distinction and gravity, as Boltzmann thought, or is it more like the connection between the left-right distinction and the subatomic processes that violate orientation symmetry?

To answer this question, we would have to characterize all those fundamental aspects of experience that we take as basic in the determination of the intuitive future-past distinction. Then we would have to explore the issue of whether we could explain all these asymmetric phenomena by using the entropic asymmetry as the uniquely asymmetric explanatory factor. Attempts at doing just this have been made, but, as yet, they are far from convincing.

Surely one of the most important intuitive distinctions between past and future is that there are traces or records of the past but not of the future. Even memory, perhaps, can be considered a system of records of the past. But why do we have records and memories of the past and not of the future?

One answer to this question, given by Reichenbach, focused on what he called macroentropy. Here it is not the order and disorder of the microconstituents of matter that are in question, but such more apparent kinds of order and disorder that would distinguish, say, an orderly array of middle-sized objects from a chaotic, disordered collection of such objects. Reichenbach argues that when we find a system having lower macroentropy than we would normally expect, we must account for this improbable macrostate. He argues that a low-entropy microsystem is not likely to be a spontaneous fluctuation of an isolated system from a high-entropy microstate but is much more likely to be a system that interacted with the outside environment in the past. Then he argues that a system's having a low macroentropy also requires outside interaction as the generator of that low macroentropy. Low macroentropy, then, allows us also to infer interaction in the past. And, he claims, it is this inference to past interaction that provides what we mean by a record or trace.

His favorite example is the footprint on the beach. We expect to find a high-macroentropy beach, that is, a smooth beach with the sand grains randomly distributed. Finding the footprint, we can infer to a past interaction of the beach with something else, the foot that made the print. So the footprint is a record or trace of the past event.

But there are many problems with this account. Sometimes records or traces are high-macroentropy states. When we expect order and find disorder, we also take this to be an indication of a past interaction. The scattered debris of an explosion is a high-macroentropy record. Sometimes we can infer from low-macroentropy to future states. Some low-macroentropy states, otherwise not expected, are *prognosticators* of future events. These situations are such that, given that those future events will occur, the present event becomes more probable. The signal on the radar screen may very well be a good indicator of a future interaction, say, of the missile hitting the target, but it is not a record of that future event.

A real justification of the Reichenbach claim would be some reason to believe that there is a general pattern of inference to past events that is characterizable in macroentropic terms and that is not matched by a similar pattern of inference to the future. Perhaps something of this sort could be done. After all, my current newspaper with its orderly type is a good indicator of what happened earlier, and there is nothing like a newspaper for the future. But why this is so remains very unclear. What is especially unclear is how the increase of microentropy into the future, the thermodynamic irreversibility of the world, is going to be used to account for the clear real asymmetry there is in the way in which we can gain knowledge of past and future. The route through macroentropy is especially puzzling because of the problem that what the macroentropy of a system is depends on how we classify events into macroevent kinds or sorts. We would view some ways of doing this as "natural," and others, as "unnatural" or perverse in some way. Any theory that tries to explain why it is that some current states ought to be counted as records of the past, but that no current states ought to be viewed as records of the future despite the ability to sometimes infer the future from them, and that tries to do so by invoking the notion of macroentropy, must do full justice to these issues of natural versus unnatural kinds of events. Needless to say, the route from thermodynamic entropy increase to an explanation of why we have memories of the past and not of the future is even more mysterious, given how little we know about just what the physical basis of memory really is.

Some approaches to supporting the Boltzmann thesis take the asymmetry of knowledge, the fact of records of the past but not of the future, as fundamental. They may then seek to derive other asymmetries, say, our belief that causation goes from past to future, from the knowledge asymmetry. Other approaches may first seek for a derivation of the causal asymmetry from the entropic, taking records to be effects of the events of which they are records, those events that are recorded being, by definition, the cause of the record of them.

A particularly ingenious attack on the causal asymmetry that seeks an explanation of it in phenomena that may be connected to the entropic asymmetry has been offered by D. Lewis. Lewis associates causation with so-called counterfactual conditionals. The idea is an old one: The cause of an event is the event such that, had it not taken place, the event considered the effect would not have occured. (The full account is more complicated than this, but the simple version will suffice for our purposes.) But how do we determine which counterfactual conditionals are true? Lewis argues that our intuitions are such that when we ask what would have happened had some actual event not occurred, or occurred otherwise than as it actually did, we rely on thinking about the kinds of changes we would be forced to make in the world had the event been other than as it was. We pick as what would have happened what happens in the world that is, in some sense, as close to our world as possible, given the posited change needed because of the event's being other than it actually was. Our standards for making such "closeness of worlds" judgments will tolerate small violations of the laws of nature, but not major ones or many of them. It will look for large regions of space and time where things remain exactly as they are in this world, but will tolerate large changes in particular matters of fact, even if these matters of fact are important to us. The standards for closeness are contrived so as to make our intuitive judgments about "what would be the case" come out right as often as possible.

One result of this analysis is to make "backtracking counterfactuals" come out false. These are counterfactuals that tell us that had some event been otherwise, its past would have been otherwise. At least they come out false in some cases. The cases are ones like that of the stone tossed into the water generating an ever-spreading ripple out into the pond in the future of the stone's impact with the water. The idea is that whereas the stone's not being tossed would have required only a minor miracle in its past (my neuron not firing and not giving me the volition to toss the stone), the stone's impact on the water is associated with a vast array of spatiotemporally dispersed facts in the future of the impact. These are all those ripple parts appearing, all the light waves being emitted from them, and so on. On Lewis's analysis, then, it turns out that had an event been other than it was, the future of that event would have been different, but the past would have been the same, because a given event is "overdetermined" by events future to it. There are many events in the future of a given event that require that event's existence but few in its past that do. And causation always goes, then, from past to future as well.

Once again there are many puzzles. For one thing, we think of causation as going from past to future, and not the other way, even in cases where no such "spreading out of order into the future" is involved. Here one might try a line due to Reichenbach, arguing that our basic idea of asymmetric causation is formed from cases where there is macroentropic spreading. The concept is then "projected" by a kind of analogy onto the cases where there is not. (But does this really seem plausible?) Once again there is the problem that all of these facts about macroorder spreading into the future are highly dependent on how the events are characterized. As before, there remains the possibility of characterizing one's macroevents in such a perverse way that one observes a spreading out of order in the wrong temporal direction. Finally, as Lewis himself states, it is not at all clear how to connect the explanation of the asymmetry of causation outlined here to the increase of microentropy of thermodynamics. Suggestions as to how this might work can be made, as there are those accounts that try to characterize phenomena like the spreading out of correlation in wave phenomena with the thermodynamical features of the emitters and absorbers of waves. Einstein attempted to explain the asymmetry of electromagnetic wave spreading in this way. But there is still much here that is not well understood.

Probably the only fair estimate of the situation at the present time is that the Boltzmann thesis is not one that is manifestly absurd or incoherent. It is also one that rests upon a strong plausibility argument. After all, if the thermodynamic asymmetry of systems in time is the one way in which radical temporal asymmetry shows up in the behavior of physical systems, doesn't it stand to reason that this grand physical asymmetry is in some way responsible for all our intuitive asymmetries in time? One thing is certain: The attempts to take time as fundamentally asymmetric in some other way, say, based upon some deep metaphysical analysis of the nature of "time itself," seem inevitably to fail to account for the entropic asymmetry. Nor is it clear how they really account for the asymmetries of knowledge and causation. However, it must be admitted that no one has ever really shown that Boltzmann's final thesis can be filled out in the detailed way essential to make it convincing.

Suppose we were able to come up with convincing arguments to the effect that all our intuitive asymmetries in time have an explanatory grounding in the entropic asymmetry. What then should we say is the connection between these two relationships: (1) the relationship one event bears to another when the first is later than the second in time, and (2) the relationship one event bears to another when the first event is separated from the second event in time and where also the direction of time from the first event to the second is that direction of time in which the entropy of isolated systems almost always increases? One suggestion that is often made is that a satisfactory filling out of the explanatory argument should lead us to claim that the two relationships are *identical* to one another.

Here the analogy is often drawn with other "discovered identities" in science. We discover that salt crystals are—i.e., are identical to—arrays of sodium and chlorine ions. We also discover that light waves are—i.e., are nothing but—a kind of electromagnetic wave. Isn't it also fair to say that we have discovered that the "down" direction in space at any location just is—just is identical to—that direction of space in which the gravitational force at that place is directed? Wouldn't it also be plausible, then, that if the Boltzmann explanatory program could be fully worked out, we ought simply to claim an identity between the future-past asymmetry in time and that asymmetry generated by entropic increase?

Some doubts that we could go that far have been voiced, however, even granted the success of the explanatory program. These doubts are related to the ones expressed in the context of the philosophical mind-body problem about the thesis that would identify such mental processes as feeling a pain or having a certain visual sensation with having a certain process going on in the brain. Those who voice these doubts are not doubting, for the context of this argument, that it might be the case that for all such felt or sensed qualia of mental life, certain brain processes were necessary and sufficient conditions. They might even agree that the mental processes were "supervenient" on the physical, meaning that any two persons with identical brain processes going on would have to have identical mental processes going on. What is denied is that the mental and physical processes can, in any reasonable way, be thought of as one and the same process.

Sometimes these doubts are expressed in a modal format harking back to R. Descartes. We can imagine a mental process of the appropriate sort without the associated brain process, it is said, or the latter without the former. So the processes are not necessarily identical to each other. But all genuine identities are necessary identities, which is not to say that their discovery might not be an empirical matter. So the contingency of the qualia/brain processes connection reveals that it is a nonidentity. The argument must go further, however, because we think we can also imagine water that is not H_2O, yet water certainly is identical to H_2O. At this point, an argument is given to explain to us why we really can't imagine water that is not H_2O, but only stuff that has many of the identifying characteristics of water and not being water. It is argued, however, that the "directness" of our access to mental qualia makes the two situations radically different.

A. Eddington offered a similar argument, to the effect that whatever the relation was between one event's being later than another and one event's being in the increasing-entropy time direction with respect to another, it could not be identity. We know, he claimed, what "afterwardness" is like. And we know what the entropic notion of one state's being more "disordered" than another is like. And we know, he claimed, that the two relations are simply not the same relation. This is just as we know that whatever the relation of mental feeling to brain process might be, it is not one of identity of what is going on.

Here, as Eddington emphasized, the special role of time in the world is important. We frequently make identifications work by a process of removing some features of the identified object out of the physical world and into the mental. Thus, when we say that a blue light wave is identical to some electromagnetic wave, we need not worry about the fact that electromagnetic waves cannot be thought of as blue. For we have already presupposed that the sensed blueness of the light wave is not a feature of the physical light wave but only a "secondary quality" in the mind, generated causally by light of a certain kind falling on our retinas. But the temporal relations among events in the world, Eddington would argue, are genuine features of those events. And that kind of temporality, he claims, must be exactly the same kind of temporality that relates the events of immediate experience to one another. For these reasons, reasons that are philosophically quite difficult to make clear but that remain persuasive nonetheless, he thinks that an identity claim is implausible between temporal relations as they are in the world, and as we immediately experience them, with such relations as those among different degrees of order, such as difference of entropy. The entropic theory of asymmetry of time has important and philosophically puzzling aspects even if the Boltzmann program as an explanatory one can be made completely plausible.

Further Readings

Reichenbach (1956) is a seminal discussion of the issues of this chapter. A contemporary discussion is Horwich (1987). Davies (1974) is an excellent introduction to the various aspects of physics. Sklar (forthcoming) is a systematic discussion of statistical physics from a philosophical perspective.

A nice introduction to probability theory is Cramer (1955). Feller (1950) gives more details and is more advanced. A brisk summary of the axiomatic basis by its inventor is Kolmogorov (1950). A survey of philosophical theories of probability can be found in Kyburg (1970) or more briefly in Chapter 3 of Sklar (forthcoming). For an introduction to objective randomness, see Earman (1986), Chapter 8.

Surveys of what philosophers say about statistical explanations can be found in Salmon (1984) and Humphreys (1989). Again, a brief sketch is in Chapter 4 of Sklar (forthcoming).

The most important papers in the history of statistical mechanics are translated in Brush (1965). Brush (1976) contains a wealth of information on the history of the subject. Ehrenfest and Ehrenfest (1959) is an early critical exposition of the subject, also very useful for historical insight.

Buchdahl (1966) and Pippard (1961) are good introductions to the concepts of thermodynamics. Gibbs's (1960) original work is a good introduction to the fundamentals of statistical mechanics. Tolman (1938) is a discursive and subtle treatment with foundational aspects emphasized. Jancel (1963) covers many of the details of foundational approaches to the theory.

The early approach to ergodic theory can be found in Farquhar (1964). The more modern approach is brilliantly summarized (at a quite sophisticated mathematical level) in Arnold and Avez (1968). Sinai (1976) is also brief and deep (but difficult). For a philosophical discussion of alternative approaches to the theory of nonequilibrium, see Sklar (forthcoming), Chapter 7.

The "subjectivist" (better, inductivist) approach to statistical mechanics can be found in Jaynes (1983), Katz (1967), and Hobson (1971). Krylov's fundamental ideas are in Krylov (1979). See also Batterman (1990) and Sklar (forthcoming), Chapter 7. For Prigogine's approach see Prigogine (1980 and 1984). See also Sklar (forthcoming), Chapter 7, and Batterman (1991).

A nontechnical introduction to the study of chaotic systems is Gleick (1987). Devaney (1986) is an introduction to the mathematical aspects of the theory. Schroeder (1991) explains the structure of many aspects of chaos theory and also discusses other areas where probabilistic reasoning has become central to scientific explanation.

A classic work on the relation of cosmology to entropy is Tolman (1934). Davies (1974) is accessible and covers many important topics. R. Penrose (1979) is a subtle treatment of entropy increase and cosmological facts. Sklar (forthcoming), Chapter 8, is a brief survey from a philosophical perspective.

On branch systems, the origin of the discussion is in Reichenbach (1956), especially Section 3. Davies (1974), Chapter 3, outlines branch systems. Skepticism about the connection of cosmic entropy increase to branch system parallel entropy increase is outlined in Sklar (forthcoming), Chapter 8.

On the issue of the direction of time, Reichenbach (1956), Section 4, is seminal. Reichenbachian-type views are defended in Grünbaum (1973), Chapter 8. Mehlberg (1980), especially Chapters 5 and 8, offers a critique. A penetrating discussion of Reichenbachian claims is in Earman (1974). Horwich (1987) offers both an account of the cosmic origins of branch system asymmetry and an attempt to ground intuitive time asymmetry on branch system asymmetry. Sklar (forthcoming), Chapter 10, and Sklar (1985), Chapter 12, explore what the structure of a reductionist account of time order must be like.

4

The Quantum Picture
of the World

The Experimental Basis of Quantum Theory

Quantum theory has presented scientists and philosophers of science with a series of perplexing questions. It seems to many that any attempt to comprehend a world described by quantum theory will require revision in our understanding of the nature of things far more radical than the revision in our understanding of the nature of space and time demanded by the theories of relativity. It has been claimed that to comprehend quantum theory we must revise our very understanding of such matters as the objective nature of reality and its independence from our perception of it, the nature of a complex system and its relation to its components, and the nature of causal and other kinds of determination in the world. What is it about this theory that seems to force upon us such a radical revision in our basic categories of nature?

It will be helpful to explore very briefly some of the highlights in the historical development of the theory. First, we must go back to the history of theories of the nature of light. In the seventeenth century, two models of the nature of light were proposed. One, espoused tentatively by Newton, was that light was a stream of particles emitted from a source and reflected off illuminated objects. The other, proposed by C. Huyghens, among others, was that light was a form of wave motion in some medium of transmission, much as sound is a wave generated by a source and transmitted as a periodic motion through the air.

The wave theory had to overcome some difficulties. How could a wave be transmitted from the sun to the earth, given a vacuum empty of matter between them? One would need to postulate some medium of transmission, the aether, to support the waves originating at the sun and arriving at the earth. Later facts about the polarization of light indicated that if light were a wave, it would have to be one whose wave motion was perpendicular to the direction of propagation of the wave. That made the constitution of this aether medium very problematic, as such waves were thought to be transmissible only in a rigid body. In the case of wave motion, one also expects diffraction phenomena. We can hear sound generated behind a wall with only a small opening, for once the sound enters the opening, it spreads out even behind the barrier. But doesn't light cast strict shadows, not showing any such spreading effects when it is interrupted by a barrier? That is what the particle theory would lead one to expect.

But in the eighteenth and nineteenth centuries, the wave theory attained what looked like a clear victory. Measurements indicated that, in accordance with the expectation of the wave theory and in conflict with the prediction of the particle theory, light traveled more slowly in media with higher indices of refraction than it did in those with lower indices. Careful observation showed, moreover, that the diffraction effects expected of a wave could be observed with light. They had previously been overlooked because the wavelength of light, unlike that of sound, is quite short compared to the size of macroscopic objects. This makes the spreading effects associated with diffraction hard to discern.

Most convincing of all in favor of the wave theory was the discovery of interference effects. A wave is a periodic phenomenon in both space and time. It has an amplitude that goes up and down periodically at any one place and up and down from place to place at a single time. Waves can be superimposed upon one another. If a crest of a wave is superimposed on another's crest, the resulting wave amplitude is increased. If a crest is superimposed on a trough, the resulting compound wave has low amplitude at that place and time. If a single wave is split into parts that are then superimposed on one another, say, by having the wave sent through two separate slits in a barrier and then having the resulting beams superimposed and allowed to fall on a screen, an "interference pattern" resulting from a systematic alternation of "constructive" and "destructive" superimpositions will arise. Such a pattern, obtainable with light, is taken as a clear indication of a wave phenomenon. If the light consisted of particles rather than waves, we would expect to find the much simpler pattern of two overlapping spreads of amplitude, one from each slit, and not the periodic system of high and low amplitudes expected from a wave.

Toward the end of the nineteenth century, Maxwell convinced the scientific community that light was a form of electromagnetic wave. Later, the idea of the aether as a medium of transmission of the wave was gradually dropped. The electromagnetic field itself was taken to be a kind of substantival entity that could be transmitted through a genuine vacuum, explaining the transmission of light from, for example, sun to earth.

The first indications that the standard wave theory would encounter difficulties came from attempts to understand the interaction of matter and light. A material body will emit and absorb light. Kept at a fixed temperature, that body will radiate light and absorb it. The body will be in equilibrium with the light, which has its energy distributed among the various possible frequencies associated with each wave, according to a fixed distribution law. This law can be experimentally determined. The changing distribution of frequencies with temperature is familiar: One can see a heated metal bar changing color as it gets hotter and hotter.

Several attempts were made to understand this important spectral distribution function. One approach, starting from the Maxwell-Boltzmann distribution law for the molecules of the heated body, gave rise to Wien's Law. This law approximated well the observed frequency distribution at high frequencies but failed at lower frequencies. Another approach also worked from the posits of the statistical mechanical theory discussed in Chapter 3, but applied statistical reasoning to the radiation itself. This resulted in the Rayleigh-Jeans Law. It worked well at low frequencies but gave impossible—divergent—results at high frequencies.

M. Planck sought a compromise law that would better suit the experimental facts, and he found one. But reflection upon its physical meaning seemed to lead to an almost inevitable interpretation. The Planck Law could be understood, on the basis of standard theoretical reasoning, as holding, if one assumed that energy was interchanged between matter and light only in discrete "packets," the energy of each packet being equal to a fixed constant multiplied by the frequency of the light emitted or absorbed. This was in strong contradiction to the usual assumptions of wave theory, that is, that energy could be exchanged between light and matter in any amount at any frequency. What was the origin of this peculiar discreteness of energy exchange?

Einstein later pointed out that another kind of interaction of light and matter, the liberating of electrons from a metal when high-energy light shone on the metal, the so-called photoelectric effect, also seemed to suggest that energy existed in the light only in discrete packets. The experimental results once again indicated that each packet would have its energy proportional to the frequency of the light it represented. The energy of the electrons liberated from the metal depended on the frequency of the light used, not on its intensity. Only the number of electrons liberated depended on the intensity of the light. It was as if each electron was liberated by interaction with a single light-energy packet ("photon") and as if the intensity of the light indicated how many photons were present at a given frequency. Light seemed, once more, to have something like a particle aspect.

Inspired by the particle-like aspects of light, a known wave phenomenon, L. de Broglie suggested that familiar particle phenomena might also have a wave aspect. The component particles making up the atom, such as the electron, would, then, under appropriate test conditions, show some aspects of a wave phenomenon such as diffraction or interference. An ingenious argument from relativity allowed de Broglie to associate with a particle not only a frequency, taken to be proportional to energy as was the case with the light-energy packets, but also a wavelength. This wavelength was taken to be inversely proportional to the particle's momentum.

Interestingly, the experimental confirmation of de Broglie's bold conjecture had already been obtained, although the importance of the data collected was not recognized until de Broglie's thesis became known. One can obtain interference phenomena from a wave not only by using a multiple slit device but also by scattering the wave off a regular pattern of scattering sources such as lines engraved on a reflecting plate, a so-called diffraction grating. The wave is scattered off each line, and the scattered waves combine, interfering with one another and producing one of the familiar periodic interference patterns so typical of the interaction of a multiplicity of coherent waves. For the electron, with its very small wavelength, the atoms of a crystal provide such a diffraction grating. Sure enough, if a beam of electrons is scattered off the surface of a crystal, the reflected electrons distribute themselves in a pattern whose angular distribution is just what one would expect from the interference pattern generated by a wave of the associated de Broglie wavelength scattered off a diffraction grating with the spacing appropriate to that of the atoms in a crystal lattice. If light, a wave, has a particle aspect, electron beams, beams of particles, show a wave aspect. (See Figure 4.1.)

Next, E. Schrödinger found the appropriate equation whose solutions would represent not only the wave associated with a free electron but also the waves associated with electrons bound in various force fields. Applying the equation to an electron orbiting the nucleus of an atom indicated that only a discrete number of energies of the electron corresponded to waves that could exist in such a bound particle situation. Sure enough, the energies corresponded to those allowable energies of electrons in an atom already posited by an existing atomic theory.

This older theory of electrons and of their behavior in the atom, the Bohr model of the atom, led, curiously, to a discovery of quantum theory that took quite a different track than the route from Planck to de Broglie to Schrödinger. The motion of the electrons in an atom results in the atom's emitting light. But the frequency pattern of the light emitted, the so-called spectrum of the atom, is quite unlike what one would expect on classical grounds. Classically one would expect frequencies to come in families of a basic frequency and integral multiples of it. This follows from some very fundamental classical theorems about the way in which the motion of a charged particle can be decomposed into basic, simple components and from the classical association of a kind of motion of a charge with the kind of light radiated from that charge.

Figure 4.1 The wave aspect of electrons as revealed by diffraction from a crystal.
A beam of electrons is shot at the surface of a crystal at an angle. The reflected
beam is detected by *D* at some other angle. The curve *C* indicates schematically the
variation in the intensity of the reflected beam as the angle of *D* to the crystal and
to the incident beam, *e*, is changed. It has a form that would be expected if the
electron beam were a wave that produced excitations that generated new waves
spreading out from each atom of the crystal lattice, waves that then "interfered"
with one another.

What one discovered instead was that the frequencies emitted could be
arranged in families characterized by *differences* of integers, rather than
simple multiples of a fundamental frequency.

Bohr offered a picture of the atom that generated this result, although the model was wildly at variance with what ought to be possible according to the then-standard theory. In Bohr's account, electrons could exist in discrete, definite energy states in the atom, as
opposed to the classical view that allowed any of a continuum of states.
In the new picture, electrons would "jump" from one energy state to
another. Each jump would emit or absorb energy in an amount equal
to the energy difference between the two states. Associated with the
energy change in the atom would be the emission or absorption of light
of a frequency associated with that energy by Planck's rule. This is in
complete contrast to the classical view—in which the electrons would
continually emit or absorb energy. Bohr's model was able to generate
the energy states for the simplest atoms by means of a group of simple
but somewhat unmotivated rules. But it proved incapable of providing
a general method for determining energy states in more complex cases
and incapable as well of giving a systematic way of determining the
intensity and the frequency of the light associated with atomic emission
and absorption.

W. Heisenberg set out to solve these problems by looking for a systematic way of treating the problem of the interaction of atoms and light. Given the incompatibility of the Bohr model with the existing theory of electron motion, he looked for a scheme that would avoid giving a dynamical picture of the electron in the atom at all. The scheme would, instead, attempt to calculate directly the desired observable quantities. Curiously, the theory ended, rather, by providing a new underpinning for dynamics as a whole. Heisenberg's procedure was to rely upon the classical method of reducing complex motion to simple motion and of associating the radiation emitted with the amount of each simple component of motion present. But now he needed a kind of twofold decomposition to correspond to the frequencies observed being characterized by two numbers, corresponding to differences in energy states, rather than by one number, corresponding to the multiple of the fundamental motion, as in classical physics.

Heisenberg, in his new formalism, duplicated by analogy the formal structure of the older rules for calculating energies, frequencies, and intensities. He thus arrived at a systematic procedure for determining the allowed energies of the electron in any atom, the corresponding frequencies of light emitted, and the intensities of light observed.

As Heisenberg, M. Born, and P. Jordan worked on the theory, they were coming up with an entirely new dynamical theory. Although the mathematics was clear, the physical interpretation of the theory was less obvious. The basic dynamical quantities of position and momentum had previously been mathematically represented by functions that assigned numbers to the particle as a function of the time. These were the position and momentum of a particle at a given time. Now, however, the dynamical quantities were represented by mathematical objects called operators. These operators mapped an abstract mathematical entity, the state of the system, from one state to another. Rules were constructed for determining, given the state of a system and given the operator corresponding to the quantity whose values one was interested in, the possible observed values of the quantity. One could thus calculate, for example, the possible energy values an electron could have in an atom of given type. Other rules allowed for the calculation of "transition amplitudes" from the state corresponding to one value of a quantity to another in a given physical situation. Thus the rate at which electrons would jump from one energy state to another in an atom could be calculated, even when the atom was subjected to outside interference. This gave the intensities of the emitted light of a specified frequency.

But what kind of physical world corresponded to this innovative mathematics? Something rather new had occurred in physics. Whereas previously a physical model had led to a mathematical description, here we had a working mathematical structure whose physical interpretation seemed quite problematic.

One answer to these questions about the physical meaning of the Heisenberg theory was soon proposed. If one calculated the possible energy states for an electron in an atom by the Schrödinger method, taking them to be the energy values possible for "standing" electron waves in the potential of the atom's nucleus (something like the standing sound waves possible in an organ pipe of specified length), one obtained predicted values identical to those obtained by the enigmatic Heisenberg rules, using the operator appropriate to energy for the atom in question. If one calculated transition rates between states by the Schrödinger method, using reasoning similar to that which tells us how one vibrating tuning fork can put another into oscillation by resonance, one obtains the same values as those obtained by Heisenberg calculating transition amplitudes by his mysterious operator calculus. Finally, Schrödinger was able to demonstrate the mathematical relation between the two theories that guaranteed they would always predict the same observable results. Mathematically, the two methods were "isomorphic" to one another, some difference in appearances owing to the fact that whereas Schrödinger packed the time evolution of the system into the evolution of its wave function, Heisenberg worked with a time-independent state of the system and packed the dynamics of time evolution into variation in time of the operators assigned to a given physical observable.

Now, it seemed, we had at least the beginnings of a physical model of the electron as wave in the Schrödinger theory. Couldn't the Heisenberg theory just be looked at as a mathematical means of dealing with the electrons and the other particles as genuine physical waves?

So Schrödinger proposed. But this simple resolution of the difficulties soon became hard to accept. The "spread out" wave function describing the electron actually took the form of a wave in physical space and time only in the case of a single particle. When a complex of particles was considered, the wave function looked like a wave only in an abstract higher dimensional coordinate space simultaneously representing the positions of all the particles as a single point. Much worse was the seeming incompatibility of the "real" spread-out wave interpretation of the electron with its manifest point particle aspects. When we apply the experimental devices used to detect the presence of an electron, we discover that all its manifestations, such as mass and charge, can be found concentrated in a very small physical region. If not "point" particles, electrons are, at least, quite small in extent. But the wave describing the presence of an electron is spread out over a large physical volume, indeed, often out to "infinity" to at least a small degree. So how can the localized particle be identified with a physically real spread-out wave?

Some hope of reconciling the particle aspects of an electron to its alleged physical wave nature arose from the fact that wave phenomena can often show a stable concentration of the wave energy in a small volume. "Wave packets," in which the overwhelming bulk of the energy of the field is concentrated in a very small volume of space, were known to exist in some cases from classical wave theory. In one exceptional case, the simple harmonic oscillator, a concentrated electron wave packet could be shown to demonstrate stability through time. But, alas, in the general case, a concentrated wave packet representing an electron could be shown to dissipate its concentration very rapidly, leading to a wave widely spread out in space. The puzzle of reconciling the spread-out wave with the localized particle remained.

We are presented, then, with a quandary. Light, which had been known for some time to show distinctly wavelike aspects of diffraction, interference, wavelength, and frequency, was now shown to have a particle-like aspect as well. Any detection of light by a material device, say, a piece of photographic film, revealed that light interacted with matter in a very particle-like way. Energy in the light appeared to be contained in discrete packets that could interact with matter only "one at a time." Matter in the form of elementary particles, which was known to be particle-like, showing mass and charge concentrated in a small physical volume, now was seen to have a wavelike aspect also. Electron beams going through small holes in barriers diffracted, as did light beams sent through very small pinholes. Electrons scattered off a crystal lattice exhibited a clear interference pattern exactly analogous to that shown by light scattered off a traditional diffraction grating.

But how could this be understood? How could such terms as wavelength and frequency apply to localized particles? How could the physical constituents described by a spread-out wave function always be found, when they were detected, to be localized in a small volume in the manner appropriate to unspread-out discrete particles?

Early Attempts to Interpret the Theory:
The Uncertainty Principle

Interpreting the Formalism: Probability,
Interference, and Measurement

A crucial insight into understanding the theory was M. Born's interpretation of the intensity of the wave function as giving a probability. Every wave has an amplitude, the "height" of the wave magnitude. The intensity of a wave, more or less proportional to the square of that amplitude, is what we normally register, for light, as the brightness of the light; it is a measure of the energy in the wave. The amplitudes of the waves of quantum wave mechanics were framed in complex numbers, but their "squares" were real numbers representing a directly interpretable physical quantity. It was Born's insight that these intensities could be taken as representative of the probability with which a physical observable would be found to have a given one of its possible values if an appropriate measurement were made. The wave function can be represented as a function of different variables, for example, as a function either of the position or of the momentum of the particle to which the wave is associated. Depending on the representation chosen, probabilities, say, for finding the particle in a region if a position measurement was made, or in a given range of momenta if a momentum measurement was made instead, could be calculated from the appropriate intensity over a region of the quantum "probability wave," as some began to call it. Probabilities of transition of a particle from one state to another could also be determined from the wave functions and their interrelations, such as the transition amplitudes associated with the intensities of emitted spectral light originally calculated by the Heisenberg method.

Clearly, Born's insight provides the first clue as to how to reconcile the "spread-outness" of the wave function and the localized nature of measured quantities. The wave represented not an actual spread-out particle, only a probability of finding the particle's localized value to be somewhere in a defined region of values.

But a simple identification of the wave function's intensity with probabilities as usually understood is fraught with difficulties. The best place to see where the difficulties lie is in the phenomenon of interference. Suppose an outcome can be obtained with a certain degree of probability in one of two ways, the two ways being causally independent of one another. Let the probabilities of the outcomes be represented as $P(O/A)$ and $P(O/B)$, where O is the outcome and A and B are the two modes by which it can be obtained. Normally we would expect, given the causal independence of A and B, that the probability of O's being obtained either by the A or by the B route is the sum of the two probabilities noted. But, in general, this is not true in the quantum situation. For example, the probability of a photon's being received at a certain point on a screen illuminated through two slits is not the sum of the probability of the photon's reaching that point given that slit 1 alone is opened plus the probability of the photon reaching that point when slit 2 alone is opened. Indeed, if both slits are opened, the probability that the photon reaches a given point can be *less* than it would be when either slit alone was opened. In wave terms this is because the wave from slit 1 and that from slit 2 "destructively interfere" with each other to give the reduced probability in question. But if the wave function is just a probability representer and not a physical wave in the world, how can such interference occur? Normal probabilities just don't "interfere" with one another.

A few simple idealized experiments show how curious the quantum world really is. First consider the two-slit experiment. Here a single beam of light is allowed to pass through a barrier having two slits that can be opened or closed, and the beam is allowed to fall on a screen. If one slit but not the other is opened, a characteristic distribution of light on the screen centered about the location of the open slit is obtained. If both slits are opened, however, as we previously noted, the pattern of the screen is not the sum of the one-slit patterns but, instead, the famous interference pattern. It is important to note that this is what is obtained even if the beam is so weak in intensity that, on the average, only one packet of energy, one photon, at a time, is passing from source through slits to screen. This indicates that the pattern obtained cannot be explained away as some normal causal interaction among the photons. It is as if, rather, each photon passes through both slits as a wave but is absorbed on the screen as a localized particle. (See Figure 4.2.)

If one modifies the experiment by placing after each slit a detector that indicates whether or not a photon has just passed through the slit, the interference pattern vanishes and the screen shows, instead, the kind of sum pattern that would be obtained if the patterns from two separate one-slit experiments were just added. That same pattern is obtained if each slit is illuminated by a separate source of light, rather than having one source pass through both slits. Here we see most of the characteristic peculiarities of the world that require the quantum formalism in order for them to be captured.

Another idealized experiment, let us call it the two-path experiment, takes a single beam of light particles and splits it into two beams, each of which travels a distinct path, and the two beams are eventually brought to a point of coincidence. The splitting of a light beam can be obtained by using a half-silvered mirror that reflects half the light incident upon it and lets half go through.

At the point where the two beams are brought back together, we can choose which detection experiment to perform. One experiment places detectors in such a way that they will trigger only if the "particle" being detected (the photon) travels one of the paths and not the other. If the beam intensity is divided evenly, this experiment will record results that are compatible with the hypothesis that it is as if the original beam splitter split a beam of particles into two halves, one beam consisting of particles that traveled path A only and the other particles that traveled path B only. But if, instead, the two beams are recombined at the new coincidence point, interference between the two beams can be obtained. In fact, an interference detector, or interferometer, of this design is a classical optical device. These interference effects reveal data in conformity with the hypothesis that it is as if the original half-silvered mirror or other splitting device actually split a wave into two components, one of which traveled path A and the other of which traveled path B, but which remained in phase with each other, allowing the components, when recombined, to exhibit the characteristic coordination phenomenon known as wave interference. It is as if each particle, if the beams are thought of as beams of particles, traveled *both* paths simultaneously! (See Figure 4.3.)

As J. Wheeler has pointed out, it is important to note that the choice of which experiment to perform at the final coincidence can be made at a time long after the beam has been split and sent on its way. This indicates that it won't do to explain these effects by appealing to the

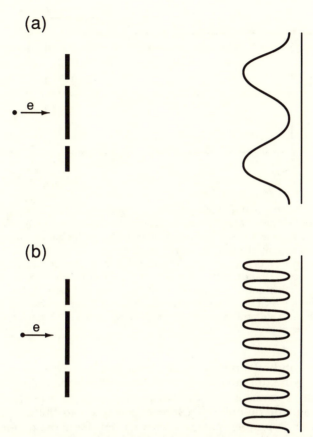

Figure 4.2 The two-slit experiment. If a beam of particles *e*, is directed at a wall with two slits and the particles are detected on a screen on the other side of the wall, the distribution of particles at the wall would be expected to have the pattern indicated in (a). Two densities of particles, each centered around one of the slits, merely add to each other. But if a wave is directed at the slit, one expects the interference pattern for wave intensity noted in (b). This is because the waves emitted from the two slits can either add to each other or cancel each other, depending on the relative distances to a point on the screen from the two slits. If a beam of electrons, *e*, is directed at a two-slit device, the pattern indicated in (b) is detected at the screen, despite the particle-like nature of electrons revealed in other experiments.

choice of experiments as somehow determining whether at the beam splitting the particle or wave aspect of the experiment was the real description of the world. It is as if at the splitting one must think of something that has both the aspects of a particle beam being divided into two distinct beams of particles and the aspects of a wave being decomposed into two component correlated waves.

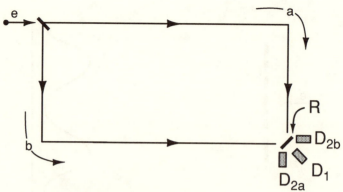

Figure 4.3   The two-path experiment. A beam of electrons, *e*, can be split so as to follow one of two paths indicated by *a* and *b* in the figure. At the far corner where the paths rejoin, one could either place a device *R*, in the path to recombine the beams and detect interference patterns by means of detector D_1 (thereby showing the wavelike nature of the electrons) or remove the recombiner, *R*, and detect by means of dectors D_{2a} and D_{2b}, the electrons as particles that traveled not both paths but one or the other only. One can choose to perform the experiment at a time later than the time at which the electron is already well on its way around the path (either around both as wave or around one or the other as particle). This is the "delayed choice" experiment.

Another kind of experiment, the Stern-Gerlach experiment, is helpful in seeing the full range of the quantum phenomena. An elementary particle may possess a quantity known as spin and a related quantity of spin magnetic moment. This bears a relation to the classical magnetization of a spinning charged particle, but like most quantum phenomena, the relation is only one of analogy. For an electron, this spin magnetic moment shows up as an internal "two valuedness" of the particle. If sent through a magnetic field that is uniform in all directions except one that is perpendicular to the direction of motion of the electron, the electron will be deflected from its path either up or down in the direction of magnetic inhomogeneity. If we pick a direction as the up-down direction then, and let the field be nonuniform in that direction, the beam of particles will be split into a beam of "up" and a beam of "down" particles.

Let a beam of particles come out of an up-down machine that absorbs all the down particles. Send the "pure up" beam obtained into a machine whose magnetic nonuniformity is at right angles to that of the up-down machine. Call this a left-right machine. One discovers that at the output end of the left-right machine, half the particles come out in the left beam and half in the right beam.

Now comes the characteristic quantum interference effects. If we block the right beam from the left-right machine and send its left beam into a new up-down machine, half the particles would come out of the up-down machine up and half down. The same thing would happen if we blocked the left beam of the left-right machine and let only the right beam into the new up-down machine. Half the electrons would come out up and half down. But if we recombined the output left and right beams from the left-right machine and sent the recombined beam through the second up-down machine, all the electrons would come out of that machine in the up beam! The left and right beams coming out of the left-right machine are correlated with each other in a way that "remembers" the original pure-up nature of the input beam. When the beams are recombined, they "interfere" with other to generate not a "mixture" of left and right particles but a beam of particles all of which are definitely up. However, just as in the two-slit case, if we had placed detectors in the left and right beam paths to note for each electron whether it came out of the left-right machine as a left or as a right particle, and then recombined the beams and sent them through the up-down machine, half the electrons would come out of that machine up and half down. Measuring the output spins from the left-right machine makes each of them definitely left or definitely right and destroys the coherence of the two beams, making the regeneration of the pure-up beam by their recombination impossible. This indicates that interference effects are relevant not only to the spatial distribution of particles but also to any observable feature they may have. (See Figure 4.4.)

The recombined beams of left and right outputs that generate a pure-up beam show a coherence of leftness and rightness that is absent in a beam one-half of which is composed of the output of a left machine and one-half of which is composed of the output of an unrelated right machine. The latter beam is said to be a "mixture" of left and right particles. The former is said to be a "superposition" of left and right particles. Such a superposition state contains information absent in a mixture state. In the case in question the information is that the output of the left-right machine is generated by its being fed a pure-up beam as input.

The interference phenomena make a simple, traditional interpretation of the wave function as a probability measure problematic. We might try to think of probability as a measure of our knowledge of a system's values. We would then try to think of assigning a probability one-half to the particles in a beam's being either left or right as asserting that each particle is either definitely left or right and that a reasonable bet as to its being the one or the other will take even odds on the outcome. Or we might try to think of the wave function as telling us that the fraction of the particles in the beam that is left is one-half and that the remainder is right. But as we have seen, such an understanding won't do by itself. For we must also understand each particle in the reassembled beam as being definitely up, and this distinguishes the beam from a quite different one composed of one-half each definite left and definite right particles. The superposition of left and right is

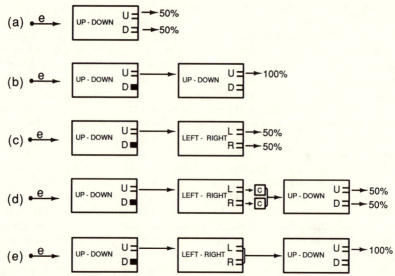

Figure 4.4 The Stern-Gerlach experiment. Quantum mechanics allows an electron to have only one of two values of spin along any chosen axis. The Stern-Gerlach apparatus can separate a beam of electrons into two beams, all of those in a given output beam having the same spin value. In (a) a "random" beam of electrons (*e*) is sent into a Stern-Gerlach machine with the axis up and down. Half the electrons come out in the up beam and half in the down beam. In (b) the pure-up output of one device is sent into another oriented along the same axis. All the electrons entering the second device come out of it in the up beam. In (c) a pure-up beam from a first device is sent into a second device whose axis of orientation is at 90° to that of the first device. A pure-up beam sent into a left-right machine has half the electrons emerge with spin right and half with spin left. In (d) the output from (c) is counted by detectors to the right of the left-right machine. The counted beams are recombined and sent into a second up-down machine. Half come out up and half down. This is what one would expect if the input beam to the last machine is half right-spinning electrons and half left-spinning electrons. In (e) interference for electron spin is revealed. This time the output beams from the left-right machine are recombined without being disturbed in any way (say, by counters). The recombined beam is fed into an up-down machine. Now all the electrons emerge from the last machine with spin up. Despite the passage through the left-right machine, the fact that the beam that went into the left-right machine was a "pure up" beam is "remembered" by the interference and reveals itself in the manner in which the final output of (e) differs from that of (d).

not the mixture of left and right, even though for both beams it is correct to assert that a left-right measurement would indicate that half the particles are left and half right upon being measured.

Reflecting on the formal interrelationship between the Schrödinger wave theory and the Heisenberg formal dynamics, J. von Neumann and P. Dirac developed formalisms that abstracted from both approaches to capture the essence of quantum theory. In each account, there are mathematical representatives of states of the world and of physical observables. Suppose a system has a definite state. The state's evolution over time when subjected to some outside causal influence is the subject of dynamics. Given the state at a time and a specification of the observable to be measured, the mathematical representatives of the observable specify what the possible outcomes of the measurement can be, and this representative of the observable combined with the state of the system determines the probabilities that one of the possible outcomes will be found to be the case.

If we know the state of a system at one time and the causal influences at later times, we can determine its state as the system evolves. But how do we determine the initial state of a system? We do this by preparing the system, a process that constitutes, at the same time, a kind of measurement of the system's values. We can determine, for example, that the initial spin state of a particle is definitely up at time=0 by knowing that the particle was emitted from the up channel of an up-down machine at $t = 0$. We can then know the spin state of the particle at later times by knowing the causal influences (electric and magnetic fields in this case) to which it was subject from the time it was emitted out of the up channel of the up-down machine. If we then choose to make a new spin measurement on the system, we can determine—from the operator appropriate to the direction of spin we choose to measure—what values can be obtained (in the case of the electron, just two, up or down in the direction chosen) and from that operator and the state of the particle at the time of measurement we can determine the probability that a given spin value will be obtained upon measurement.

Attributing the appropriate state to the particle just after preparation relies upon von Neumann's famous Projection Postulate. This states that if a measurement has just been performed that reveals a given value for an observable, then the state of the system immediately after that measurement is the one appropriate to the system's having that exact value for the measured quantity. (Actually this needs patching up to account for the fact that sometimes measurement destroys a system and for the fact that a measurement doesn't usually determine all of a system's compatible quantities, but for our purposes it will do.) A major argument of von Neumann's is that only such a state attribution will assure us that if the measurement was immediately repeated, we would be certain of obtaining the same value as we did in the first measurement. The formalized theory presented by von Neumann and taken as the orthodox version of quantum theory is curious, then, in presenting two different rules for determining the change of a system's state over time. One, the dynamic rule, tells how the passage of time itself and outside influences, such as the interaction of the system with some other system, will lead to a dynamic evolution of the state of the system. The other rule tells us that whatever the state of a system prior to a measurement, after the measurement takes place, the state of the system will correspond to the system's having the value of the observable just measured. The state of the system upon measurement is "projected" to the so-called characteristic state corresponding to the observed or measured value obtained by the measurement. When measurement takes place, the dynamic rules of state evolution are put aside. As we shall see, the notion of measurement as a special process outside of ordinary dynamics becomes one of the great problem areas for quantum theory.

The Copenhagen Interpretation

The great physicist Niels Bohr attempted to frame an overall picture of the world that would do justice to the strange new quantum phenomena and to design the appropriate theoretical structure. His so-called Copenhagen Interpretation is not easy to summarize neatly. Some have viewed it as a new philosophy of being and knowledge whose importance goes beyond a clarification of the quantum aspects of the world. Others have been more skeptical. Einstein once called it "the Heisenberg-Bohr tranquilizing philosophy—or religion?" and went on to say that it "provides a gentle pillow for the true believer from which he cannot easily be aroused," i.e., that it "covered up" the problematic aspects of the quantum picture instead of offering a coherent, intelligible account of the quantum phenomena.

Bohr takes the purpose of science to be to determine the interrelations among observable quantities of the world. For the purpose of understanding the quantum theory, what is observable is taken to be, not "sense data directly perceivable by the mind," as in traditional positivist philosophy, but, rather, the results of observations with typical measuring devices. Nonetheless, Bohr's philosophy does share some aspects of traditional positivism, with its emphasis on a once-and-for-all class of "the observables" and on theory as merely an instrument to get the correlations of observables with one another correct. Bohr asserted that in our description of these observable results of measurement, we will always remain restricted to the typical "classical" means for describing the world developed by prequantum physics. Thus such things as the position of a particle, its momentum, charge, and angular momentum, and so on, are the quantities we read off from our measuring apparatus. A measuring apparatus is something once again characterizable in classical terms. It has definite "output" states that are correlated to the measured quantities of the microsystems. A deposited mark of metallic silver will, for example, indicate that a photon was absorbed in some limited region of a photographic film, a definite flash of a detector tube may indicate the passage through a region of a charged particle, and so on. In our recording of the results of measurement, we will have no place for quantum "superposition" states, only for states as classically described.

The purpose of the quantum states is to allow us to make probabilistic predictions about the outcomes of the measurement process. A classical reading tells us that a system has been prepared in a given quantum state. The dynamical rules allow us to follow the evolution through time of the quantum state assigned to the system. At a later time, we can use that quantum state to make probabilistic predictions about the values, classically described, that would be obtained from any measurement we choose to perform. But it is wrong, on this view, to think of systems between measurements as having classical states at all. If we can infer from the quantum state that a specific outcome of a particular measurement would occur with certainty, then, perhaps, we can attribute that classical value to the system even when it is not being measured. But, in general, where only probabilities less than certainty can be given for a variety of possible values for the outcome of a measurement, it is wrong, on this view, to think of the unmeasured system as having any one of the possible outcome values. This is quite unlike the classical probability situation, where we think of the system as having a definite but unknown value, the probability being only a measure of our ignorance of the actual state.

This view of the nature of measurement and of the limited legitimacy of attributing classical physical states to systems was combined by Bohr with what he called the idea of "complementarity" to resolve some of the paradoxes of quantum theory. Complementarity is a difficult notion to fully pin down. Bohr himself sometimes extends the notion in quite dramatic ways, speaking, for example, of the mental and physical descriptions of mind and brain as complementary. But even in the quantum theoretic situation, the term is used quite broadly. The wave and particle aspects of a system are spoken of as complementary to each other. Sometimes two aspects of a system's dynamical description—like position and momentum—are what are taken as complementary. The general idea is that a system can be described classically in more than one way. In classical physics, a system is either a wave or a particle, and a system has both a definite position and a definite momentum. In quantum theory, however, the pairs of features becomes curiously linked. Both complementary aspects of the system are necessary for its full characterization. But it is impossible to describe the system simultaneously in terms of both complementary features. We can characterize the wave aspects of a system, or we can characterize its particle-like aspects. But we cannot think of a system as both wavelike and particle-like. We can think of a system as having a definite position or a definite momentum, but, according to Bohr, it is impossible to attribute simultaneous definite position and momentum to the particle.

The "joint exhaustiveness but mutual exclusiveness" of complementary features reveals itself physically when we think about possible ways of using measurement to attribute a feature to a system. We can set up an interference device to find the wave aspects of a system, its wavelength and frequency, for example. Or we can use particle detectors to determine its particle aspects, noting which slit the particle actually comes through. But setting up one of these experimental devices precludes constructing the other. It is physically impossible to construct a measuring device that will simultaneously determine both of two complementary descriptive features to be attributed to a system. It is legitimate, then, to think of a system as wavelike, meaning that if a wave-revealing experiment were to be performed, the system would reveal its wavelike aspects. And it is legitimate to think of the system as particle-like, for parallel reasons. But we are relieved of the burden of attributing contradictory aspects to the system because of the fact that nothing that we can do in the way of measurement will reveal the contradictory aspects simultaneously.

Bohr goes on to maintain that it is illegitimate to even think of the quantum system between measurements as having the feature we want to attribute to it in some absolute, nonrelativized, sense. Relying on analogy with Einstein's relativistic demonstration that length and time interval were attributable to things only relative to the choice of a particular motional reference frame, Bohr argued that the attribution of states to systems—in the sense of attributing to them such features as wave or particle aspects—was relative only to a choice of measuring apparatus. Relative to an interferometric experimental device, the light was wavelike. Relative to a photon particle–detecting device, it was particulate. Not relative to a specified choice of experimental device it wasn't anything at all. (Naturally, Einstein did not take kindly to the analogy to relativity, saying that even a good joke could be repeated too often!).

Bohr then argued that in any experimental situation, it was essential to distinguish between the system being measured, which was, until the measurement was performed, to be described only in quantum states that expressed potentialities toward observable values being obtained in the form of probabilities, and the measuring apparatus. The measuring apparatus was, according to Bohr, correctly characterized in classical terms both as to its construction and purpose prior to the measurement and as to its final state that revealed the correct measured value to be attributed to the system. Whereas quantum theory was universal in the sense that any physical system in the world obeyed the basic laws of quantum theory, in any measurement situation one had to "split" the world into two components, the measured system and the measuring apparatus. The former was rightly characterized in quantum terms, but for the remaining measuring portion of the world, the correct description was framed in the traditional classical physical concepts. Further, measurement could not be assimilated to ordinary physical interaction, for although the dynamical laws of quantum mechanics governed the latter, the former process obeyed the distinct rule of the Projection Postulate.

But where in the world was the line to be drawn between quantum measured system and classical measuring apparatus? The answer was that it could be drawn at any level. For some purposes it was useful to think of the elementary particle alone as the quantum system and all of the physical world remaining as measuring apparatus. But we could also, consistently, treat any portion of the measuring apparatus as a physical system in interaction with the elementary particle, with the whole joint system of particle and that fraction of the apparatus to be characterized as a quantum system. If we did this, we would narrow the classically described apparatus down to that remaining after the portion initially reacting to the particle had been placed in the quantum realm. Nothing in physics made a hard and fast dividing line between the quantum nature and the classical measuring device. The division could be drawn at any level. But the very intelligibility of the quantum picture demanded that it be drawn somewhere. It would be incoherent to think of the whole universe as a pure quantum system, for the very intelligibility of the attribution of a quantum state to a system required thinking of the system as being measured by a classically described measuring apparatus outside the quantum system itself.

The Copenhagen Interpretation is an extraordinarily ingenious attempt to do justice to all the peculiar aspects of the new quantum theory. It encompasses everything from the need for apparently incompatible descriptions of one and the same system as wave- and particle-like, to the special role played by measurement and the Projection Postulate in the theory's formalism. But it certainly is not a view of the world easy to understand. Most suspicious of all is the special role reserved for classically described measuring devices as essential to interpreting the theory. How can there be such things if, as the theory claims, everything really is a quantum system? And what is the special role reserved for measurement processes? Aren't they just interactions of a system with another physical system? Aren't such interactions describable by the standard rules of quantum theory? Why should there be a special rule for measurement processes at all, if measurements are nothing but another variety of physical interaction? And is the Copenhagen view, with its radical relativism of the physical states of systems to choices of measuring apparatus, capable of providing us with a "realistic" characterization of what the world is really like in its "own nature"? We will return to these issues shortly.

The Uncertainty Principle

It was soon realized that quantum theory in each of its formal guises led to a variety of relations among the features of a system, which were summarized as the Uncertainty Relations. A simple illustration of these results can be found in the wave picture of Schrödinger's version of quantum mechanics. We can ask about the probability of finding a particle located in some specified spatial region, calculating the probabilities by the degree to which the wave function is confined to that region. Alternatively, we can rewrite the wave function as a function of the particle's momentum, thereby finding a new function that can be used to determine the probability of finding the particle having its mo-

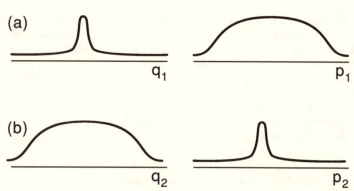

Figure 4.5   The Uncertainty Relations. In any quantum state of a particle, there is a certain probability that the particle will be found in a specified region of space and a certain probability that its momentum will be found to be in a specified range of momenta. In (a) a state is outlined in which the position of the particle is tightly circumscribed by a narrow probability distribution (graph q_1). The corresponding distribution of probability for momentum (graph p_1) shows a very "spread out" probability distribution. In (b) a state is outlined in which the probability distribution for momentum (graph p_2) is now sharply peaked. Now the position probability distribution (graph q_2) shows a broadly "spread out" probability, in accordance with the uncertainty relations.

mentum in a specified range. From classical wave physics, it was realized that there was a reciprocal relationship between the degree to which a wave function had spatial spread and the degree to which it would be spread out in "frequency space" when the wave was reformulated as constituted of various pure frequency components. Translated into quantum terms, this reciprocal relationship results in the observation that the less spread out in position a probability distribution is for a particle when calculated from its quantum state, the more spread out the probability distribution will have to be for calculating its momentum. No quantum state could simultaneously generate probabilities very highly concentrated about both a single point in space and a single momentum value. (See Figure 4.5.)

From the Heisenberg perspective, this kind of inverse relationship showed up in the fact that the mathematical representatives of observable quantities, the operators in his mathematical formalism, were "noncommutative." This means that the product of two of them in one order was not, in general, equal to the product taken in the reverse order. This relationship holds between other conjugate quantities as well, and not just between position and momentum. When one moved to the abstract representation of quantum theory of von Neumann and Dirac, it was possible to find some very general mathematical relations that summed up the Uncertainty Principle.

The degree of uncertainty is taken as the product of a measure of the spread-outness of probability of the two quantities, as these probability distributions are calculated from the quantum state. Sometimes the uncertainty varies from physical state to physical state. In other cases, for example, that of position and momentum, there was a fixed, minimal uncertainty that holds universally. But what does this "ineliminable uncertainty" mean physically?

In exploring this problem, Heisenberg offered an imaginative account of uncertainty, taking it as an indication of an ultimate limitation on our ability to fix all of the properties of a system to an arbitrary degree of exactness by any experimental technique. The basic idea here was that any measurement performed on a system must, inevitably, physically disturb the system measured. Fixing one quantity to a specified degree of precision would, then, so disturb the system as to reduce our knowledge of the value of some conjugate quantity by allowing it, after the measurement, to have any of a large range of values.

A famous Heisenbergian thought experiment to illustrate his interpretation of the Uncertainty Principle is a kind of microscope designed to determine to a high degree of accuracy the spatial position of a particle at some specified time. How could such a position determination be made? Only, Heisenberg argued, by causing some detecting signal to interact with the particle in question. One could, for example, illuminate the particle with light and look for the scattered light bounced off the particle. Seeing where the light was scattered by the particle would provide information concerning the particle's location.

But the classical treatment of the use of light in microscopy relates the ability of the light to resolve small spatial differences to the wavelength of the light. Shorter wavelength light can determine spatial differences to a finer degree than can long wavelength light. But in quantum theory, the shorter wavelength is associated with higher frequency and therefore with higher energy for the minimal packet of energy of the light, the photon. To observe the particle, at least one photon must be scattered off it. The higher the energy of that photon, the greater the range of values of the "kick" it might give the particle, modifying its initial momentum to some new value. Following through on the details gives a picture in which a microscopic effort to place the position of the particle within a narrow range is accompanied by an inevitable causal interference in the life of the particle that diminishes the precision we are able to have about the momentum of the particle subsequent to the position measurement.

Even in prequantum physics, theoretically any measurement of a system must interfere with the state of the system to some small degree. But in the classical picture, such interference can be reduced to as small an amount as one chooses. For Heisenberg, at least in this interpretation of uncertainty, the essential element of quantum theory was the now inevitable minimal interference in the system, the irreducible disturbance of its state, a disturbance that could not be reduced by any physical means, and that must accompany any attempt to determine the value of a given property of the system to within a small range of values.

From this perspective, uncertainty is thought of as a limitation on our ability to discern the exact simultaneous values of two conjugate properties of a system. That is, we think of the system as having, for example, precise simultaneous values of both position and momentum, but of our being unable, because of the inevitable interference of measuring process with system, to exactly determine those existing joint, precise values.

Bohr was never satisfied with such an interpretation of uncertainty. He insisted from the beginning that the specification of the quantum state of a system constituted a complete description of each individual system of which that quantum state was correctly predicable. It was wrong, he argued, to think of the quantum state as holding of a collection of particles, with each particle actually having a fuller, if not completely knowable, precise state of the classical sort. Rather, he argued, the quantum state, with its intrinsic "spread-outness" of values of classical quantities represented by the spread-outness of the probability distributions associated with those values, was a total description of the actual state of the particle. For any such quantum state, as we have noted, there would be connections between the degree to which the probability distributions for conjugate quantities were spread out. Any fixing of a quantum state that made the position spread very narrow would automatically generate a quantum state whose momentum probability distribution was broad. But, Bohr argued, it was too conservative to interpret this inverse relationship as merely being a limitation on our ability to precisely fix conjugate values simultaneously. Instead, one had to think of each individual particle as having—at best—spread-out values of a classical quantity, if one insisted on thinking of a particle as having any classical properties at all between measurements.

Heisenberg was moved to accept the more radical Bohrian "ontological" reading of uncertainty. That is, he accepted the view that uncertainty reflects irreducible spread-outness of features of systems, not merely a limitation on our knowledge of joint properties to degrees of arbitrary precision. We shall later see some of the reasons for his adopting this more radical stance. Einstein, however, was dismayed by the radical Bohrian theory and for some time sought to find good physical reasons to reject it.

A series of fascinating debates between Einstein and Bohr ensued. Einstein set himself the project of trying to find an experimental situation in which the limitations on precise specification of conjugate quantities given by the Uncertainty Relations could be violated. He designed ingenious thought experiments to try to show that one could determine two conjugate quantities to within a degree of joint precision that the Uncertainty Relation declared impossible. For each of Einstein's suggestions, however, Bohr argued that the experimental procedure in question ultimately required the determination of two basic quantities by one of the procedures that could be shown, using Heisenbergian arguments, to limit our knowledge of the joint quantities necessary according to the familiar uncertainty limitations. If one accepts Bohr's counterarguments, it would seem that it was impossible to find a way around the Uncertainty Relations by means of some actual experimental overcoming of their limitation. This still leaves it open, however, even if the Uncertainty Principle is true, exactly how the relations are to be understood. Are they to be understood in the older, more modest, Heisenbergian sense, as a limitation on what we can determine, or in the more radical Bohrian mode, which denies the very existence of precise values for two conjugate quantities?

What Is Measurement in Quantum Theory?

The Measurement Problem

The basic formalism of quantum theory is clear, and its application to the world of observation and experiment is, in practice, no more controversial than that of any other formal physical theory. But the theory presents us with a host of perplexing interpretive problems. Members of the scientific community who agree without hesitation on the results of the quantum theory applied to the physical world find themselves at odds with one another when they try to explain just how they "understand" what the theory tells us about the fundamental structure of the world.

In the theory, systems between measurements are described as having a quantum state. Presumably, then, this state somehow or another "represents" the state of nature of the system. But what is that physical state of the system, and how does the quantum state represent it? Should the quantum state be thought of as a description of individual systems, say, of the one photon in the two-slit experiment? After all, the fact that the interference results hold even if the particles are sent through the slits one at a time suggests that each photon somehow or another must be thought of as "being aware" of both slits in the manner the quantum state describes. But how can such a localized particle be correctly described by a spread-out wave function?

The probabilistic use of the wave function first suggested by Born hints at an interpretation that would make the wave function descriptive, rather, of a collection, or "ensemble," of systems, in the manner reminiscent of the role of probability distributions over possible microstates of systems in the statistical mechanics described in Chapter 3. Such an interpretation is also suggested by the most obvious reading of the Projection Postulate. If the wave function is a probabilistic description of a collection of systems or, in related interpretation, a representation of our partial knowledge of the full state of an individual system, then the reason seems clear for dropping one wave function in favor of that corresponding to a system whose exact value for a given observable is known as soon as that value of the observable has been obtained in a measurement. If measurement increases our specific knowledge about a particular system and if the wave function is relative to that knowledge, it is no wonder that a kind of nondynamic "collapse" of the wave function occurs upon measurement.

But this interpretation too is fraught with difficulties. How do we explain the famous interference effects so paradigmatic of the quantum situation? Partial knowledge of whether the photon went through slit one shouldn't "interfere" with partial knowledge that it went through slit two. Interference phenomena are characteristic, rather, of real, spread-out physical waves. There are other difficulties with the simple ensemble or partial-knowledge interpretation of the quantum wave function as well. The normal supplement to thinking of a representation as being "partial," in the manner of a statistical ensemble description of a system, is to entertain the notion that further description is possible; the further description will locate the specific system as a member of a more restrictive collection of systems. Indeed, the normal expectation is that there will be a description of a system that pins it down as the unique member of the "unit class" of one and only one physical system. Thus, for example, if in statistical mechanics we have a description of a system as being a member of a collection of systems characterized by their common temperature, we think that more-complete descriptions of the systems are possible, the ultimate one being that which specified exactly the full microstate of the system at any given time.

But Bohr was insistent that the quantum state of a specific system was a *complete* description of the state of that system. Although such a description specified only probabilities for the outcomes of the various observations that could be performed on the system, it was the "finest" description possible of the system. If this is so, then thinking of the wave function as characterizing a collection or characterizing partial knowledge in the sense of traditional interpretations of probability is misleading. The question of whether Bohr was right remains controversial. Nevertheless, as we shall see, many results have shown that if Bohr is wrong, it will not be a trivial matter to explain in exactly what manner a quantum description could be filled in to give a fuller description of the state of an individual system. Some questions that arise here involve the possibility of further describing the state of a system in traditional classical terms. Is it possible, for example, to think of a particle in a quantum state that is a superposition of two spin states as actually having one of the component spins, although it is unknown to us which one? Other debates concern the possibility of filling in quantum description of a system with a more detailed characterization of the system sufficient to pin it down in a nonstatistical manner, even in a way that eschews the classical descriptive terms. For the moment, it suffices to say that neither a simple interpretation of the quantum state of a system as a traditional physically spread-out state like a classical wave, nor a simpleminded interpretation of it as a traditional probability measure of a collection specified by only partial knowledge of the state of a system, seems to do justice to the role the quantum state plays in the theory.

The quantum theory makes use not only of the newly introduced quantum states but of the older classical states as well. Bohr interprets the wave function as specifying the probabilities of outcomes upon measurements of various quantities. But, as Bohr points out, these outcomes are specified in the older classical terms. A particle comes out of the Stern-Gerlach apparatus used to determine its spin component either "definitely in the up beam" or "definitely in the down beam." A photon that has gone through the two-slit apparatus is finally located as having impinged in some definite region or other of the photographic screen. Alternatively, if detectors had been placed at the slits, the photon is detected as "definitely having gone through slit one and triggered detector one" or "definitely having gone through slit two and triggered detector two."

But if all physical states are properly described according to the laws of quantum mechanics—and the theory does claim this universality— then how can there be room in the universe for measuring instruments whose detection states are characterized in old-fashioned classical terms? Are there really two different kinds of systems in the world, quantum systems and classical systems, the former to be described in wave-function terms and the latter in classical terms? Or is the practice of characterizing the results of measurements in classical terms something to be "explained away" in the context of quantum theory as, perhaps, a kind of legitimate but misleading "approximative description" of the actual state of the measuring apparatus? If one takes the line that the classical descriptions of measuring apparatus are not a false description of them but, instead, the actual characterization of their true physical state, then the question of whether it might not be legitimate to think of the measured quantum systems as having such classical states arises.

Finally there is the question of the nature of the measurement process. As we noted, the formal theory makes a strict demarcation between the two processes, dynamic evolution and measurement. Suppose we know the quantum state of a system at one time. How are we to determine the quantum state to attribute to it at some later time? If the system is not observed at any point in time between the two times, according to the theory, we are to follow out the evolution of the wave function describing the quantum state of the system by using the famous Schrödinger equation. This equation is the parallel in quantum theory to the dynamical equations of classical dynamics that told us how the classical dynamical state of a system would evolve over time, given that the system was subjected to certain forces and had a specified internal construction. Just as in classical physics, then, there is a kind of "determinism" of the quantum state's evolution. A system subject to specified forces and of a given nature will, if it has a definite quantum state at one time, have at a later time a definite quantum state related to the first by the laws of dynamics.

But this is not so if the system is measured in the time interval! For, the theory says, when measurement takes place, dynamic evolution is to be ignored and, instead, the Projection Postulate is to be applied. The wave function describing the system prior to the measurement is to be discarded, and in its place a wave function is introduced corresponding to the value of the observable quantity obtained in the measurement. (If the measurement doesn't determine the values of all the observable quantities that could be determined for the system, a modified version of the Projection Postulate, Lüder's Rule, is used instead. Like the Projection Postulate, though, it is plainly not a mere instance of ordinary dynamical evolution.)

Now if we could get away with the interpretation of the wave function that made it, like some classical probability distributions, a representation of our partial knowledge of a system, we could understand measurement and the Projection Postulate quite simply. Measurement would be any process that added to our knowledge of the state of the system. No wonder, then, that upon measurement the function describing our partial knowledge of the system would "jump" in the discontinuous manner determined by the Projection Postulate. But, as we have seen, such an interpretation of the wave function fails to do full justice to its other, physical state–like, aspects, such as interference. If we think of the wave function as some sort of physical state of the system, it becomes much harder to understand the place of the peculiar process called measurement in the formalism and to understand the nondynamical change of the wave function in measurement processes.

What, from this latter perspective, differentiates a measurement process from any other ordinary dynamical interaction? How is the system related to a measuring apparatus any different from the system merely physically interacting with some other physical system? That interaction has a perfectly clear description within the theory. It is one aspect of the dynamics of systems, in this case, the dynamics describing two systems initially independent of each other and later in physical interaction. But the evolution of the new joint system (the original system combined with the physical system with which it has come into interaction) is, according to the theory's formalism, nothing like that process described by the Projection Postulate at all. Most crucially, in ordinary dynamical interaction, the "interference" effects of the system's originally being in a superposition of states are preserved when the system interacts with some new physical system. The correlations that characterize the interference process are simply transferred to the new joint system.

But in a measurement process, as described by the Projection Postulate, interference is destroyed. In the "collapse of the wave packet" that the Projection Postulate describes, the interference terms just vanish. An electron described by a wave function spread all over space is, after the electron is measured and found to be in a limited spatial region, described by a wave function confined entirely to that region. A photon described as being in a superposition of coming through slit one and slit two is, after the detector in front of slit one is triggered, described by a "pure" slit-one wave function. Why are measurements different from ordinary physical interactions?

Bohr's Solution and Its Critics

We have earlier noted Bohr's exciting and subtle attempt to do justice to the paradoxical nature of the quantum world. In the Copenhagen Interpretation, measurement is taken as a "primitive" notion. A system interacting with the outside world can be measured and not just enter into dynamical interaction. The results of measurement processes are taken as constituting the real hard facts about the world, and theory is taken as a device whose sole role is to provide correlations between the value based on one measurement process that prepares a system in a given quantum state and the value of some observable quantity upon a later measurement. In between measurements the system is not to be thought of as having some actual but unknown classical values at all. Rather it has merely "potentials" to reveal observable values with specifiable probabilities relative to a chosen measuring apparatus. Because some quantities—complementary ones—are not capable of simultaneous measurement, it is pointless to ask about the probabilities of the system's having such joint, incompatible, values for complementary observables.

But is the Copenhagen Interpretation acceptable? One objection to it originates with Schrödinger and Einstein. Like Einstein, Schrödinger was one of the great inventors of the quantum theory and at the same time one of the most severe critics of its "orthodox" interpreters.

First, remember that for Bohr it is incorrect to think of a system not yet measured as having any classical state, except, perhaps in the unusual situation that the system is certain upon measurement to show one particular value. Next, remember that for Bohr any measurement consists of a quantum system's being measured by an apparatus that must be described in classical terms. Finally, remember that in Bohr's account of measurement, the line between system (described by a quantum state) and apparatus (described by classical states) can be drawn at any level. Although there must be a partition somewhere between measured quantum system and measuring classical apparatus, the line between the one and the other is not something fixed by the physics of the situation but can be taken to be anywhere in the chain from microscopic system to ultimately observed value. Indeed, various consistency results from quantum theory show that the same probabilities for the various outcomes will be inferred whether we take a system A as measured by a complex apparatus $B + C$ or, instead, think of the apparatus C as measuring the complex system $A + B$.

Figure 4.6 Schrödinger's cat. In a sealed box an apparatus is set up in which a particle beam, e, is split into two beams with the probability of a particle going one or the other way being equal. If the first particle follows the route through D_1, a barrel of explosive is set off, destroying a poor cat on top of it. If the first particle goes to D_2, switch S is opened, saving the cat from the possibility of being exploded. How should an observer outside the box and unable to know what has happened in it describe the cat after a period of time in which it is certain that at least one particle has gone to D_1 or one has gone to D_2? According to the Copenhagen Interpretation, the observer should think of the cat not as alive or as dead but, rather, "in a superposition of live and dead states," just as an electron coming out of a left-right Stern-Gerlach machine but undetected must be thought of as in a "superposition of spin-left and spin-right states" until detection. But is such a description of the cat (or of any macroscopic object) tenable? If not, at what point prior to the outside observer's making an observation on what is left inside the box should that observer consider the cat to be "definitely alive" or "definitely dead"?

Now let a box contain a beam-splitting mirror and a weak source of photons. Put detectors in the paths of the device and wire them up so that if detector one fires first, it triggers an explosion by means of an amplified signal that blows up a cat in the box. Moreover, arrange things so that if detector two fires first, the explosive device is disconnected. Schrödinger asks us to consider the following: Until the photon is measured as having been on one path or the other, we must think of it as being in a superposition of having been on both paths, each with associated weight one-half. Now we could take measurement as having occurred as soon as one or the other of the detectors is first triggered. At that point in time, then, the photon will definitely have been on path one or definitely have been on path two. The superposition of path states will collapse to a single pure path state. (See Figure 4.6.)

But we can also think of the measurement as occurring only when we have looked in the sealed box to see what occurred. The line between quantum world and classical apparatus, that is, could be properly drawn with our being measuring apparatus and with the entire contents of the box, including photon source, beam splitter, detectors, amplifiers, explosive devices, circuit-breaking devices, *and the cat*, being all components of a single, complex quantum system. If we draw the line that way, then Bohr's view commits us to believing that until we look in the box, the photon remains in a superposition of path-one and path-two states. But so does the rest of the system coupled to the photon and its detectors remain in a superposition. In other words, until we look in the box, it is incorrect to say that the cat is either alive or dead. Instead we must speak of it as being "in a superposition of live and dead states." However, as Schrödinger implies, such a view of something both macroscopic and animate is an absurdity. It may be possible (if difficult) to think of a photon as in a superposition of path states or an electron in a superposition of spin states, but isn't it just manifestly absurd to think of the cat as neither alive nor dead but "in a combination of both states with equal weight"? Remember now, being in a superposition cannot be interpreted, according to Bohr, as being in one definite state or the other, with our being ignorant of which. It is an actual "combination" of the two states.

Notice, of course, that Schrödinger in no way shows that Bohr's account leads to observations falsified in the world. At the point at which we look at the cat, of course, the wave packet collapses and we find the cat alive or dead. Indeed, Bohr would undoubtedly be happy to swallow the consequences of his theory. All objects in the world obey quantum mechanics, from the smallest to the largest. And so all are capable of the kind of interference effects that force us to regard systems as being in superposition states. Once again, for Bohr these states are only potentialities toward outcomes with given probabilities upon measurement. The cat exists, like the photon when unmeasured, in a state of potential that requires reference to superposition. For, in principle, experiments could be performed that would reveal the interference latent in the cat's state just as we could remove the detectors and substitute a screen revealing the interference latent in the superposition of path states that is the photon's quantum condition.

Idealist Solutions

But for others, it seems absurd to think of the cat as in a superposition of live and dead states. Carrying Schrödinger's suggestion one step further, E. Wigner introduces "Wigner's Friend." Replace the cat in the box with a scientist. According to Bohr, until we look in the box, we should think of the scientist as in a superposition of live and dead states, although, of course, the scientist can—at a time we are thinking of him as in such a superposition—view himself as determinately blown up or not. But, Wigner says, this is absurd. This leads Wigner to a view of measurement and of the world that is quite surprising coming from a physical scientist, but almost inevitable as an optional way to think of the quantum perplexities.

What is special, Wigner asks, about a measurement, as opposed to an ordinary physical interaction of two physical systems? In a real measurement, some measurer must become "aware" of the value determined by the measuring process. Wigner's view reminds us of that of the philosophical dualists, who thought of a human being (and, perhaps, other sentient beings) as a joint creature composed of both a physical body and a mind—a kind of nonphysical entity "attached" to the body, perhaps by mutual causation through the brain. Thus he thinks of a measurement as having taken place when and only when some mind is affected by the system measured. The effect on mind can be very indirect, happening through the means of much intermediate physical apparatus (including the sense organs, nerves, and brain of the body).

But we can't think of measurement as merely a subject's gaining information and hence changing his "partial knowledge function." As we have noted, the view of the wave function as merely a summary of our knowledge of a system and of its collapse upon measurement as just the familiar discontinuous change of a knowledge function when new knowledge is acquired doesn't do justice to the other features of the wave function. These are the interference features that make the wave function seem much more like a knowledge-independent representation of a state of a natural system. For Wigner, rather, measurement is a two-way interaction of mind and physical world. The world causally affects the mind, telling it what the determined measured value of the system is; the world does this by indicating to the mind in which possible state the physical measuring apparatus ended up. But the mind also acts on the world. For the very fact that the physical system is in a definite classical state and no longer in a superposition is an effect of the interaction of mind with matter.

For Wigner, then, the measurement has clearly taken place once the scientist in the box knows whether or not he is being blown up. Presumably, if cats have minds, the same thing is true for Schrödinger's cat. The Bohrian view, which allows even scientists and cats to constitute part of a quantum system relative to an external measurer—such as the scientist outside the closed box—is rejected.

Not surprisingly, Wigner's account of the world, with its dualist metaphysics of physical world and observing minds, is not one that appeals to many. In addition to tolerating what many would consider a quite extravagant metaphysics, the account of measurement offered is itself problematic. The collapse of the wave function caused by the action of mind on physical system is something left unexplained and outside the competence of physics to explain. Along with the lawlike processes of nature governed by the standard laws of physics, in particular, by the dynamical law of evolution given by the Schrödinger equation, one now has an "extraphysical" process in which something from the "outside," the mind of the observer, interferes with the lawlike workings of physical nature. Couldn't we find an account of measurement that avoids going to the lengths tolerated by these idealist accounts, but that also avoids both the introduction of primitive notions of measurement in the manner of Bohr and Bohr's curious ineliminable separation of quantum system from the classical measuring apparatus?

Measurement as a Physical Interaction

One group of approaches looks for the characterization of a measurement process, as distinguished from ordinary physical interactions, not by making it a distinctive kind of process in the metaphysical manner of either the Bohr approach or the idealist approach, but by trying to characterize a measurement interaction as a specific subclass of ordinary physical interactions. Within this school, one group of approaches focuses on the fact that in a measurement process, the quantum system interacts with a "macroscopic" measuring instrument, and in the measuring process, a microfeature of the system being measured is correlated with a macrofeature of the measuring apparatus in a manner that reveals the microquantity's value.

In an operation that detects which slit a particle passes through, for example, the particle may be detected as it comes out of the slit by some electronic discharge device (like a Geiger counter) that amplifies the passage of the particle through the detector. This might work by means of inducing from the passage of the particle a cascade of a large number of charged particles, and by finally revealing the presence of the microscopic particle by a large, macroscopic voltage discharge involving vast numbers of particles acting in concert. In a Stern-Gerlach machine, the particles having differing components of spin in the direction being measured are first separated from each other spatially by macroscopic distances by the inhomogeneous magnetic field of the device. Then they are detected in either the up beam or the down beam by a device similar to the one described above. In the case of Schrödinger's cat, the apparatus reveals the route taken by the particle by amplifying the quantum choice made into macroscopically distinguished states of integral live cat and dispersed, dead, blown-up cat.

There are two important features, then, we must note about measurement. The first is that the final state of the measuring apparatus is one involving large numbers of particles and is identifiable on a macroscopic scale. The other is that the final states of the apparatus are macroscopically distinguishable (they are "pure" and not superposition states) and perfectly correlated with the microscopic states of the quantum system being measured.

Next, this school argues, we must realize that in truth the macroscopic apparatus is, just like the original quantum system, an ordinary physical system in the world. From this point of view the macroscopic system must be describable by quantum theory, and its interaction with the quantum system being measured must be determined by the ordinary quantum laws of the interaction of two physical systems. But at this point the interpretation faces a difficulty. Quantum theory tells us that if one system interacts with another, and if the first system was in a superposition state before the interaction took place, the combined first and second system after interaction has occurred must be in a superposition state. This is true even if the second system was originally in a pure state or in one of the mixed states corresponding to its being in one pure state or another with different degrees of probability in the older sense. If a left-spinning particle interacts with an up-down spin-detecting apparatus, the particle enters the interaction in a superposition of up and down spin states. The ultimate state of the particle-plus-measuring-apparatus system must be, then, a superposition state. It is the superposition of the two pure states—"particle is spin up and machine says spin up" and "particle is spin down and machine says spin down." But if this is so, how can the interaction represent a measurement in which the outcome is supposed to be either a definite "particle is up and machine says up" or a definite "particle is down and machine says down" state?

Here an attempt to solve this is frequently offered in terms of the fact that a measurement interaction may be viewed for various purposes as if the final superposition doesn't exist at all, even though, properly speaking, the measurement interaction does result in a superposition state. Instead, the final superposition state can be replaced by a related mixture state. The fundamental idea is that although the interaction of system and measuring apparatus must, according to the laws of quantum mechanics, retain those interference-like correlations that distinguish a superposition of states from a mixture of the two states, this interference and its effects may be in practice irrecoverable after the interaction has taken place.

What is it that tells us that the state of a spin-left particle sent through an up-down spin machine and not detected must be described later as in a superposition of up and down states and not in a mixture of them? If one were to examine the output of the up-down spin machine for up-down spin, one would discover half the particles with spin up and half with spin down. This is the prediction one gets from describing the particle as being either in a superposition or in a mixture of up and down spin states with equal weight. But if one sent this output into a left-right spin detector, the particles would all come out left. That is what the superposition description predicts, but not what the mixture description predicts. That reveals the remaining interference.

But if the particle coming out of the up-down machine is detected as it comes out, it will be impossible in practice to reveal any difference between the mixture of "particle up, apparatus says up" and "particle down, apparatus says down" states and their superposition. To do so would require a process that kept exact track of all the microstates of all the particles in the causal chain initiated by the interaction of the system particle and the detector. Such an ability to reveal the remaining interference correlation is beyond any real possibility. Hence for predictive purposes about the probabilities of outcomes of further experiments involving the particle or the apparatus, the mixture description will suffice as an approximation of the true superposition description. The interference correlation has dissipated itself into the vast numbers of degrees of freedom of the innumerable particles that make up the macroscopic apparatus. This dissipation occurs in the amplifying process that reveals the microstate of the particle being measured. So superposition, although actually present, can be treated as if it vanishes when measurement takes place.

This way of looking at the measurement process has many virtues. One need not introduce minds to interact with the physical world while one remains outside it and outside the ability of a comprehensive physics to describe the world. Nor does one require the curious flexible bifurcation of the world into system and measuring apparatus that the Copenhagen Interpretation demands. Instead, there is only one physical world with ordinary physical interactions in it. Some of these interactions have the features necessary for the true quantum description to be replaceable by a false but adequate approximation. These features are the macroscopicity and complexity of the measuring apparatus and the appropriate perfect correlation between its indicator states and the microscopic states of the system being measured. Measurement is, on this view, just one special kind of physical interaction and, when exactly described, falls under the laws of quantum dynamics and not outside them, as in the idealist or Copenhagen interpretive views.

But this way of looking at measurement has problems of its own. The arguments are designed to show that one can replace a superposition wave function with a mixture wave function for predictive purposes when a measured quantum system interacts with a sufficiently large and complex measuring apparatus. But the measurement of an individual quantum system results in a system determined to have, not the mixture wave function, but the pure wave function of one of its components. If we measure the up-down spin of a particle originally in a state that is a superposition of up and down states, we discover the particle upon measurement to be definitely up or definitely down. This is the "collapse of the wave packet." To argue that the original superposition of up and down states, now converted to a superposition of combined system and apparatus states, can be replaced by a mixture state seems to be implicitly taking the line that the wave function ought to be thought of as a description, not of a single particle, but of a collection of particles. For it is to a collection of measured particles, some now definitely up and some definitely down, that the mixture state is properly attributed.

But how can this implicitly ensemble view of the wave function be reconciled with the facts that seemed to indicate that each individual particle had the quality of a superposition wave function? Of course, the reply can be made that these curious interference-like correlations of a particle, the things that incline us to say that each individual photon "goes through both slits," remain characteristic of the quantum world. What is being argued for here, it will be said, is that we can understand why in a measurement process we frame our theory to speak as if the interference disappears, when we know that it really does not. The argument is, once again, that the size and complexity of the measuring apparatus assure us that the actual existing remaining interference potentials can never be observationally realized by any practicable experiment.

There is, perhaps, a deeper objection, but one that has at least a potential answer. Born, puzzled over what the wave function meant, offered the famous insight that its intensity was to be taken as the probability of some value obtaining for the system. Faced with the questions about how quantum probabilities differed so radically from classical probabilities, Bohr offered the subtle emendation of Born's insight and spoke of probabilities relative to a choice of one or another of a set of complementary measuring procedures. But these interpretations, and the idealist ones as well, presuppose that at some point results of measurements are truly characterizable in classical terms. For we can interpret the quantum state as "potential" for the system to reveal classical aspects only by retaining the classical concepts for describing the outcomes of measurements.

The interpretation that we are concerned with now, however, must handle the role of classical concepts in the interpretation of the theory in a more complex way. That is because, according to this interpretation, there really are no states of the physical world correctly describable in classical terms. The full state of the world—system and measuring apparatus as well—is always to be characterized in the most correct way in terms of a quantum wave function. But if the wave function is itself to be understood in terms of probabilities of states classically described, how can this dilemma be resolved?

A story can be told that will perhaps explain how it is that we can come to understand the meaning of the quantum state function through a route that "in passing" involves classical concepts, even if, in our final understanding, these classical concepts have no legitimate role in characterizing any states of the physical world. The story will have to be that our early, prequantum, understanding of the world is a false one, but its adequacy for many purposes in characterizing the states of the world can itself be ultimately explained by the relation of this false picture to the true quantum picture. This relation is to be grounded on the theory of the measurement process noted above, where the classical characterization of the measuring apparatus is explained as a "false but adequate manner of speaking." The story will tell us that, based on a conceptual apparatus that is part of and dependent on a false view of the world, we construct the correct quantum theory, initially understanding its concepts by fitting them into the earlier classical framework. Then, having the quantum apparatus in our grasp, we reconstruct the earlier classical framework as the false but useful picture of the world that it is. Having used the classical framework as a ladder, we throw it away when we have reached our goal.

Perhaps. But there are many questions here. Do we really believe that objects are really always in superposition states? Do we believe that there is really nothing to the cat's being, truly, fully alive or fully dead, but that it remains always in a superposition of states? How are we truly to understand such a claim? Will there be an ultimate retreat to the idea that the classical concepts are still adequate to characterize what we directly experience as some sort of feature of our immediate awareness, if not of any real physical object? This would make the classical states something like the "secondary qualities" of traditional Lockean metaphysics, that is, features that are truly predictable only of the contents of direct awareness and not of physical objects "as they are in themselves."

Kochen's Interpretation and Stochastic Interpretations

It should be noted that there are other interpretations of the measurement process that share with the one we have just been discussing its basic claim that measurement is to be thought of as one species of physical interaction in general and not, as in Bohr's view or the idealist view, as a process distinctive from ordinary dynamical evolution of systems. But not all such views of the measurement process will explain the adequacy of the Projection Postulate, that is, the usefulness of viewing the wave function as collapsing and losing all its interference terms, as a result of the size and complexity of the measuring apparatus and the consequent dissipation of interference into irrecoverability.

S. Kochen, for example, has offered another account of the place of measurement in dynamics. Once more, it is in the nature of the interaction of measured system and measuring apparatus, as described by quantum dynamics, that the ground is found for rationalizing the place of the Projection Postulate in the theory. No role is retained for a classically described measuring apparatus, as in Bohr's theory, nor is there any invocation of some special realm of being outside physics and, hence, outside quantum mechanics, as in the idealist interpretations. But the macroscopic size and complexity of measuring apparatus don't play a crucial role either. The nature of the interaction establishing correlations between the pure states of measured system and measuring apparatus is, however, still important.

Kochen's interpretation rests upon an important theorem of quantum mechanics. Let two systems interact. There will then exist properties of each of the two component systems that have a special nature. If the wave function for the combined system is expanded out in terms of pure states of the individual systems that are based on these special properties, then that wave function will have its interference terms disappear. In terms of these properties, then, the wave function for the combined system will be like one characterizing a "mixture." The special properties are determined by the nature of the component systems and by the nature of their interaction. In many cases there will be only one such family of special properties. Although the tradition in quantum theory has been to express the wave function of the interacting system in terms of the pure states relevant to the isolated system and apparatus by themselves, this new expression chooses a "basis" for representing the state dependent upon the nature of the interaction. (The mathematics here is reminiscent of the ability in classical physics to represent coupled dynamical systems in "normal coordinates." If two pendulums are coupled by a weak spring, for instance, energy travels back and forth from one pendulum to the other, leading to time-varying states of the individual systems. But there exist new coordinates in which the motion can be expressed. These depend upon the interaction. The state of the entire coupled system is stationary when viewed in this new, more complex, coordinate representation.)

The idea of this new interpretation is that the system and apparatus when in interaction can be viewed, relative to each other, as having one or another of the definite values of the properties that form the basis for this special way of representing the wave function. Thus, a spinning particle interacting with the Stern-Gerlach up-down measuring machine can be said to be definitely up or definitely down relative to the measuring apparatus with which it is interacting. Similarly, the machine can be said to be definitely in a "reveals up" state or definitely in a "reveals down" state relative to the particle whose spin it is measuring. It is the dynamics of the interaction that determines in any measurement interaction what features of system and apparatus can be claimed to be definite.

But even this definiteness is only a definiteness of system *relative* to apparatus and of apparatus *relative* to system. The particle is definitely up or down as "witnessed" by the measuring apparatus and the apparatus definitely saying up or down as witnessed by the system measured. In this new interpretation there is no "collapse of the wave packet" in the sense that is intended by the Bohrian or idealist interpretation. In this aspect it is similar to the interpretation discussed earlier that relies upon the size and complexity of the measuring apparatus. Quantum mechanics has universal reign, and the theorems that tell us that in interaction superposition never really disappears remain valid. One can see this if one considers the state of the combined measured system and measuring apparatus relative to the entire outside environment, that is, relative to the universe exclusive of the interacting particle and measuring device being considered. As witnessed by the outside world, the combined particle and apparatus has the full quantum state of an interacting system, with all the correlational interference features that entails.

Kochen calls the witnessing of the combined system-plus-apparatus by the outside world "passive witnessing," as there is no dynamical coupling of system-plus-apparatus to outside world. The witnessing of system by apparatus and of apparatus by system he calls "active witnessing," as there is a dynamic coupling between system and apparatus. It can be true, then, that a spin-left particle, after an interaction with an up-down measuring machine has either a definite spin up relative to the measuring device or a definite spin down relative to that device. And the device will have a definite up or down reading relative to the particle. Nonetheless, the information that the particle was originally spin left remains, and the interference of the basic states for the combined system (up for particle and says up for machine, down for particle and says down for machine), interference that contains the information that the particle was originally spin left, remains and is in principle revealable by a sufficiently subtle observation.

This interpretation, then, attempts to do justice to our intuition that after the measurement, the particle and apparatus have definite states. They do if the states are those appropriate to the dynamics of the interaction and if the particle and apparatus are thought to have these pure states as witnessed by each other. And it attempts to do justice as well as to the quantum mechanical claim that superposition is never destroyed. That is because superposition remains present in the state of the combined system and measuring apparatus as witnessed by the outside world. Of course, there is much more to be said in the way of trying to show that this interpretation will do justice to all of the observational facts without invoking the radical dichotomy of measurement and dynamical interaction of the Bohrian viewpoint.

Some other recent interpretations work by postulating a realm of physical process going on at a level below that of the quantum state. At this deeper level, it is proposed that a kind of random, or stochastic, activity occurs. With an appropriately clever formulation of such additional physics describing new physical processes, one can hope for a theory in which in certain circumstances the underlying randomlike physical process can "drive" a system originally in a quantum state that is a superposition state into a quantum state that is "almost" a pure state corresponding to a single value for the measured quantity. Naturally, these physical circumstances are supposed to be the ones that correspond to what we take to be a measurement process in the orthodox account. In all these theories, however, the new state is not really the completely collapsed wave state that quantum mechanics predicts after a measurement has taken place. Such a theory must, then, also contain elements that tell us why it is legitimate to adopt the Projection Postulate and assume that the state after measurement is a pure state, when it really is not. Here the usual arguments are made to the effect that for all practical purposes the predictions made using the real state and the approximating pure state will be the same.

"Many Worlds" Interpretations

Still another interpretation, originally offered by H. Everett and J. Wheeler, tries to do justice to the puzzling features of measurement by advocating a new metaphysics for the world. Unlike Bohr's radical metaphysical revisionism, one that denies in some sense an objective reality to the physical world altogether, retaining a reality only relative to a choice of measuring device, the new metaphysics is objectivist. But the real world it posits is one that seems to our intuitions strange indeed.

In the Bohrian account of the measurement process, there is a "throwing away" of part of a wave function whenever a measurement is performed. The particle, spinning left, comes into the up-down measuring machine in a superposition of up and down states. But once the measurement has taken place, the particle is either definitely up (and the measuring device says definitely up) or the particle is definitely down (and the machine says definitely down). But according to quantum dynamics, just prior to the "collapse of the wave function" the particle-and-apparatus complex was in a superposition of combined "up and says up" and "down and says down" states. Suppose the measurement gives the value "up" for the particle. What happened to the "down and says down" component of the wave function? It simply vanished from the world. And with it, the interference-generated possibilities latent in its joint presence with the other component of the wave function vanished as well.

But Everett and Wheeler take it that both components of the wave function continue to exist after the measurement has taken place. How can this be? When a particle is detected after coming out of an up-down spin-measuring machine, isn't it either definitely up or definitely down? How could it be both? The answer given by this interpretation is that in each measurement the universe splits into a multiplicity of worlds, one for each possible outcome of the measurement process. There is a world in which the particle comes out of the machine in the up-spin state. In that world, the machine also gives the spin-up reading, for the detection states of the measuring apparatus are, once again, supposed to be exactly correlated with the value of the measured quantity in question. But along with the world having a spin-up particle and a measuring device giving an up reading, there is also a world with a spin-down particle and a machine reading spin down. The wave function of the spin-left particle entering the machine and then interacting with it could be written as a superposition of "spin up and says up" and "spin down and says down" states. In the "many worlds" interpretation we are looking at now, each component of this superposition represents what goes on in some of the many actual worlds that "split" from one universe each time a measurement takes place.

Naturally the interpretation requires a way of handling the probability of outcomes. It also requires various consistency results to try to convince us that the picture of measurement it is providing will give observational results consistent with the known results summarized in the standard formalism of quantum mechanics. Naturally, also, the interpretation is not without its critics. For one thing, the metaphysical picture is, not surprisingly, considered grotesque and extravagant by many. After all, we experience only one of the possible resultant states as the outcome of a measurement, not a manifold of all possible outcomes. That is why we spoke of "collapse of the wave packet" in the first place. What reason, other than a preference for symmetry over experience, do we really have for supposing that all the other outcomes occurred as well, hidden from us because they are experienced by other "branches" of us that exist in other branches of the universe? The theory also has its internal problems as to when the splitting takes place. Does it occur with every interaction? Only upon measurement interactions? If the latter, what distinguishes them from ordinary dynamical evolutions in a way that would justify the metaphysics of universe splitting? And along what dimensions does it take place? A wave function can be decomposed into different components. Do all of these decompositions represent splittings? How? Or is there a preferred decomposition that governs how the universe splits, say, determined in the manner that the Kochen interaction interpretation determines the special measured property and measurement property?

In recent years some have combined the "many worlds" view and the idealist view of measurement into a "many minds" interpretation (D. Albert and B. Loewer). Here there is only one physical world, described always by the evolving wave function that follows the evolution dictated by the Schrödinger equation and that never collapses. But any mind taking in the value of a measured quantity splits into a manifold of minds, each of which experiences one only of all the possible outcomes of the measurement process. Once again, consistency proofs are offered to try to convince us that in such matters as communicating our measurement results to others and receiving communications from them (mediated through the physical world) or in repeating measurements, we will obtain the familiar predicted probabilistic results of the quantum theory.

Quantum Logics

We have been exploring approaches designed to explain the curious features of the world implied by quantum mechanics; these approaches rely upon programs that explain the phenomena by looking at metaphysical features of the world. Whether the programs posit a flexible duality of quantum system and classical measuring apparatus, as does Bohr's theory; a remaining role for classical concepts in the realm of the mind outside of physical reality, as do the idealist approaches; a view of the world as one in which quantum dynamics reigns universally, as do the approaches that rely upon the size and complexity of the measuring apparatus or Kochen's interaction interpretation; or a radical expansion of our ontology to explain the phenomena, as do the many worlds–type approaches; all seek the resolution in some modification of our traditional views on the nature of the physical systems of the world.

A somewhat different approach looks for the resolution of the problems in a modification of our traditional thought concerning some of
the most pervasive and general modes we have for describing the world.
Perhaps a radical reinterpretation of the most general schemata we have
for assimilating phenomena in the world will be needed, it is argued,
to make sense of the mysterious quantum features we have noted.

One such approach emphasizes the important role that probability
plays in the theory. Some of the puzzling quantum features can be
summarized by pointing out how radically quantum probabilities differ
in their operation from the more familiar probabilities of classical physics. Take, for example, the two-slit experiment. We think of light as
composed of localizable photons because detectors placed at the slits
determine that all of the light energy goes through either one slit or
the other, photon by photon, and never through both. Shouldn't we,
then, think of the probability of a photon's arriving at the screen as the
result of two "independent" processes, the photon's arriving at x after
going through slit one and the photon's arriving at x after going through
slit two? But then the classical rules of probability lead us to expect the
probability of a photon's arriving at x if it goes through either slit one
or slit two to be the sum of the two separate probabilities. Of course,
it is not, for we have the now-familiar interference effects. Perhaps,
then, we ought to reject our traditional rules for combining probabilities
conditional on independent causes.

Another deviant feature of probability in quantum theory can be seen
when we think about so-called joint distributions. Suppose we have a
population of human beings whose heights are distributed according
to some probability distribution for heights. And suppose also that there
is a distribution of eye color, again characterizable by a probability distribution. Then it makes sense to ask about the joint distribution for
height and eye color together. If there is a certain probability of a human being over six feet tall, and a certain probability of a human having
blue eyes, then there is a joint probability of being a blue-eyed person
over six feet tall.

But, as we know, such joint probability distributions are not always
possible in quantum mechanics. There may be a probability for a particle's being found in a particular region of space and also a probability
distribution that determines the particle's momentum being found within
a specified range of momentum values. But there will not be a joint
probability for the particle's being found both in a definitive spatial range
and in a definitive momentum range. Bohr handles this by pointing
out the physical impossibility of making the position and momentum
measurements simultaneously. Position and momentum are, in his terms,
complementary to one another. And for complementary observables,
one cannot expect from quantum mechanics well-defined joint probability distribution functions. Now the suggestion is being made that
perhaps this absence of joint probability functions can be grounded in
some new, nonstandard, theory of probability.

An even deeper diagnosis of the conceptual problems of quantum mechanics seeks the core of the issues in questions about the very nature of logic itself. Logic gives us the basic rules governing the entailment relations our propositions about the world bear to one another. Standard logic tells us, for example, that a proposition and its negation cannot both be true, that one or the other must be true, that if two propositions are true, their conjunction is true as well, and so on. Could a revision of our standard logic itself help us to make sense of the quantum phenomena? We have thought of logic as being something immutable and independent of our experimental knowledge of the world. But, after all, we thought of geometry that way until the past two centuries as well. Perhaps logic is just as much an empirical matter as chemistry or as geometry is now taken to be.

One suggestion in this vein was made by H. Reichenbach, who thought that by allowing for propositions that were neither true nor false some of the features of quantum systems could be well represented. A statement about the position of a particle was either true or false after a position measurement had been performed. But for a particle in a quantum state between measurements in which position had no definite value with probability one, could we not say that statements about position had "indeterminate" truth value, being neither true nor false?

A much more fruitful suggestion for a logical revision to help us with quantum mechanics has its origins in the work of G. Birkhoff and J. von Neumann. Their work has both an uncontroversial and a controversial aspect. The uncontroversial one comes from a general project of trying to discern in quantum theory the most basic features that lead to the puzzling quantum phenomena. We have already noted that the theory was originally developed in two formalisms that at first appeared to have little to do with each other, Heisenberg's matrix mechanics and Schrödinger's wave mechanics. Schrödinger showed the formal equivalence of the two theories, and Dirac and von Neumann went on to present the theory in a more abstract manner, which took from the two approaches their common core.

But even these standard formulations of quantum theory might contain, along with the essential elements, elements that are inessential and merely artifacts of a particular way of presenting the theory. Could we find a way of pinning down the most essential elements of the theory, those that would have to appear in any "representation" of the physical facts?

Birkhoff and von Neumann pointed out that one way of doing this is to focus on the relations between states of systems, relations that could be considered a kind of "logic" of propositions about the system. Suppose a particle will definitely, i.e., with probability equal to one, pass through a filter that lets only spin-up particles through. Then we can say that "spin up" is true of it. If a particle will definitely pass through a filter that lets both spin-up particles and spin-down particles through, we will say that "spin up qor spin down" is true of it. If a particle will definitely pass through both a p filter and an s filter we will say "p qand s" is true of it.

Now consider the "distributive law" of traditional logic, the law that says that if p is true of something and if r or s is true of something, then either p and r are true of the system or p and s are true of it. If a man is tall and either blue-eyed or brown-eyed, then the man is either tall and blue-eyed or tall and brown-eyed. Does 'qand' distribute over 'qor' the way 'and' distributes over 'or'? It does not. Consider a particle that is "spin left qand (spin up qor spin down)." As all the relevant particles pass through the (up qor down) machine, "up qor down" is true of every particle. The particles that are "spin left qand (spin up qor spin down)" are, then, just the definitely spin-left particles. But no particle will have probability one of going through a spin-left machine and probability one of going through a spin-up machine. For spin left and spin up are complementary properties, and no system can definitely have both of these properties at one time. The same is true of spin left and spin down. So nothing is "spin left qand spin up" and nothing is "spin left qand spin down," and thus nothing is "(spin left qand spin up) qor (spin left qand spin down)." Although lots of particles are "spin left qand (spin up qor spin down)," i.e., all that are spin left, no particles are "(spin left qand spin up) qor (spin left qand spin down)." Therefore, 'qand' does not distribute over 'qor' the way 'and' distributes over 'or'.

One can formulate a logic of propositions of the ordinary sort using ordinary 'not', ordinary 'and', and ordinary 'or'. Such a logic has the distributive property noted above and is called a Boolean algebra. One can formulate a formal structure of the kind appropriate to 'qand' and 'qor' (along with an appropriate quantum negation). It is called an orthocomplemented modular lattice. (Actually the structure needed for quantum mechanics is, for reasons not of interest here, a little weaker, a "weak" modular lattice.) The uncontroversial use of such a new "logic" is this: One can capture the essential elements of the superposition structure that is so characteristic of quantum systems by representing the structure of propositions about quantum systems as a modular lattice. Then one can explain why the standard formulation of quantum mechanics works as well as it does by showing that it "represents" the lattice of propositions. (In a parallel fashion, one can justify the introduction of classical phase space in classical mechanics as a representation of the Boolean algebra of propositions about classical systems.)

Matters become more controversial, indeed very controversial, when the proposal is made (at one time by H. Putnam, for example) that quantum "logic" ought to be interpreted as logic in the full sense. The idea here is that just as general relativity showed us that the Euclidean geometry once thought to hold of the world was actually false and had to be replaced on empirical grounds by non-Euclidean geometry of spacetime, so quantum mechanics tells us that the standard, Boolean, logic we were used to is incorrect as the logic of the world. The empirical facts lead us to realize that the true logic of the world is that characterized by the nondistributive logic of quantum mechanics and not the distributive logic we thought correctly described the relations among propositions about the world. From this point of view, 'qand' really is 'and' and 'qor' is 'or'. It is just that some things we thought true about 'and' and 'or' are false, with other truths taking their place.

It is easy to see why such a view would have an appeal. Consider a beam of particles, all of which were prepared in the spin-left state. The beam was then sent through an up-down spin-measuring machine with both the up and down channels open. The emerging beams were then recombined. We would like to say of this beam that it is a definite spin-left beam. We would also like to say of the particles in it that they are either spin up or spin down. But we don't want to say of any particle in the beam that it is either "spin left and spin up" or "spin left and spin down," for spin left and spin up are complementary properties, as are spin left and spin down. So no particle can be definitely spin left and definitely spin up and no particle can be definitely spin left and definitely spin down.

But in quantum logic we can affirm that the particles in the beam are all spin left, and that each particle in the beam is "either spin up or spin down," as long as we read the 'and' as 'qand' and the 'or' as 'qor'. Paradox is avoided because, given the nondistributivity of 'qand' over 'qor', saying that each particle is "spin left and (either spin up or spin down)" with these new readings for the connectives does not imply that we are committed to the truth of any particle in the beam being "spin left and spin up" or "spin left and spin down."

But does quantum mechanics really show us that we ought to replace our standard logic with a new logic? And does doing so really eliminate the paradoxical aspects of the quantum world? One objection is that although 'qand' and 'qor' play a useful role, it would be grossly misleading to think of them as replacing 'and' and 'or'. One problem is that 'and' and 'or' in their traditional meanings still play a role in the quantum description of the world. A mixture beam of particles that came through the up-down machine, particles that have been detected as they emerged from the appropriate channels of the up-down machine prior to the beams' being recombined, is one in which the particles are correctly described as being "either spin up or spin down" with 'or' receiving its classical meaning. Only the superposition beam of the particles that went through the channels undetected and then merged into the recombined beam is correctly described as "spin up qor spin down." So it is misleading to think that in giving a quantum picture of the world 'qand' and 'qor' replace, rather than supplement, 'and' and 'or'. Another standard objection to the replacement thesis is that the argumentation used in the discussion itself assumes the rules of standard logic.

Even internally, in its attempt to reconstruct the quantum description of the world, the logical revisionist approach has its difficulties. It is true that in quantum logic 'p qand (r qor s)' is not equivalent to '(p qand r) qor (p qand s)'. But even in quantum logic the latter *entails* the former, that is, if the latter is true, the former must be true as well. It is only in the direction from former to latter that the entailment doesn't hold. Now suppose we apply standard probability theory to our new logic. It is a basic result of probability theory that if t entails w, then the probability of w is at least as great as that of t. After all, if t's being true guarantees that w is true, surely it is at least as probable that w is the case as it is that t is the case.

In the two-slit case in quantum theory, this connection between entailment and probability would seem to suggest, given quantum logic and standard probability theory, that the probability that a particle lands at a point x on the screen, given that the two slits were open, should be at least as great as the probability that it lands at x, given that one or the other of the slits is open, but not both. The former probability is the probability assigned to the assertion 'lands at x and either came through slit one or came through slit two'. The latter probability is that of 'either lands at x and came through slit one or else lands at x and came through slit two'. And, once again, this latter phenomenon entails the former. But the phenomenon of interference allows for the probability of landing at x when both slits are open to be *less* than the probability of landing at x given one of the slits open, much less than the sum of the probabilities derived from the two slits' individually being open. This at least seems to indicate that quantum logic, by itself, won't resolve all our dilemmas about the quantum paradoxes.

Summary

We have now surveyed, in a very quick and superficial manner, a variety of the attempts to "make sense" of the peculiar nature of the world revealed by the quantum theory. The reader should realize that each of the interpretations noted here is a subtle and sometimes rather complex attempt to do justice to the range of facts that quantum theory reveals to us. Each interpretation needs careful examination of its virtues and of its critical weaknesses before it can be judged adequate or inadequate to the task it has taken on.

The very range of questions that remain without definitive answers is intimidating. What, exactly, is the role of classical concepts in the quantum description of the world? Are they the primitive and ineliminable concepts needed to describe the part of the world on the measurement side of a flexible "cut" between quantum system and classical measuring apparatus? Are they the ineliminable terms by which the experience of minds outside of the physical realm is to be described? Or are those classical concepts the false, but usefully fictitious, ways that are legitimately applied to describe truly quantum states in special circumstances—where the concepts serve to "approximately" characterize states of systems? Further, to what extent can they be applied to systems between measurements? Are they totally inapplicable to these systems, or is there some way in which we can legitimately think of systems in their evolution as characterized by classical values, even if these are unknown to us?

And what is the nature of the quantum state represented by the wave function? Is it a characterization of individual systems or only of a collection of systems? Is it the characterization of some real physical aspect of the world, or should we think of it, instead, as a kind of intermediate calculating device, not representing some physical reality? Given the role of that wave function in calculating probabilities of measurement outcomes, can it be thought of as something very much like a pre-quantum probability, say, a measure of proportion in a collection or degree of rational belief? Or do the interference phenomena make it clear, rather, that it is something more like a physical wave function? Further, is the quantum state of a system relative to a particular measurement process, as Bohr insists?

What about the peculiar measurement process? Must it be thought of as an ineliminable component of the theory, not in any way assimilable to ordinary dynamic evolutions or interactions of systems? Is the "collapse of the wave packet" a description of a real physical phenomenon or something like the change in a classical probability distribution when the agent's knowledge base changes? Exactly what characterizes those situations that are measurements, as opposed to those that are ordinary physical interactions? Is some Bohrian distinction between system and classical apparatus the clue? Is the presence of a "mind" acting on the world essential? Or is the measurement process just a special instance of a standard quantum interaction characterized either by the size and complexity of one of the interacting systems or by the special nature of the interaction relative to some preferred property of system and apparatus? Must we posit a radical new ontology of pluralizing universes to do justice to the facts about measurement?

Plainly, there is a complex of interconnected questions here. Developing the questions themselves in detail has thrown much light on just how peculiar the quantum picture of the world really is. Understanding some of the interpretations of measurement requires delving deeply into both the observational facts about the quantum world and the formalism of the theory that attempts to do justice to these facts. The reader who goes on to probe the more detailed, and sometimes formally quite sophisticated, literature on these issues ought to remember, however, to keep certain basic facts in mind. It is always a good idea to keep reminding oneself of the fundamental peculiarities of the basic experiments. Light going through a two-slit screen shows an interference pattern easily explained if the light were a spread-out wave that passed its energy through both of the two slits. The individual parts of the wave then recombine on the far side of the slit screen. Yet every experiment designed to detect the energy of the light finds that energy in a localized form. Detectors placed at the slits show photons passing through one slit or the other, never through both simultaneously. The light absorbed on the photographic film always reveals itself in the interaction of one photon with one silver iodide molecule, never a spread-out wave of energy. Electrons too, when detected, reveal themselves as localized particles. Yet when electrons are diffracted off a crystal lattice, even if they are diffracted only one at a time, the diffracted beam received at the detectors reveals the typical interference pattern expected from a wave interacting with a diffraction grating. How can each individual electron, if it is just a "point" particle, "know" on meeting the crystal that it is interacting with a spatially distributed regular array of scattering atoms in the crystal lattice?

It is facts like these and their analogues for other features, such as the interference effects noted in spin-measuring experiments, that require the radical revision of our physical formalism from that of classical physics to that of quantum mechanics. It is no wonder that such peculiar facts require not a revision of detail, say, by modifying some of the laws of forces governing systems, but a radical rethinking of what it is to be a system in the world, what it is for such a system to have value, and what it is for value to be revealed by a measurement process. As we shall see in the rest of the chapter, this is not the end of the mysteries with which quantum theory presents us.

The Problem of Hidden Variables and Determinism

Determinism and Indeterminism

The influence of the Newtonian mechanistic dynamical picture of the world led to a new emphasis on an old doctrine, determinism. The idea of determinism—that the state of the world at one time and the laws of nature together completely fix the state of the world at all later times—is hardly new. Ideas of that sort had been part of ancient Greek speculation. But the model of a system of particles interacting with each other by forces in such a way that a given initial condition of the system generated its later condition for all time in the future, following out Newton's famous laws of motion, provided renewed impetus for this deterministic view of the world. The physicist Laplace's famous statement to the effect that were he to know the state of the world at one time, he could infer its state for all future times represents this view.

Naturally such a doctrine had its disturbing consequences as well. If, as T. S. Eliot puts it, "time past and time future are in time present, and time present in time past," if all that is to be is already fixed by that which has been, where is there a role in the universe for "free choice"? How can our decision making, determining for us as it does—at least to a degree—what our future life will be, be thought of itself as anything but the working out of the state of the world prior even to our birth, something, surely, not in our control? I will have nothing more to say about those much debated philosophical issues.

Let us look more closely at determinism. Even in classical physics, it is far from clear that a simpleminded determinism can be said with any assurance to hold of the world. In the case of Newtonian particle mechanics, there are possibilities of multiparticle collisions. If the particles are thought of as point particles with the usual force laws holding, we cannot, in general, project the state of the world future to the collision from the state prior to the collision. There is also the possibility, at any time, of particles "coming in from infinity" in such a way as to make the state at a later time not determinable from a sufficiently earlier state. In general relativistic contexts, issues of the complexity of the topology of spacetime may even make the notion of "the state of the entire world" at a time dubious. The study of the possibility of "Cauchy surfaces", i.e., of world states "at one time" sufficient to determine world states at all later times, is an intricate theoretical issue. Again, as we saw in Chapter 3, there is the issue of radical instability of motion even in the Newtonian account. A system may be so constituted that there will be states as close as one likes to any of its initial conditions; but these states can lead to future states of the system radically divergent from those that the given initial condition leads to. No matter how accurate our measuring devices may be, we may be unable to determine the initial state of a system to a degree of accuracy in any way useful for predicting its future state, after even miniscule time intervals. Indeed, there are those who argue that such radical instability makes it unreasonable for us to think of the system as having some exact initial condition that fully determines its future evolution, although this view is, to be sure, a minority one.

Despite these qualms, there are clearly aspects of Newtonian mechanics, and of other classical physical theories such as the theory of electromagnetism, that lead one to think of the world described by them as genuinely deterministic. And these results from physics have an impact on the philosophical views that try to describe the world as one in which everything that occurs is determined to occur by some past occurrence and by the lawlike connections between the states of the world at one time and its states at some other time.

The idea that every event had its cause, that for each occurrence in the world a "sufficient reason" for that occurrence could be found in past events, was taken to be a fundamental metaphysical posit by Leibniz. Kant argued that the principle of "universal causation" was a rule of the working of human understanding. He was responding in part to Hume's skepticism that anything could be found in the world corresponding to the metaphysician's notion of the "necessary connection" of events to one another (anything, that is, over and above the actual matter-of-fact regularities of occurrence and the psychological expectations generated by them). According to Kant, we could know a priori that the world of our experience was subject to the principles of cause and effect. (Actually it is far from clear that the doubts about determinism arising from quantum theory that we will be exploring really would dismay Kant, given the role he reserves for the principle that "every event has a cause.")

One group of philosophers found the principle that every event has a cause to be true universally but not as a metaphysical truth in the manner of Leibniz or a "transcendental" truth in the manner of Kant. For them, the principle that every event was such that a past event could be found sufficient to guarantee the occurrence of the given event was a "methodological injunction." It was a decision on our part never to give up the search for an earlier explaining event. If some event occurred for which we could find no earlier causally explaining event, could we not always take the line that we simply hadn't looked hard or long enough? After all, what could assure us that there was no such explaining event? Our mere inability to have found one yet could always be taken, these philosophers alleged, as an indication not of the nonexistence of a causally adequate explaining event but simply of our inability to pin it down.

Perhaps the most interesting impact of quantum theory on these issues is the claim of many that for the first time we have a theory of the world that allows us to deny, for a given event, that *any* past event could ever be found that was causally adequate to explain why the given event, rather than some specifiable alternatives to it, occurred. Here, it is claimed, reasons exist for denying the existence of the needed cause, not just reasons for thinking that such a cause had merely eluded our grasp. We will move on to explore the kinds of arguments offered to back up such a claim. The reader should be aware, however, that lurking in the background there are all sorts of puzzling philosophical issues that we will not be exploring. For example, the very notion of determinism presupposes the notion of a scientific law, a generalization connecting events at one time to those at some other time. But as B. Russell pointed out, if we allow any kind of description of events as legitimate and any generalization using such descriptions, it becomes a trivial matter that every event can be "lawlike" connected to some earlier event. Thus there remain for us many important, purely philosophical, issues, if we want to be clear on what an assertion that the world is deterministic really means.

Arguments Against Hidden Variables

But let us return to our central concern. What would inspire one to say that quantum mechanics shows the world to be indeterministic? Suppose that a system is prepared in a given quantum state at a certain time. Now suppose that over a time interval that system remains isolated from any interaction with the world external to it. Is the quantum state of that system at the end of the time interval fully "determined" by its quantum state at the beginning of the interval? The answer is that it is. The dynamical evolution of the quantum state is governed by the Schrödinger equation. And this equation completely determines the quantum state at the later time from its form at the beginning of the time interval. So nothing in the evolution of the quantum states themselves suggests any new indeterminism due to quantum theory.

It is, rather, in determining the values of the outcomes of a measurement that the indeterminism might arise. Given the observable quantity we are using the measurement to determine, a class of possible outcomes for that measurement process is fixed. But the quantum state attributed to the system just allows one to infer that a given one of these outcomes will arise with a certain probability. Only in very exceptional cases will the quantum state assign a probability of one to one possible outcome and a probability of zero to each of the other possible outcomes. So knowing that a system has been prepared in a given manner at one time, and even knowing that the system has not been interfered with in a given time interval, will not generally let us predict that one and only one value of an observable will be obtained if that observable is measured at the end of the time interval.

But, of course, that is still compatible with determinism holding in the world. For although the quantum state doesn't fully determine which of the outcomes will be obtained, that might still always be determined by some factor not taken into account by the quantum state. There are arguments designed to convince us that the quantity obtained upon a measurement must not be thought of, in general, as a quantity possessed by the system prior to the measurement. Consider a particle known to be in a spin-left state, for example. If a left-right measurement is performed on that particle, we know that the particle will definitely turn out to be spin left. If an up-down measurement is performed on the particle, half of the particles will be found to be up and half will be found to be down. But no particle is "definitely left and definitely up" and no particle is "definitely left and definitely down." It would be misleading, then, to think of the collection of particles as being a collection, prior to measurement, in which 100 percent are spin left, 50 percent are spin up and 50 percent are spin down. Considerations like this led many to suggest that the measurement process doesn't "determine a preexisting value for a quantity" but, rather, "brings the quantity into being." As we shall see, even thinking of measurement this way, at least thinking of it as some sort of causal process that, when it acts on the system, brings the measured state of it into being, has its own difficulties.

Nonetheless, couldn't we think of the particle before being measured as having some "hidden variable" quantity that fully determines the measured value that is the outcome of the measurement? Think of the particle that is definitely spin left. Couldn't there be some other factor true of the particle that fixes its nature either to be such that upon up-down measurement it is found to be in the up state or to be such that upon up-down measurement it is found to be in the down state? This factor is not taken account of in the quantum state of the system, in the fact that the system is definitely spin left. The spin-left quantum state generates the appropriate probabilities of being found spin up or spin down if an up-down measurement is made. But that by itself doesn't mean that a hidden factor, one ignored by the quantum formalism, doesn't exist. Bohr explicitly denied that such a factor could exist, insisting that the quantum state was a complete description of the quantum system. But dogmatic insistence by itself, even by someone as knowledgeable as Bohr, isn't argument. Einstein, as is well known, was adamant in his insistence that the indeterminism of the quantum formalism indicated that the theory was incomplete. He could not believe, he asserted, that the Lord "played dice" with the universe. Could the quantum states, like classical statistical states, have underneath them a more detailed description of systems that reintroduced full determinism into the description of the world?

To see why many have denied the very possibility of hidden variables that reintroduce determinism, we need to follow out a long argument that has been developed over many years. First we need the notion of the expectation value of a quantity in a given quantum state. In a specific quantum state, a given observable might have many possible values upon measurement. Each possible value will have its probability of occurrence. Multiply each value by its probability and add up the products for each of the possible values. The result is the average or mean value of the measured quantity for a system in the given quantum state. It is called the expectation value for that quantity in that quantum state.

Now, some quantities can be written as functions of other quantities. Most simply, for example, the square of the momentum of a particle is a simple function of its momentum. Some quantities are functions of a number of distinct quantities. For example, the total energy of a particle is the sum of its potential energy and its kinetic energy. Now, if observable C is a function of observables A and B, for example, how will the expectation value of C in a given state be related to those of A and B? If A, B, and C are all simultaneously measurable, surely the expectation value for C must be the same function of the expectation values for A and for B that the observable C is of the observables A and B. For we could measure the A, B, and C values for a system simultaneously and get the C value in two different ways, one directly and the other by computing it from the values obtained from A and B. The results must be consistent for simultaneously measurable quantities.

But now suppose A, B, and C are not simultaneously measurable. In the example given above, for example, total energy, kinetic energy, and potential energy are generally not simultaneously measurable. Potential energy is a function of position and kinetic energy a function of momentum, and potential and kinetic energy are typical examples of

Bohrian complementary quantities. We can prepare a system in a given quantum state. It will then have expectation values for potential energy, kinetic energy, and total energy. Even if these are not simultaneously measurable, will the expectation value for the total energy for systems in that quantum state be equal to the sum of the expectation value for potential energy in that quantum state and the expectation value for kinetic energy in that quantum state, as total energy is definable by the sum of potential and kinetic energy? The answer is yes, even if the quantities are not simultaneously measurable. It is a simple theorem of quantum theory that expectation values will behave this way for all observables in any quantum state.

But we are not now interested in quantum states so much as as we are in the alleged "deeper" underlying states, where all the hidden variables not taken into account by the quantum state have definite values. For each of these states, the outcome of any observation relative to the specification of the deeper state is that one value of the observed quantity has probability one and all other values have probability zero. Could there be such states? An argument of von Neumann's was designed to show that there could not be. Von Neumann assumed that for such hidden-variable states, the same relation among expectation values holds as the one that holds in quantum states, that is, that the expectation value of a quantity C will be the same function of the expectation values for quantities A and B as the observable C is of the observables A and B. This is called the "linearity assumption." Given this assumption, he was able to prove that the existence of such hidden-variable states would result in a violation of the interrelations of probabilities for outcomes predicted by quantum mechanics. The postulation of hidden variables would, then, be incompatible with the predictions made by quantum mechanics. Here is an argument to the effect that hidden causes do not exist. It argues that it isn't simply a case of the quantum theory's not making deterministic predictions about systems. The claim is that if there were such an underlying level of fully determining parameter values, even if they were unknown to us, their very existence would ensure that the statistical predictions quantum mechanics does make would have to be wrong.

For many years von Neumann's argument was taken by many as a decisive refutation of the compatibility of determinism with quantum mechanics. He had shown us, it was argued, that if determinism held, quantum mechanics must be wrong. Quantum mechanics could not, then, be looked upon as a statistical theory that rested on top of an underlying deterministic account of the world, as classical statistical mechanics is thought to rest on top of an underlying deterministic dynamics of the microstates of the systems it describes.

Later, however, doubts arose about the legitimacy of the von Neumann "no hidden variables" proof—not about its mathematical reasoning, of course, but about the legitimacy of a basic assumption on which it rests. This is the linearity assumption when extended beyond quantum states to the hidden-variable states, in particular, when it is applied to observables not simultaneously measurable. Is it so obvious that it must be the case that even for observables that cannot be simultaneously measured, the expectation value for *C* in a given hidden-variable state must be the sum of that for *A* and that for *B*, as long as the observable *C* was the sum of observables *A* and *B*? Could we not imagine the following: There is a hidden-variable state. Every system in the same hidden-variable state will give the same, determined, value when total energy is measured. It will also give the same, determined, value when potential energy is measured. And the same, determined, value when kinetic energy is measured. But the total energy of systems in that state will not be the sum of the potential and kinetic energies. If we could simultaneously determine all these values for a single system, this would seem absurd, but, as Bohr long insisted, we cannot perform the three measurements at one and the same time on any one system.

That the von Neumann assumption was too strong received further confirmation. His very strong result showed that hidden variables could never be possible, even for the simplest possible observable quantities. Yet for the very simplest cases, hidden-variable-type theories *can* actually be constructed. Consider, once again, the particle that can have only two spin-component states in a given choice of an axis direction, like the electron that must be up or down in its spin-component value along any up-down direction one chooses to measure. Let an electron beam consist of electrons that are all definitely spin left. If we put them through an up-down measuring device, measuring their spin component at right angles to their known spin-left direction, half will come out spin up and half will come out spin down. The up-down direction is perpendicular to the left-right direction. Choose any other direction distinct from the left-right and from the up-down direction. Quantum theory will assign definite probabilities to the electron spin component coming out in one of the two possible directions along the new axis chosen.

It turns out that a very simple hidden-variable theory can be offered to account for the probabilistic relations among these spin components for the case of a single particle whose spin component in a given direction can have only one of two values (up or down in that direction), such as the electron. Suppose the particle is definitely spin left. One can then imagine a further parameter describing the particle; the value of the parameter can vary over a certain range. Pick any direction in which the spin component is to be measured. Assume that if the hidden parameter is in a certain subset of its range, the particle will be found to be spin up in that direction. A model can be constructed with the following features: For each direction in which the spin is measured and for each possible outcome of that measurement, up or down in that direction, a set of values of the hidden parameter is assigned. When the particle has a definite spin in one direction, a probability distribution over the hidden parameter values is then determined. The probability that a particle will be found to be spin up, say, in some chosen direction, will then be the probability, according to this distribution, that the parameter value falls in the subregion of parameter values corresponding to this result in this direction. One and the same probability distribution for the hidden parameter will give the *correct* probability for each outcome in each possible direction, as predicted by quantum mechanics. In other words, for the special case of a single particle with just two possible spin-component states in any direction, all of the probabilistic predictions of quantum mechanics can, in fact, be duplicated by a simple hidden-variable model that has each outcome determined by the value the hidden variable has in a particular case. The probabilities of a given outcome for a system in a given quantum state, then, will simply be fixed by the probabilities of the underlying hidden variable's having its value in the appropriate subrange of possible hidden-variable values.

Now, nothing in this argument is designed to show that the results of quantum mechanics for this special case are, in fact, explained by any such real physical hidden variable. Rather, the argument is designed to show that there is nothing *inconsistent* in the postulation of such a hidden-variable, deterministic, model of the phenomena and of the probabilistic predictions of quantum mechanics in this special case. But if the von Neumann argument were to be taken as conclusive, if von Neumann's very strong postulate were to be assumed, then hidden variables would be inconsistent with the quantum mechanical results even in this simple case of a single particle with just two possible spin-component values in any direction. So the argument seems to show that von Neumann's assumption is too strong to be legitimate.

But this is certainly not the end of the story. If von Neumann assumes too much in his proof of the "impossibility of hidden variables," perhaps an argument that assumes less, indeed one that assumes only postulates that seem intuitively necessary for any genuine hidden-variable theory, will serve to ground the impossibility proof in a sounder way. Such arguments have, in fact, been constructed. Suppose hidden variables exist. Then in any state fully specifying the values of all the hidden variables, we ought to have fully specified all the outcomes of a set of observations—of which all *can* be simultaneously performed. That is, if there is a maximal set of possible simultaneous measurements (or a multiplicity of sets), for each such set of possible measurements, the value of the hidden variables should determine one and only one outcome of each measurement as occurring. These outcomes must be compatible with quantum mechanical predictions if the hidden variable theory is to underpin quantum mechanics and not replace it as a rejected, false theory. Can such a hidden-variable theory exist? Notice here that the von Neumann idea that, even in hidden-variable states, the linearity relation for expectation values for even incompatible observables will hold is not being assumed. All that is assumed is that the right quantum mechanical relations will hold between the out-comes of any set of measurements all of which are simultaneously per-formable. And this is assumed for each such simultaneously perform-able set of observations.

That no hidden-variable theory can meet even this more modest re-quirement follows either from a theorem of A. Gleason or, more di-rectly, from the work of Kochen and E. Specker. Their work shows that no such hidden-variable theory will reproduce the results of quantum mechanics for any system even one step beyond the system discussed above: the single particle with two possible outcomes to an observation. For that simplest case, we know that a hidden-variable model is con-sistent with quantum mechanics. But even for the next-simplest case, no hidden-variable theory will be found that meets the requirement demanded above.

An illustration of the theorem, originated by Kochen and Specker, will give the reader a basic idea of how the proof works, although the detail of the proof will not be given here. A system exists that has the following features: In any direction a spin-component-squared mea-surement of the system will give either value 1 or value 0. In any triple of three directions, each of which is at right angles to the other two, the system will, when measured, have spin-squared value 1 in two of the directions and spin-squared value 0 in the third of these directions. And for any such triple of mutually perpendicular directions, the three measurements are simultaneously performable according to the quan-tum theory. Could there exist hidden variables that more completely characterize the system, going beyond the quantum characterization that gives us the relations among the values noted above but provides only probabilistic predictions as to whether a given direction will have the 1 value or the 0 value? For a given fully specified hidden-variable as-signment, whether a given direction has value 1 or 0 must be com-pletely determined, and the quantum relations among these values noted above must be obeyed by this fuller characterization of the system.

No such hidden-variable theory is possible. The argument that this is so uses only results of elementary geometry. It can be shown that it is simply impossible to assign values 1 and 0 (or any other pair of dis-tinct values) to directions from a given point in such a way that for any triple of three mutually perpendicular directions, two of the directions are assigned the value 1 and one of the directions is assigned the value 0. Thus no hidden-variable theory could fully determine the correct value of the spin-squared value for every set of three mutually perpendicular directions. And no hidden-variable theory could be such that the right quantum mechanical relations held among the outcomes of *every* set of possible simultaneous measurements one could make on the system.

Yet the proponent of the view that quantum mechanics is an incom-plete statistical theory that requires a complete deterministic underlying theory won't give up quite so easily. If you examine how the above proof of "no hidden variables" works, you discover that the fundamental move is to notice that any one direction from a point can be considered as a member of innumerable triplets of perpendicular directions. So the value of the measured quantity in one direction must be consistent, according to the predictions of quantum mechanics, with the values in two other directions perpendicular to it for many triplets of directions. It is because of this that the proof can show the inconsistency of hidden variables with quantum mechanics. Beginning with one assignment of *1*, *1*, and *0* to three perpendicular directions, one can find a number of other triplets of directions containing one or more of the direction in the original set. Then one continues that process, until some direction originally assigned value *1* is forced to be assigned value *0*. (See Figure 4.7.)

But what if we declare that the value of the measured quantity in a given direction relative to a choice of the other two perpendicular directions is just not the same physical quantity as that value relative to another choice of two perpendicular directions? Then having that value *1* for each such "relative" physical quantity and *0* for the other won't be a blatant contradiction. But how could we, from a physical point of view, argue that such a relativization of the quantity in question was reasonable? The answer lies in the fact that although values of the quantity in the three perpendicular directions are all simultaneously measurable, the values of that quantity in other directions are not necessarily simultaneously measurable with all the three quantities. So although one could determine three values in three perpendicular directions in one measurement, one could not determine all values for all directions simultaneously. Perhaps, then, the change in the measuring apparatus that measured the value in one direction, *A*, while at the same time determining the value of that quantity in two other directions, *B* and *C*, to the different apparatus needed to measure the value in direction *A* and in two different directions perpendicular to it, *D* and *E*, causally affects the system. This might give the result that the value of the quantity in the *A* direction relative to the *B* and *C* measurement is differently determined by the underlying hidden variables from the way that quantity in the *A* direction is determined by those hidden variables when the values in the *D* and *E* directions are also being measured. Couldn't we imagine that the very act of changing the measuring apparatus acting on the system itself causally interacts with the hidden variables of the system to make the difference? After all, the result of the measurement of the value in the *A* direction is the joint causal result of the hidden variables of both the system and the measuring apparatus. So measuring *A* in conjunction with a measurement of *B* and *C* might very well give a value in the *A* direction different from the one obtained by measuring the value in the *A* direction in conjunction with a measurement in the *D* and *E* directions. Still, in both cases, it is the values of the underlying hidden variables that com-

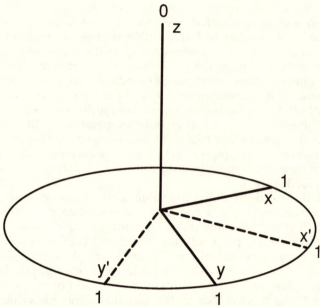

Figure 4.7 A system used in an argument against hidden variables. There is a quantum system that is such that for any three mutually perpendicular directions a certain quantity must have value *0* in one of those directions and value *1* in the other two directions. Could a single set of hidden variables determine all those values? The argument that this could not be so relies upon the fact that any given direction is a member of innumerable triplets of mutually perpendicular directions. For example, *z* in the figure is a member of the triplet (*z, x, y*) but also of the triplet (*z, x', y'*). One can show that it is impossible to assign *0*'s and *1*'s to all directions from a point so that for every triplet of mutually perpendicular directions, one direction gets value *0* and the other two value *1*. But whereas the values along any three mutually perpendicular directions are "simultaneously measurable" (say, along *z, x,* and *y*), the values will not in general be simultaneously measurable along, say, *x* and *x'*. This leads to a view of hidden variables in which the values determined may vary with the set of simultaneously possible measurements chosen.

pletely determine what all of those measured values will turn out to be.

If we adopt such a "contextual" view of the nature of a measured quantity, then the proof outlined above, the proof that the interrelationships among measured values predicted by quantum theory are incompatible with any possibility of these values being fully determined by underlying values of hidden parameters, will not stand. Can we find another kind of proof of "no hidden variables" that is immune to the kind of reasoning used above to make contextualism seem not too implausible from a deterministic, causal point of view? The answer is that we can, and it is to those arguments that we now turn.

The Inseparability of Systems

The Einstein, Podolsky, and Rosen Argument

Bohr and Einstein represented, respectively, the most eminent spokes-men for two opposing views about the quantum theory. For Bohr, the quantum theory provided an ultimate description of the world. To be sure, any quantum account of the world needed to be supplemented by those detailed theories that told us what sorts of forces acted be-tween the elementary particles, the basic constituents of the world, but as far as the underlying description of the basic states of nature and their dynamic evolution went, the quantum description was rock bot-tom. If a system was prepared in a given quantum state, by means of one of those kinds of measurements that determined for the system after the measurement the values of some members of a compatible, simultaneously measurable, set of observables, that quantum state was a complete description of the state of the system after the preparation process. Any inferences to be drawn concerning the possible outcomes of a future measurement of the system, or concerning the likelihood of these outcomes occurring, would have to be drawn from our knowl-edge of the quantum state of the system. If these inferences to future-measured outcomes were at best probabilistic, as they usually are in quantum mechanics, so be it. Quantum mechanics showed us that the world was, at its deepest level, genuinely indeterministic. Contrary to the deterministic ideal, supported at least to a degree, as we have noted, by the results of classical physics, the world was irreducibly "tychistic," or chancelike, in its nature.

Einstein, in contrast, was adamant in his view that quantum me-chanics could not be a complete theory of the world. As a statistical theory, making at best probabilistic predictions about the world, it ought to be understood as requiring an underpinning in the form of a deter-ministic theory of systems that relied upon a description of them at a deeper level than that provided by the quantum description. A system prepared in a quantum state, then, had to have other factors true of it, even if we did not know what they were, much less what were the particular values of these hidden features the particular system pos-sessed. These underlying factors would determine with certainty the outcome of any measurement applied to the system, and the merely probabilistic predictions derivable from the quantum state of the system would have to be seen as a reflection of the fact that the quantum state provided only a partial, not a complete, description of the state of the system.

For Bohr, a measurement process "brought into being" the value of the quantity measured. Prior to measurement, the system did not have the value of the quantity measured, unless it was in a very special quantum state in which that value was certain upon measurement to begin with. And prior to measurement, the system was not characterizable by any other inner parameters that would fully determine that the outcome in fact obtained was the one to be obtained when the system interacted with the appropriate measuring apparatus. For Einstein, this was unacceptable. If the system in fact turned out to have a specific value when the measurement was performed, something in the world characterizing the antecedent state of the system (and, perhaps, of the measuring apparatus) had to account for the value coming out as it did, and not with one of the other possible results.

In 1935 Einstein, in collaboration with B. Podolsky and N. Rosen, published a seminal paper attempting to cast doubts on the Bohrian way of looking at things. This paper inspired a long discussion of the kind of "thought experiment" Einstein proposed. Ultimately, these studies led to a series of results that seem to provide the gravest difficulties for an understanding of quantum mechanics from the Einsteinian point of view.

Einstein's idea is to consider a system that is composed of two component parts. These might be, for example, two nuclear particles joined together in a two-particle nucleus. Systems can be so constructed that the value of a quantity for one of the particles in the joint system is exactly correlated with the value of that quantity for the other component. Indeed, the system may be such that for a whole family of properties, if particle one has a given value for one of the properties in the family, particle two must have one and only one correlated value of that property. Einstein originally used position and momentum features for his model, but we will use, instead, the model of two particles with correlated spins. This is the system usually used to explain the thought experiment and its consequences. The particles might be, for example, electrons that have the familiar spin properties we have noted in the previous sections. For any given direction, the spin component of each particle will have one of two values, either "up" in that direction or "down" in that direction. The joint systems we will be interested in are ones in a "singlet" state. In this state, the particles are so correlated that if the spin of one is up in a given direction, the spin of the other must be down in that direction. (The name singlet comes from spectroscopy, where singlet states correspond to spectral lines that remain undivided when the system is placed in an external magnetic field. Other coupled systems might be in, for example, a "triplet" state, where the spectral line splits into three lines when the system is immersed in a magnetic field.)

Next, we are to imagine the joint system's being split into its two components. Each of these moves off in space until the originally component particles now constitute two particles well separated in space. At the same time, the splitting is supposed to be done by some method that does not disturb the spin correlations the particles have to each other. This can be done by an appropriate physical intervention on the system from the outside. Under these circumstances, what is the correct description of the particles, according to quantum mechanics, after

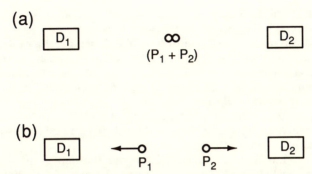

Figure 4.8   The inseparability of quantum systems. In (a) a system is shown that is composed of two particles (P_1 and P_2). The system is such that the spin values of the particles in any direction will, if measured, be found to be in directions opposite to each other, whatever axis is chosen along which to make the measurement. In (b) the particles are separated and sent away from each other in opposite directions. The separation is done in such a way as to retain their spin "anticorrelation" with each other. One can choose to measure the spin of particle P_1 in any direction, using detector D_1, and to measure the spin of particle P_2 in any direction using detector D_2. The values obtained bear definite probabilistic correlational relations to each other in quantum mechanics. One can show that no positing of a set of hidden variables that would determine the outcomes of the measurements at D_1 and D_2, whatever measurement is chosen in each case, will give the right predictions for the probabilities of all correlations predicted by quantum mechanics. Further, it is now difficult to think of the choice of measurement on one of the particles as affecting the hidden variable determining the outcome for measurement of the other particle, because the two measurements are done at such vast distances and proximities in time that they make causal interaction between them impossible.

they have been separated? The answer is that they must, together, still be considered a joint system in a singlet spin state. Properly speaking, there is no quantum state for one particle that neglects the other, although a kind of "reduced" state for one without the other can be constructed for some purposes. (See Figure 4.8)

What are the predictions we can make about spin measurements on the particles, given their joint quantum state? Well, for any direction we can predict the probability that one of the particles will, if its spin is measured in that direction, be found to be spin up or spin down. In this case, each of those probabilities is one-half. These probabilities would follow both from the full quantum state of the joint system and from the reduced states we can attribute to each particle alone. But something else follows from the nature of the joint state. This is the perfect correlation of the particles. No matter how far apart the particles become in space, assuming that nothing interacts with them from the outside between the splitting of the original system and the measurements performed, we can always infer that if one particle is found by a measurement to be spin up in a given direction, it is certain that the other particle will be found to be spin down if its spin is measured in the same direction. Further, if one particle is measured in a given direction and the result noted, definite probabilities for the outcome of a spin measurement on the other particle will be found in any other direction chosen. These conditional probabilities of the outcome of a measurement on particle two, given the result of a measurement on particle one, follow from the full quantum state of the joint system. They are eliminated in the reduced descriptions constructible for the particles one at a time, which is why those reduced descriptions fail to specify the full quantum state of the world.

Now, says Einstein, let us look from the Bohrian point of view at the state of particle two before and after the state of particle one is determined by a measurement. According to Bohr, prior to a measurement's taking place, neither particle has a definite spin. Nor, according to Bohr, do they have any property that would determine their having a specific spin value in a specific direction if measured. Rather, prior to measurement, the particles have only their disposition to come up with a given spin value in a given direction with probability one-half, along with the disposition to have their spin values, if both are measured, correlated in the way described by a singlet-state wave function. But suppose particle one has its spin measured in a given direction, say, A. Suppose the "up" value is obtained. At that very instant, according to Bohr, the second particle, be it light-years away, instantaneously "jumps" into the quantum state appropriate for having the direction "down" for its spin in the A direction. This is true because once the spin on particle one has been determined to be up in the A direction, it is certain that the spin of particle two is down in that direction, and the only wave function to give that probability to particle two would be a "pure down in the A direction" wave function. This wave function for particle two is quite different from assigning to particle two, in conjunction with particle one, a previous wave function appropriate to particle two's being part of a joint system in a singlet state.

Now, says Einstein, if we think of the wave function as a complete physical characterization of the particle, this kind of change is absurd. Bohr thinks of the measurement as "bringing into being" a value for the observation for the system, a value that did not exist prior to the measurement's having taken place, and not as revealing a preexisting (or at least predetermined) value for that quantity. This may be plausible if we physically interact with the system when we measure it, but it seems absurd if the system is left completely alone by us in our measurement. That is what happens in the coupled system case we are considering. We measure the spin value on particle two by interacting our measuring device with particle *one*. The measurement we perform determines the spin value in the A direction for particle one. That immediately tells us what the spin value is for particle two, i.e., what value of spin in the A direction a measurement of particle two would now show. But as we did absolutely nothing, in the physical sense, to particle two in the measurement process, whatever it is that determines that particle two will have a definite spin value in the *A* direction if it is measured *must have already been true of particle two prior to our measuring particle one.* But prior to our measurement of particle one, the wave function describing the particles did not assign a definite spin value in the *A* direction to particle two. And, I repeat, particle two must have had such a determinate spin value in the *A* direction even prior to our measurement on particle one. Therefore, Einstein and his collaborators conclude, the quantum state of the joint system prior to the measurement did not contain a full description of the actual state of the world. It did not, for example, assign a definite disposition of particle two to show one and only one value of spin in the *A* direction, a disposition that particle two must have had "all along," according to the argument just given.

They conclude, then, that quantum mechanics is an incomplete theory. The wave function, they argue, must be taken as representing, not the entire physical state of a system, but only our partial knowledge of that state. The instantaneous change of the wave function upon measurement is no longer mysterious. Suppose we know that a penny is either here in a matchbox on Earth or else in a matchbox on a planet of Alpha Centauri. We can represent that by a probability function that assigns, say, probability of one-half to each possibility. We now look in the matchbox on Earth and see the penny. Of course, the probability that the penny is in the other matchbox drops instantly to zero. But that is not some mysterious physical change of the matchbox on the distant planet, only a change in what we know about it. But if the distant matchbox turns up empty, it must have been empty even prior to our looking in the matchbox on earth.

Bohr will have none of this argument. It is true, he replies, that the wave function assigned to a system is relative to some choice of measurement. Prior to the measurement's having been performed on particle one, the wave function appropriate to characterize particle two is the one that characterizes it as a component of the original singlet-state compound system. Relative to the original preparation measurement, this is the correct wave function to describe the world. After particle one has been measured and found to have a definite value of spin in the *A* direction, the correct wave function to describe the world is the one that assigns to each particle a definite spin in the *A* direction. It assigns particle one the spin value determined by the measurement, and it assigns particle two the spin value it must hold because of the perfect correlation of spins of the two particles. So measuring particle one does change the wave function attributed to particle two. But this does not imply either that the wave function is merely a summary of our knowledge and not a full specification of the physical state or that measuring particle one has a "causal" effect on particle two. Rather, it is a feature of the relativity of the wave function to the measurement process. It is this relational aspect of quantum mechanics, that states

exist only relative to measurements, that Bohr reaches for in his explanation of the situation, arguing that the relativity of wave function to
measurement performed is something analogous to the relativity of length
of a rod to state of motion of an observer in relativity. Changing one's
state of motion relative to the rod changes the length of the rod relative
to oneself as an observer. But this not a causal change in the rod, as
the aether theory would have it. Nor is it the fact that length is some
subjective feature of the rod. Length is relative to reference frame. Similarly, Bohr claims, the wave function is physical but relative.

Bell's Theorem

Could any argument serve to help determine which of these attitudes
toward the wave function is correct? At least we might hope to do the
following: We might be able to determine whether the postulation of
hidden variables that fix the states of the two separated systems individually, as well as the state of the distant particle independent of the
measurement we choose to perform on the closer particle, is consistent
with all the probabilistic predictions made by quantum mechanics. We
now turn to the claim that such a postulation, one in keeping with
Einstein's picture of the wave function as an incomplete description of
the world underlain by a more complete, deterministic level of description whether known to us or not, is *not* in fact consistent with quantum
mechanics. A theorem of J. Bell's, and some extensions of it, are designed to show that the picture Einstein suggests as the correct understanding of the wave function assigned to correlated systems cannot
be correct.

How does the proof work? To begin with, let us assume that Einstein
is correct. In the case of the two correlated particles with possible spin
values as described above, let us assume that as soon as the particles
are separated from each other, each particle carries with it a hidden-
parameter value. The hidden-parameter value associated with a particle
will fully determine, for that particle, whether it comes out up or down
in any spin measurement performed on it in any direction we choose.
Let us also assume that events far apart in space and close together in
time, so that by relativity no causal signal could be sent from the one
to another, cannot affect each other. One consequence of this is the
following: Suppose we measure particle two in direction B. The outcome of this measurement must not depend on any choice on our part
of direction in which we choose to measure the spin of particle one.
After all, we could arrange the two measurements once the particles
have separated by some distance, so that one measurement cannot
causally affect the other. So choosing the direction in which we will
measure the spin of particle one should have no effect whatever on the
outcome of a spin measurement of particle two in the direction chosen
to make that measurement.

Now suppose we choose to make such pairs of spin measurements
on a large class of pairs of particles, all prepared in the same way, with

the same spin correlations predicted by quantum mechanics. We assume each outcome is fully determined by the value of the hidden parameter carried by each of the particles in each of the experiments. We also assume the probabilities for outcomes of measurements in one of the particles are independent of which spin measurement we choose to make on the other particle. The probability that a given value will be obtained by a measurement on a given particle in a given direction should, then, depend only upon the probability with which the various possible values of the hidden parameters for each particle are distributed.

Let us introduce the following notation: (, , ; , ,) is a symbol with six open places. The three places before the semicolon correspond to particle one and the three after it to particle two. Each of the three places on each side of the semicolon corresponds to a direction, A, B, and C. We will consider measurements of the spin component of each particle in each of these three directions. A "+" symbol in a place means that the value of the spin for that particle in that direction is determined by the hidden parameters to come out in the up direction. A "−" means that it is determined to come out down. (Which of the two directions counts as up and which as down for each of A, B, and C is arbitrary.). A "0" in a place means that the hidden parameter has a value that determines the spin in that direction to come out up or down, i.e., any value consistent with the pluses and minuses assigned to the other places. Remember that the particles have perfect correlation, so that if a plus appears, say, in the first place on the left of the semicolon, that will force the first place to the right of the semicolon to have the minus value. For example, the symbol (+,0,0;0,0,+) will stand for the probability that a measurement of the first particle in the A direction is determined to come out with the particle spin up in that direction, *and* a measurement of the second particle in the C direction is determined to come out in the up C direction.

Consider the following equation:

Eqn. A-C: $(+,0,0;0,0,+) = (+,+,-;-,-,+) + (+,-,-;-,+,+)$

Here we rely on the following two arguments: (1) if the value for one particle in a direction comes out plus, the value for the other particle in that direction is forced to be minus; (2) given the determined values for the spins of particles one and two in the A and the C direction, there are only two remaining possibilities for the value of these spins in the undetermined B direction. Because all these probabilities are well defined and independent of the measurement we choose to make on either particle, it stands to reason on the basis of elementary postulates of probability theory that the total probability of particle one's coming up plus in the A direction and particle two's coming up plus in the C direction is the probability of that happening and also particle one's coming up plus in the B direction (with particle two's coming up minus in that direction) plus the probability of the specified result happening and particle one's coming up minus in the *B* direction (and particle two's coming up plus). This is because given the specified result, these two other possibilities for the *B* direction result are exclusive of each other and exhaust all the possibilities that can occur.

By exactly the same reasoning there is a second equation:

Eqn. B-C: $(0,+,0;0,0,+) = (+,+,-;-,-,+) + (-,+,-;+,-,+)$

and a third equation:

Eqn. A-B: $(+,0,0;0,+,0) = (+,-,+;-,+,-) + (+,-,-;-,+,+)$

Now comes the observation that makes the postulation of so-called local hidden variables underlying quantum mechanical probabilities dubious. If we look at the right-hand side of Eqn. A-C, we note that the first term in it appears on the right-hand side of Eqn. B-C and the second term appears on the right-hand side of Eqn. A-B. Now the remaining terms on the right-hand side of each of these latter two equations must be greater than or equal to zero because they represent probabilities and probabilities are never negative numbers. So if we add the left-hand side of Eqns. B-C and A-B, we must obtain a number that is at least as great as the left-hand side of Eqn. A-C. In words, this comes down to the following: "The sum of the probabilities that particle one comes out up in the *B* direction and particle two comes out up in the *C* direction with the probability that particle one comes out up in the *A* direction and particle two comes out up in the *B* direction cannot be less than the probability that particle one comes out up in the *A* direction and particle two comes out up in the *C* direction. This must be true for all directions *A*, *B*, and *C*."

But it turns out that there are directions of *A*, *B*, and *C* such that this inequality is violated by the probabilities predicted by quantum mechanics! In quantum mechanics, the probabilistic correlation of direction *A* with direction *C* can be greater than the sum of the correlation of direction *A* with some other direction, *B*, and the correlation of that other direction, *B*, with direction *C*. It seems that the postulation that all the probabilities above are well defined is incompatible with quantum mechanical predictions about probabilities of joint outcomes. And the postulates behind the existence of these probabilities seem, then, to be incompatible with the quantum mechanical probabilistic predictions. These postulates are, first, that there are hidden-parameter values that determine the outcomes of all possible spin experiments on the separated particles and, second, that the outcome of a measurement on the second particle is independent of the choice of spin measurement we made for measuring the spin of the first particle (and vice versa). It seems as though we are obliged to think that performing a particular measurement on the first particle has a determining effect on the distribution of probabilities for the outcome of measurements on the second particle. This effect cannot be assimilated to the classical case of there being an already-determinate probability for each outcome on the second particle, independent of the experiment we performed on the first, with the experiment on the first particle serving only to allow us to make deeper inferences about the second by a kind of probabilistic conditionalization.

Suppose we assume that the hidden parameters carried by each of the particles do not determine with certainty the outcome of each possible measurement performable on the particles; they fix the result only indeterministically and probabilistically. Here, then, the hidden variables wouldn't restore determinism to the physics. But couldn't they at least restore "locality"? Couldn't we think of each particle, after the separation, as carrying its own probability of having a specific outcome for any measurement performed on it, even if the particle is not carrying a fully determinate outcome for each possible measurement? Alas, if an additional, natural, "locality" assumption is made, this version of "stochastic local hidden variables" is inconsistent with quantum mechanics as well. The additional assumption is that the probability determined for the outcomes of all possible measurements on particle two by its hidden, stochastic variable is independent of the *outcome* of any measurement that we perform on particle one. In the case of deterministic hidden variables, we assumed that the outcome on particle two was independent of the choice of experiment made on particle one. Now we assume as well that the probability of an outcome on particle two is independent of the result we might obtain for an observation made on particle one. Surely this is a reasonable assumption if we are trying to construct a theory that meets with the Einsteinian desideratum that the state of particle two, once separated from particle one in every ordinary causal fashion, is independent of whatever happens to particle one.

Even in the case of a probabilistic hidden-variable theory, the assumption of locality for the hidden variable, naturally interpreted, is at variance with the quantum predictions. There is a kind of "entanglement" of the once joined and now separated systems that cannot be reduced to the mere, classically intelligible, fact that they each, independently of one another, carry a record of their past existence as components of a joint system with specified properties. It is true that together they carry a record of that previous state, but it seems that this record cannot be factored into independent features of the two particles taken as distinct, independent physical systems.

The idea that performing an experiment at one place seems, according to quantum mechanics, to produce an effect on the probabilities of outcomes of another experiment at some distant place conjures up the possibility of communication that exceeds the limits placed on the transmission of energy by the famous relativistic claim that light is the fastest signal possible for the transmission of a causal signal. But careful examination of the situation shows that there is nothing that an experimenter can do at particle one's place to modify any results an experimenter at particle two's place will obtain and that could be used to inform the second experimenter that, for example, the first experimenter had in fact chosen to measure the spin of particle one in a particular direction or had gotten specific results when he did so. The correlations between the spins of the particles that would be obtained if two particular measurements were made on two particular correlated particles separated out from the same original singlet-state conjoined system, the correlations predicted by quantum mechanics, are not reproducible by local hidden variables of either the deterministic or stochastic sort. But none of these facts about correlation could be used to violate the relativistic limits on the velocity of transmittability of a causal signal.

It seems false, then, that the probabilities of the separated components of a once unified system could be fixed, either deterministically or merely probabilistically, by features local to this isolated system and in such a way that the probabilities of outcomes on measurements of the individual systems will obey all the correlational results on outcomes ordered by the laws of quantum mechanics. And it is false if one makes the fundamental assumptions presupposed by these "no local hidden variables" arguments. Attempts exist at making end runs around these arguments by, for example, relying on nonstandard probability theories. But the oddity of the world these theories entail is at least as extreme as the apparent nonlocality of systems that is usually taken to be the consequence of the arguments.

But might quantum mechanics be wrong in its predictions about the correlations of states of separated systems? It does not seem likely. Some experimental work has been done (not with the kind of particles we used in our example, but with polarized photons of light, for which a related "no hidden variables" result can be proved). It seems to show, to no one's great surprise, that the correlations between the states of the once united particles are just as quantum mechanics predicts.

So following out Einstein's clever idea of invoking systems that once causally interacted but that, at the time measurements were performed on them, constituted widely separated systems that could not be thought of as in causal contact with each other has had quite the opposite effect from the one that Einstein intended. Einstein thought it absurd that a measurement at one place and time could determine a real change at another place and time not causally connectable to the first, and that this showed that the quantum state ought to be taken as a representation of our partial knowledge of the state of the world and not a complete description of that state. But the Bell Theorem results seem to indicate, rather, that no understanding of quantum mechanics as a statistical theory superimposed on an underlying local hidden-variable theory is plausible. They go beyond the results discussed in "Arguments Against Hidden Variables" in that, in the cases we are now considering, the hidden-variable theorist's way out of the dilemma—first taking observables as contextual and relative to other quantities observed and then thinking of the other measurements simultaneously performed as causally acting on the hidden variables that determine the outcome of the measurement in question—does not seem to be available. If we admit that the choice of what measurement to perform on one particle at a given time, and the outcome obtained for that measurement, cannot causally affect the hidden-variable values for the other particle at a vast distance and whose measurement is close in time to that of the first measurement, this way around the "no hidden variable" results is now blocked.

Summary

The results outlined in "The Einstein, Podolsky, and Rosen Argument" and "Bell's Theorem" cannot, by themselves, determine which of the possible metaphysical interpretations of quantum mechanics and of the measurement process is the correct one. They do, however, seem to weigh in favor of those interpretations that propose more radical revisions in our understanding of the nature of the world and against those that claim that we can understand the new theory with only fairly minor revisions in our concepts of what the world is like. There were, for example, those interpretations of the Uncertainty Principle that took it to be a limitation merely in our possible knowledge of the state of a system. We could not know, these interpretations argued, simultaneous exact values of position and momentum of a particle. But we could suppose, the argument continued, that such values still existed. But the fact that no noncontextual hidden variables of any kind could generate the right probabilistic results for all possible measurements on a system would seem to militate against this view and argue in favor, rather, of the more radical Bohr line that the features attributed to a system when it was measured and found to have certain values of an observable quantity were "brought into being" by the measurement and not already present in the system.

The even more surprising results in "Bell's Theorem" seem to allow us to go a little further. It is one thing to think of the measurement as "bringing into being" the observed state of the system by means of a kind of causal process, the result of causal interaction between the measuring apparatus and the system measured. After all, we are aware of the fact that even in prequantum physics an act of measuring a quantity on a system can change the state of the system. Putting a thermometer into a liquid in order to measure the temperature of that liquid will change the temperature of the liquid in the process. Couldn't the "effect of measurement on the system measured" be thought of in this vein? The difference between the classical and the quantum case would then reside in the fact that in the prequantum case, it is in principle possible to make the disturbance of the system by the measuring apparatus as small as one likes but that in quantum mechanics, the ir-

reducible limit on the minimum amount of energy transferred in a measurement process (due to the quantum nature of energy transfer from
system to system) might make it impossible to reduce such distur-
bances to "almost zero." Such a way of looking at uncertainty had its
proponents, especially in the earlier interpretation of the Uncertainty
Principle.

But, as we have seen, quantum mechanics seems to demand that a
measurement can have an effect on a system even if measuring apparatus and system are not in causal contact in any way. Measuring
the spin on particle one changes the quantum state of particle two. As
we have seen, this change cannot be reduced to the simple modification in probabilities that comes about from an increase in our knowledge of the world for which a classical model would do. The nonexistence of local hidden variables seems to have that conclusion. So Bohr
seems to be right when he maintains that states of the world, quantum
states of systems, have a kind of relativity to choice of measurement
and measurement outcome that is assimilable neither to a causal modification of the system by the measurement nor to the quantum state's
being thought of as only a partial description of the system, a com-
pendium of our knowledge about it whose change upon measurement
is understandable in a classical way. The results of the "no hidden variables" theorems add weight to the claim that quantum mechanics will
force upon us a radical reunderstanding of the nature of the world,
once we have anything like a coherent understanding of it at all.

What such a reunderstanding would consist of is far from clear. At
a minimum it would seem that quantum mechanics places a very different light on the old question of whether Leibniz was right in thinking that every event that occurred had a "sufficient reason." If most
interpreters of quantum mechanics are right, there is simply no causal
reason at all why one nucleus of a radioactive element decayed in a
given time interval whereas an identical nucleus of the same kind did
not. Worse yet, as we have seen, stochastic or probabilistic causes seem
ruled out, if causation—even if it is indeterministic—is supposed to be
a purely local relationship in which states of affairs are determined only
by what goes on in their spacetime vicinity. Along with the notion of
the causal chain of occurrence in the world goes our notion of what it
is to explain why phenomena occur. We can explain the correlations
observed in the spin measurements of the distant particles by referring
back to their origin as components of a singlet-state compound system.
But unlike the usual classical explanation of such correlations, we can't
explain this correlation by showing how the historical origin of the particles provides for each, independently of the other, a definite probability of occurrence, the correlation being the consequent joint probability distribution for a pair of outcomes, each of which is probabilistically
accounted for. Instead, the correlation is an "irreducible" fact, and the
explanation of it is direct and not through such independent probabil-

ities, for we know that any assignment of these would be incompatible with the correlations that actually occur.

Finally, although more indirectly, the "no hidden variables" results lend weight to the claims that a full understanding of the world described by quantum mechanics will require a radical rethinking of our metaphysical picture of the world. For some, this means a change from the presupposition of the classical mechanistic picture of a single, material, world to one in which rather old-fashioned idealistic assumptions of the existence of mental states ontologically independent of physical underpinnings play a role. For others, it means the rather more radical denial of a unitary physical world and its replacement by some version or other of a "many worlds" ontology, in which at every moment each of a variety of possible outcomes of a process is realized in different "branch universes." For others, the even more radical change still would be the denial altogether of any notion of an objective world existing independently of our attempts to come to know it, replacing this traditional objectivist view with some kind of version of a Bohrian picture, in which the world is described by quantum states, but these states are themselves relative to the choice of a measurement to be performed.

Once again, the reader should think over the physical phenomena that led to these rather wild speculations in the first place. It is important to remember such phenomena as the dual nature of light as both wave showing interference phenomena and particle showing energy transfer in a highly localized way; the presence of interference phenomena for the fundamental material particles of the world as evidenced, say, by electron scattering off a crystal; the appearance of interference in other aspects of the world than the spatial, as in the spin experiments that show the retention of memory of the original spin of a particle in one direction even after the beam of particles has been split into pure beams of particles with spins up and down in some other direction; the correlated results of possible simultaneous measurements on a system not compatible with their being determined by any noncontextual hidden variable for the system, for quite elementary geometric reasons; and the existence of distant correlations whose explanation does rest in a past local interaction of the separated systems but that cannot be reconstructed as explainable by local parameters carried by each of the separated systems individually. These experimentally demonstrable features of the world are not parts of an esoteric formalism but quite distinctive features reproducible in the laboratory. The more one reflects on them, the harder it is to come up with some plausible unitary explanation for them that will not resort to a quite radical rethinking of the nature of the world.

Further Readings

Three basic introductions to the philosophy of quantum mechanics that are easily accessible are Pagels (1982), Squires (1986), and

Rae (1986). Gibbins (1987) also surveys with some philosophical sophistication the basic material. Heisenberg (1930) remains a classic of brilliant elementary exposition. Hughes (1989) contains an exposition of the formalism of the theory, with a careful explanation of why it plays the role it does. D'Espagnat (1971) is a sophisticated treatment of many major problems that uses a greater amount of formal apparatus than the easier works. Jammer (1974) is encyclopedic in scope, surveying most of the important threads in interpretation throughout the history of the subject.

Jammer (1966) is a comprehensive history of the origins of quantum theory, emphasizing the development of the major concepts. Ludwig (1968) contains translations of the original papers in the field of quantum theory. Bohm (1951) also has clear expository chapters on the experimental basis of the theory and on its early development.

There are numerous introductory texts on quantum theory. Bohm (1951), Dicke and Wittke (1960), and Gottfried (1960) are all excellent. Classical formal presentations of the theory are Dirac (1930) and von Neumann (1955). Introductions to the mathematics needed to formulate the theory can be found in Hughes (1989) and Jordan (1969). More-advanced material is surveyed in Jauch (1968).

On the early interpretations of the theory, Jammer (1974), Chapters 2 through 6, is comprehensive. Heisenberg (1930) is also essential reading. An introduction to the debate, along with many of the original important papers, is contained in Wheeler and Zurek (1983).

On measurement, the readings in Chapters 2 and 4–6 of Wheeler and Zurek (1983) are vital. D'Espagnet (1971), Part 4, is thorough and clear. Jammer (1974), Chapter 11, covers the major theories.

Kochen's "relative state" formulation of the theory can be found in Kochen (1985). A thorough exposition and discussion of this approach is Healy (1989). A related interpretation can be found in van Fraassen (1991). Proposals that tie quantum measurement to the kind of irreversibility discussed in Chapter 3 of the present book can be found in Chapter 5 of Wheeler and Zurek (1983). The view that measurement is the result of "random kicks" to the system from a "deeper" physical level can be found in Ghirardi, Rimini, and Weber (1986). A critique of this view and of the Kochen view can be found in Albert and Loewer (1990). The "many worlds" interpretation of quantum theory is discussed in Section 11.6 of Jammer (1974) and 2.3 of Wheeler and Zurek (1983) as well as Chapter 20 of d'Espagnat (1971).

Reichenbach's version of "quantum logic" is in Reichenbach (1944). A survey of the main themes in quantum logic is in Chapter 8 of Jammer (1974). Chapters 9 and 10 of Gibbins (1987) both expound the nature of alleged quantum logics and offer a critique of those philosophical positions that take quantum "logic" to be a revision of logic properly so-called. Hughes (1989) is also a good source on this topic.

For the variety of hidden-variable theories, see Jammer (1974), Chapter 7, and Belinfante (1973). On the inseparability of systems, d'Espagnat (1971), Part 3, is excellent. Important original papers of Bell are in Bell (1987).

5

Reflections on the Interdependence of Philosophy and Science

We have now explored quite a variety of topics on which the resources of contemporary physics and those of the philosophy of science can both be brought to bear. The wealth of examples, and the way in which physics and philosophy play an intricately intertwined role in trying to get to the bottom of the issues raised, ought to convince the reader that physics and philosophy are two highly interdependent ways of seeking to understand the world and our place as knowers of it.

Traditionally, philosophy has attempted to describe the nature of the world in terms of utmost generality. Eschewing the detailed description and classification of the multitudinous phenomena of nature, leaving that as a task for the special sciences, philosophy has worried about the nature of being at the levels of greatest abstraction. Do particulars alone exist, or must we posit universals, properties, as having existence of their own? Is the substance of the world exhausted by material being, or must we also tolerate some realm of nonmaterial existence in order to account for the phenomena of mind? These are the sorts of questions we expect philosophers to ask.

Philosophy has also taken as its domain the critical examination of the specific sciences. Although science infers the nature of the future and the unobserved from the limited data made available by our observations up to the present, philosophy is concerned with the justification of the inductive reasoning that allows for such projection of alleged knowledge beyond the realm of the observed. Science collects the results of observations, results framed in the terms ultimately derived from the language of everyday experience. Then it explains these results by referring to a realm of unobserved theoretical entities and properties of them. Philosophy, in contrast, asks about the legitimacy of such extrapolation beyond the realm of the observable into the realm of the unobservable. How can such inferences be rationalized or justified? Even more profoundly, how can concepts that purport to refer to the unobservable even be meaningful to us, given the role that the association of concept with experience allegedly plays in the grounding of meaning?

Philosophy of science is often characterized as reserving for itself issues in the realm of methodology. Whereas the actual accumulation of observational results and their assimilation into general explanatory theories are to be the task of the scientist in his special discipline, it is the philosopher of science who is to explore the methods by which science goes about its task. How are theories formulated, tested, accepted, and rejected in science? What role does confrontation with the data play? What role is played by such elements as ontological simplicity or formal elegance in the ongoing process of theory construction and selection? What are the means by which the scientist offers understanding of the world on the basis of observations and theorizing? How are explanations formulated by the scientist? What are the resources behind explanatory schemes, and how does the existence of a scientific explanation give us further understanding of the nature of the world? But, as we have seen, the need for revolutionary theories in physics that treat of the phenomena of nature at the levels of highest generality and greatest depth has forced scientists themselves to confront issues of just the kind that have traditionally been reserved for philosophers.

When we are dealing with the most fundamental issues concerning space and time and their place in nature, issues concerning the kind of being that can exist and that can be invoked in our explanatory accounts come to the fore. This was already obvious in the seventeenth century when, as we have seen, such great thinkers as Newton and Leibniz wrestled with the metaphysical questions that seemed inextricable from their views on the nature of space and time. Now, with the revolutions in our views of space and time forced on us by the special theory of relativity and the general theory of relativity, these old issues about the substantivality of space and time have resurfaced. Even more profoundly, as we have seen, thinkers such as Bohr, coming to grips with the strange phenomena to which quantum mechanics must do justice, have found it necessary to deal with issues concerning the very objectivity of the world as an entity allegedly independent of the actions taken by those trying to come to know its nature. The old philosophical issues of the autonomy of the world from our sensible and intellectual grasp of it, issues puzzled over by, for example, Kant, become part of an attempt to understand the formalism of the theory designed to handle the queer facts about the interaction of matter and radiation with which quantum mechanics must deal.

We have also seen that the critical, epistemological approach of philosophy has played a role in the foundations of some of these contemporary physical theories. Although the revolutionary spacetimes of the special and general theories of relativity arise in part from the need for new accounts of space and time that will do justice to the newly discovered experimental facts about the behavior of light, the motion of particles, and the measuring results of rods and clocks, an equally important role in the formulation of these theories is played by the critical examination of concepts from the epistemic point of view. This critical program is most notable in the work of Einstein. Time and again he advances the theoretical discussion by asking us to reflect upon the meanings of our basic terms dealing with space and time. He asks us to consider how these terms function in our theories, emphasizing especially the degree to which our assumed theories are grounded on facts of the world that are genuinely epistemically accessible to us. Using a critical examination of terms and hypotheses that depends on an exploration of the limits of our epistemic awareness of the world, Einstein reinvigorates the physical theories available for dealing with the spatial and temporal structure of the world. In the attempt to resolve the apparently paradoxical features of the world described to us in quantum mechanics, we again find such thinkers as Bohr and Heisenberg trying to convince us that a correct understanding of the theory, and of the world it describes, requires us to stand back and reflect upon our ability to come to know the world. This reflection is from a critical-epistemological perspective.

As one example of how results in physics require rethinking of methodological issues, we might consider the way in which statistical mechanics indicates that there are modes of explaining phenomena that seem to require models of statistical explanation of striking originality. The role of probabilities in statistical mechanics; the ground for their attribution to microstates of particular kinds of systems; their role in accounting for the macroscopic phenomena dealt with by thermodynamics; and the relationship of these probabilities to the statistical-like consequences derived from the underlying laws of dynamics; all these indicate that a rethinking is in order. We must think hard about the relationship of initial conditions to laws, and of the role both play in explaining why what happens in the world happens. We have also seen how the consequences of quantum mechanics, such as the proofs of the impossibility of local hidden variables, suggest that science has forced upon us a new attitude toward what constitutes a complete explanation of the discovered correlations of phenomena with one another when these phenomena are not in causal interaction at the time they occur. Indeed, the very nature of causation and how it is to be sought and invoked in science take on a different appearance in the quantum context.

We cannot hope, then, to do philosophy without reference to the results of physics. That this is true for metaphysics, the investigation into the nature of the world at the levels of greatest generality, seems most obvious. It is plain that our understanding of the fundamental kinds of things and properties we must posit in order to comprehend the nature of the world must take account of that which science tells us about the world. Time and time again philosophy that tries to reason a priori, without reliance on the data of observation and experiment, and to come to conclusions about how the world must be has seen itself embarrassed by the revelations of science. This has shown us that the aprioristic philosophers have been quite limited in their imaginations when they attempted to delimit the realm of possibilities for the nature of the world. Without the results of physics, what philosopher would have considered the wide variety of possibilities for the nature of space and time, of causation, and of the kinds of objectivity and its lack that the radical new theories of physics have posed as possibilities for our consideration?

But it is not only metaphysics that must pay attention to the results of science. Many philosophers in the theory of knowledge have argued in recent years that hopes for an aprioristically formulated and rationalized theory of inference to the truth is also a dubious proposition. In deciding what rules are the reasonable ones to use in seeking out the truth, they have argued, you must rely upon your best insights into the nature of the world whose truths you are trying to ferret out. But, if this is so, surely we must take into consideration those theories from the sciences, be they foundational physics or neuropsychology and the cognitive sciences of perception and thought, that tell us what we know about the nature of the world we are trying to discover and about our relation to it as perceivers and theorizers. As we have seen, our very idea of what it is to comprehend that world, to understand its workings, and to provide explanatory accounts of what goes on in it will itself depend on the very nature of that world. So in both its epistemological and its methodological tasks, philosophy will need to refer continually to what the advanced sciences, including foundational physics, tell us about the world.

It is important to note that this dependence on the sciences is no mere dependence upon them as sources of raw data alone. To be sure, the observational results that push the science of physics into the invention of the radical and novel theories we have been looking at are crucial in their impact on philosophy. But it is also the ability of the practitioners of these sciences to imagine novel conceptual schemes that take account of the new data that provides to philosophy an ever richer spectrum of new conceptual ways of dealing with the world. It is the imaginations of scientists like Boltzmann, Einstein, and Bohr that are the source of wholly new ways of thinking about the nature of reality, our knowledge of it, and our ability to give an explanatory account of it. They provide an ever fertile source of enrichment for the philosopher seeking new ways of dealing with both old and new problems presented by the world of experience.

But if philosophy must pay close attention to the results of foundational physics, it is clear that foundational physics has a dependence on philosophy as well. As we have explored the roots of the foundational theories at the core of modern physics, we have seen again and again that the formulation of these theories is no trivial extrapolation by obvious reasoning from the observational data. Instead, the formulation of an appropriate theory and the rationalization provided for that choice, when a particular theoretical stance is adopted and defended against criticism, depend upon the kinds of reasoning that philosophers have explored and puzzled over. This can be seen clearly, for example, in the rationalizations behind the special and general theories of relativity offered by Einstein and in the attempts of Bohr to provide a coherent understanding of the quantum mechanical formalism. Here such philosophical issues as the distinguishability of those consequences of a theory testable by observation from those immune to such confrontation; the role of critical examination of the meanings of the nonobservational concepts of the theories; the rationale for principles of theory choice that rest upon considerations such as that of ontological simplicity; the suitability of generalizations to provide genuine explanations for phenomena; and the question as to when an explanation can be considered ultimate; all play a crucial role *within* the scientific dialectic that leads to theory formulation and acceptance. It is as though traditionally philosophical issues must become part of scientific thinking itself when the scientific theories in question are of such great generality and fundamentality as those we have discussed in the preceding chapters.

At one time, theoretical physicists usually received some training in philosophy and its history. In those days, explicit reference to the kind of philosophical reasoning backing up scientific reasoning could be found in the works of some of the greatest scientists. Einstein and Bohr provide two noteworthy examples. Although the specialization of academic training in recent decades has made such familiarity with traditional philosophy less common among scientists, even the most theoretical scientists, the need for the kind of philosophical thinking we have been discussing as part of scientific thinking has now become clear. This is so whether the scientist wants to confront that fact or not. Evidence of this can be seen in the kind of quasi-philosophical thinking that has become part of cosmological speculation and theorizing about the Big Bang in scientific cosmology.

The fact that the scientific theories are themselves based on thinking of a philosophical sort, whether this is explicit in the scientific history or only implicit and waiting for the historian and philosopher to dig it out, means also that one must be wary of too naive an attempt to resolve traditional philosophical issues by referring to the results of science. Arguments to the effect that some given result of science conclusively resolves a traditional philosophical question in one direction or another all too frequently lose sight of the way in which implicit philosophical presuppositions have been built into the theory that is being used to resolve the debate. Had other philosophical choices been made in the science itself, the implications of the science for philosophy might look quite different indeed.

In any case, it is quite clear that at its levels of highest generality and in its attempts to deal with nature at its most fundamental level, science is a discipline not radically distinguishable in its nature from philosophy. And the best way of doing philosophy is to use a method that, like science, always refers back in its theorizing to the nature of things as revealed to us by that refined experience we call scientific observation and experiment.

References

Albert, D., and B. Loewer. 1990. "Wanted Dead or Alive: Two Attempts to Solve Schrödinger's Paradox." In A. Fine, M. Forbes, and L. Wessels, eds., *PSA-1990*, vol. 1. East Lansing, MI: Philosophy of Science Association.

Alexander, H., ed. 1956. *The Leibniz-Clarke Correspondence.* Manchester: Manchester University Press.

Anderson, J. 1967. *Principles of Relativity Physics.* New York: Academic Press. (*)

Arnold, V., and A. Avez. 1968. *Ergodic Problems of Classical Mechanics.* New York: Benjamin. (**)

Barbour, J. 1989. *Absolute or Relative Motion?* vol. 1, *The Discovery of Dynamics.* Cambridge: Cambridge University Press.

Batterman, R. 1990. "Irreversibility and Statistical Mechanics: A New Approach?" *Philosophy of Science* 57:395–419.

———. 1991. "Randomness and Probability in Dynamical Theories: On the Proposals of the Prigogine School." *Philosophy of Science* 57:241–263.

Belinfante, F. 1973. *A Survey of Hidden Variable Theories.* New York: Pergamon. (*)

Bell, J. 1987. *Speakable and Unspeakable in Quantum Mechanics.* Cambridge: Cambridge University Press.

Bohm, D. 1951. *Quantum Theory.* Englewood Cliffs NJ: Prentice-Hall. (*)

———. 1989. *The Special Theory of Relativity.* Reading, MA: Addison-Wesley.

Brush, S. 1965. *Kinetic Theory.* Oxford: Pergamon Press.

———. 1976. *The Kind of Motion That We Call Heat.* Amsterdam: North-Holland.

Buchdahl, H. 1966. *The Concepts of Classical Thermodynamics.* Cambridge: Cambridge University Press. (*)

Cramér, H. 1955. *The Elements of Probability Theory and Some of Its Applications.* New York: John Wiley.

Davies, P. 1974. *The Physics of Time Asymmetry.* Berkeley: University of California Press.

d'Espagnat, B. 1971. *Conceptual Foundations of Quantum Mechanics.* Menlo Park, CA: Benjamin. (**)

Devaney, R. 1986. *An Introduction to Chaotic Dynamical Systems.* Menlo Park, CA: Benjamin-Cummings. (**)

Dicke, R., and J. Wittke. 1960. *Introduction to Quantum Mechanics.* Reading, MA: Addison-Wesley. (*)

Material requiring some background in mathematics and theoretical physics (e.g., at the undergraduate level) is marked (*). Material requiring a more extensive familiarity with the technical concepts and methods is marked (**).

Dirac, P. 1930. *The Principles of Quantum Mechanics*. Oxford: Oxford University Press. (*)

Earman, J. 1974. "An Attempt to Add a Little Direction to 'The Problem of the Direction of Time.'" *Philosophy of Science* 41:15–47.

————. 1986. *A Primer of Determinism*. Dordrecht: D. Reidel.

————. 1989. *World-Enough and Space-Time*. Cambridge, MA: MIT Press.

Eddington, A. 1920. *Space, Time and Gravitation*. Cambridge: Cambridge University Press.

Ehrenfest, P., and T. Ehrenfest. 1959. *The Conceptual Foundations of the Statistical Approach in Mechanics*. Ithaca, NY: Cornell University Press. (*)

Einstein, A., et al. 1923. *The Principle of Relativity*. New York: Dover.

Farquhar, I. 1964. *Ergodic Theory in Statistical Mechanics*. New York: John Wiley. (*)

Feller, W. 1950. *An Introduction to Probability Theory and Its Applications*. New York: John Wiley. (*)

Friedman, M. 1983. *Foundations of Space-Time Theories*. Princeton: Princeton University Press. (*)

Geroch, R. 1978. *General Relativity from A to B*. Chicago: University of Chicago Press.

Ghirardi, G., A. Rimini, and M. Weber. 1986. "Unified Dynamics for Microscopic and Macroscopic Systems." *Physical Review* D 34:470–479. (*)

Gibbins, P. 1987. *Particles and Paradoxes*. Cambridge: Cambridge University Press.

Gibbs, J. 1960. *Elementary Principles in Statistical Mechanics*. New York: Dover. (*)

Gleick, J. 1987. *Chaos: Making a New Science*. New York: Penguin Books.

Gottfried, K. 1960. *Quantum Mechanics*. New York: Benjamin. (*)

Graves, J. 1971. *The Conceptual Foundations of General Relativity Theory*. Cambridge, MA: MIT Press.

Grünbaum, A. 1973. *Philosophical Problems of Space and Time*, 2d ed. Dordrecht: Reidel.

Hawking, S., and G. Ellis. 1973. *The Large Scale Structure of Space-Time*. Cambridge: Cambridge University Press. (**)

Healy, R. 1989. *The Philosophy of Quantum Mechanics*. Cambridge: Cambridge University Press.

Heisenberg, W. 1930. *The Physical Principles of the Quantum Theory*. New York: Dover.

Hobson, A. 1971. *Concepts in Statistical Mechanics*. New York: Gordon and Breach.

Horwich, P. 1987. *Asymmetries in Time*. Cambridge, MA: MIT Press.

Hughes, R. 1989. *The Structure and Interpretation of Quantum Mechanics*. Cambridge, MA: Harvard University Press.

Humphreys, P. 1989. *The Chances of Explanation*. Princeton: Princeton University Press.

Jammer, M. 1954. *Concepts of Space*. Cambridge: Cambridge University Press.

————. 1966. *The Conceptual Development of Quantum Mechanics*. New York: McGraw-Hill.

————. 1974. *The Philosophy of Quantum Mechanics*. New York: John Wiley.

Jancel, R. 1963. *Foundations of Classical and Quantum Statistical Mechanics*. Oxford: Pergamon Press. (*)

Jauch, J. 1968. *Foundations of Quantum Mechanics*. Reading, MA: Addison-Wesley. (**)

Jaynes, E. 1983. *Papers on Probability, Statistics and Statistical Physics*. Dordrecht: Reidel.

Jordan, T. 1969. *Linear Operators for Quantum Mechanics*. New York: John Wiley. (*)

Kant, I. 1929. *The Critique of Pure Reason*, trans. by N. Kemp Smith. New York: Macmillan.

————. 1950. *Prolegomenon to Any Future Metaphysic*. New York: Liberal Arts Press.

Katz, A. 1967. *Principles of Statistical Mechanics*. San Francisco: Freeman. (*)

Kochen, S. 1985. "A New Interpretation of Quantum Mechanics." In P. Lahti and P. Mittelstaedt, eds., *Symposium on the Foundations of Modern Physics*. Teaneck, NJ: World Scientific Publishing. (*)

Kolmogorov, A. 1950. *Foundations of the Theory of Probability*. New York: Chelsea. (*)

Krylov, N. 1979. *Works on the Foundations of Statistical Physics*. Princeton: Princeton University Press.

Kyburg, H. 1970. *Probability and Inductive Logic*. London: Macmillan.

Lucas, J., and P. Hodgson. 1990. *Spacetime and Electromagnetism*. Oxford: Oxford University Press.

Ludwig, G. 1968. *Wave Mechanics*. Oxford: Pergamon Press.

Mehlberg, H. 1980. *Time, Causality and the Quantum Theory*. Dordrecht: D. Reidel.

Mellor, D. 1981. *Real Time*. Cambridge: Cambridge University Press.

Misner, C., K. Thorne, and J. Wheeler. 1973. *Gravitation*. San Francisco: Freeman. (**)

Møller, C. 1952. *The Theory of Relativity*. Oxford: Oxford University Press. (*)

Nerlich, G. 1976. *The Shape of Space*. Cambridge: Cambridge University Press.

Newton-Smith, W. 1980. *The Structure of Time*. London: Routledge and Kegan-Paul.

Pagels, H. 1982. *The Cosmic Code*. New York: Bantam Books.

Penrose, R. 1979. "Singularities and Time Asymmetry." In S. Hawking and W. Israel, eds., *General Relativity: An Einstein Centenary Survey*. Cambridge: Cambridge University Press.

Pippard, A. 1961. *The Elements of Classical Thermodynamics*. Cambridge: Cambridge University Press.

Poincaré, H. 1952. *Science and Hypothesis*. New York: Dover.

Prigogine, I. 1980. *From Being to Becoming*. San Francisco: Freeman.

————. 1984. *Order Out of Chaos*. New York: Bantam Books.

Putnam, H. 1967. "Time and Physical Geometry." *Journal of Philosophy* 64:240–247.

Rae, A. 1986. *Quantum Physics: Illusion or Reality?* Cambridge: Cambridge University Press.

Reichenbach, H. 1944. *Philosophic Foundations of Quantum Mechanics*. Berkeley: University of California Press.

————. 1956. *The Direction of Time*. Berkeley: University of California Press.

————. 1958. *The Philosophy of Space and Time*. New York: Dover.

Rietdijk, C. 1966. "A Rigorous Proof of Determinism from the Special Theory of Relativity." *Philosophy of Science* 33:341–344.

Rindler, W. 1977. *Essential Relativity*. New York: Springer-Verlag. (*)

Salmon, W. 1984. *Scientific Explanation and the Causal Structure of the World*. Princeton: Princeton University Press.

Schroeder, M. 1991. *Fractals, Chaos, Power Laws*. New York: Freeman. (*)

Sinai, Y. 1976. *Introduction to Ergodic Theory*. Princeton: Princeton University Press. (**)

Sklar, L. 1974. *Space, Time, and Spacetime*. Berkeley: University of California Press.

————. 1985. *Philosophy and Spacetime Physics*. Berkeley: University of California Press.

————. Forthcoming. *The Physics of Chance*. Cambridge: Cambridge University Press.

Smart, J., ed. 1964. *Problems of Space and Time*. New York: Macmillan.

Squires, E. 1986. *The Mystery of the Quantum World*. Bristol: Adam Hilger.

Stein, H. 1991. "On Relativity Theory and Openness of the Future." *Philosophy of Science* 58:147–167.

Synge, J. 1956. *Relativity: the Special Theory*. Amsterdam: North-Holland. (*)

Taylor, E., and J. Wheeler. 1963. *Spacetime Physics*. San Francisco: Freeman.

Tolman, R. 1934. *Relativity, Thermodynamics and Cosmology*. Oxford: Oxford University Press.

————. 1938. *The Principles of Statistical Mechanics*. Oxford: Oxford University Press. (*)

Toretti, R. 1978. *The Philosophy of Geometry from Riemann to Poincaré*. Dordrecht: Reidel.

————. 1983. *Relativity and Geometry*. Oxford: Pergamon Press. (*)

van Fraassen, B. 1970. *An Introduction to the Philosophy of Time and Space*. New York: Random House.

————. 1991. *Quantum Mechanics: An Empiricist View*. Oxford: Oxford University Press. (*)

von Neumann, J. 1955. *Mathematical Foundations of Quantum Mechanics*. Princeton: Princeton University Press. (**)

Wald, R. 1984. *General Relativity*. Chicago: University of Chicago Press. (*)

Wheeler, J., and W. Zurek, eds. 1983. *Quantum Theory and Measurement*. Princeton: Princeton University Press. (*)

Winnie, J. 1977. "The Causal Theory of Space-Time." In J. Earman, C. Glymour, and J. Stachel, eds., *Foundations of Space-Time Theories, Minnesota Studies in the Philosophy of Science*, vol. 8. Minneapolis: University of Minnesota Press.

About the Book
and Author

The study of the physical world had its origins in philosophy, and, two-and-one-half millennia later, the scientific advances of the twentieth century are bringing the two fields closer together again. So argues Lawrence Sklar in this brilliant new text on the philosophy of phsyics.

Aimed at students of both disciplines, *Philosophy of Physics* is a broad overview of the problems of contemporary philosophy of physics that readers of all levels of sophistication should find accessible and engaging. Profesor Sklar's talent for clarity and accuracy are on display throughout as he guides students through the key problems: the nature of space and time, the problems of probability and irreversibility in statistical mechanics, and, of course, the many notorious problems raised by quantum mechanics.

Integrated by the theme of the interconnectedness of philosophy and science, and linked by many references to the history of both disciplines, *Philosophy of Physics* is always clear, while remaining faithful to the complexity and integrity of the issues. It will take its place as a classic text in a field of fundamental intellectual importance.

Lawrence Sklar is professor of philosophy at the University of Michigan. He is the author of *Space, Time, and Spacetime* (winner of the Franklin J. Matchette Prize) and *Philosophy and Spacetime Physics* as well as many articles on the philosophy of physics.

237

Index